'Jenny Tough writes with the same talent, imagination and sheer courage that she displays in her athletic endeavours. This book will broaden the horizons of all who venture between its covers.'
– Emily Chappell, author of *Where There's a Will*

'I love that *SOLO* is part self-help and part adventure story. Jenny shows us all that the journey to self-belief comes with just as many ups and downs as the mountains she traverses and that, with a little trust in ourselves (and a few good cups of coffee), the next seemingly insurmountable pass is never beyond our reach.'
– Anna McNuff, author of *Bedtime Adventure Stories for Grown Ups*

SOLO

A true story of spirit,
adventure and the
life-changing power of
running alone

JENNY TOUGH

ASTER*

ASTER*

First published in Great Britain in 2022 by Aster, an imprint of
Octopus Publishing Group Ltd
Carmelite House
50 Victoria Embankment
London EC4Y 0DZ
www.octopusbooks.co.uk
www.octopusbooksusa.com

An Hachette UK Company
www.hachette.co.uk

First published in paperback in 2023

Distributed in the US by
Hachette Book Group
1290 Avenue of the Americas
4th and 5th Floors
New York, NY 10104

Distributed in Canada by
Canadian Manda Group
664 Annette St.
Toronto, Ontario, Canada M6S 2C8

ISBN (US): 978-1-78325-592-4

Printed and bound in the UK

1 3 5 7 9 10 8 6 4 2

Typeset in 10.75/16.5pt Farnham Text by Jouve (UK), Milton Keynes

This FSC® label means that materials used for
the product have been responsibly sourced.

Publisher: Stephanie Jackson
Senior Editor: Pauline Bache
Editorial Assistant: Louisa Johnson
Interior Design: Juliette Norsworthy
Illustrator: Abi Read
Senior Production Manager: Peter Hunt

You're tougher than you think.

I believe in you.

Contents

Foreword

Mountains have always been a sanctuary for me.

For as long as I can remember, big mountain environments have been the places where I feel most at home, most like myself, and most inspired and curious about the world. I grew up in Calgary, on the doorstep of the Canadian Rockies, and – although I left my hometown at 18 – I always felt that I'd found my way 'home' when I travelled in mountains, wherever they were on the planet.

Throughout my adult life I've pursued challenges on mountains around the world, ultimately carving out a career as an adventurer and athlete – although adopting the latter title has always come with crippling impostor syndrome. But my journey into running and mountain sports was not a smooth or even a positive one.

I began running as a teenager as a way of burning calories and attempting to 'fix' my body. I was *fat*, in my eyes, and getting dressed for school every morning was turning into a daily crisis. I covered myself in baggy sweaters and retreated socially. At nights after school, I took my golden retriever, Tessa, out for runs around the neighbourhood. I only had my school shoes and clothes entirely inappropriate for Calgary winters, and I hated every minute of it. I hated running and I hated my body. I quietly resented my skinny friends who didn't 'have to' exercise. I saw running's sole purpose as punishment for eating: a weight-loss function.

Tessa, on the other hand, loved it. She brought the 'positive mental attitude' that I lacked, and spurred me to carry on.

Over time, I got distracted from my negative mindset, and started exploring the neighbourhood more on our runs. I got lost a few times and ran further than I had previously thought possible. I sometimes ran in the morning or on spare periods at high school when I could go home and take Tessa out. It didn't happen overnight, but running slowly became enjoyable. That endorphin rush is nature's way of convincing you that running is good and you should try it again. In addition to the endorphin hit, running slowly started aiding my self-esteem.

I noticed that on days when I ran, I was a happier person. More creative and focused, too. And I needed more of it. In my last year of high school, I ran a 10k fun run and found a confidence I had never possessed before. I set myself new goals, picked up training plans and achieved them. I ran a half marathon and then a full marathon. And then again, again and again.

Running became an important pillar of my life. Far beyond

burning calories, it was a place to maintain my whole health – and it has got me over every hurdle my life has posed so far. It is also a place that has brought me endless joy, especially after I discovered trail running, where my love for mountains and nature finally met my love for endurance running.

I built my life around travel and adventure, finding myself in my second home of Scotland in my early twenties. Scotland became a base for me to explore the world and find my footing as an independent person. I travelled as much as I could during that decade, frequently combining adventures with athletic pursuits like cycling, paddling, sailing, running, skiing – whatever I could get my hands on. A pair of running shoes would always be in my backpack, and anywhere I landed I would go for a run as a means of exploring. Running became my favourite gateway to adventure, although I didn't realize it at the time.

I set myself up as a freelance writer, too. I had no idea what I was doing or how to do it, but the lifestyle afforded me the schedule (if not the budget) to travel almost at whim. Over time my adventures grew in scale, and I raced occasionally as a way to really push myself.

But the *expedition* world always felt out of reach – just a little too high for someone like me. That world was for the star adventurers, the rugged bearded men who were members of exclusive clubs and had extensive qualifications. I was just a girl with too many backpacks. I had nothing in common with that elite world of international expeditions.

I *wanted* in, but I couldn't even find the door.

*

I daydream about exploring all the time. I look at maps and I read about cultures far away from my own. This is how many of my adventures begin – by daydreaming and pulling at the threads of curiosity.

One day, an idea began to form.

Long-distance, unsupported, multi-day (or, more accurately, multi-week) running was not a qualified 'thing' when I started this project. It wasn't something that I could buy a guidebook for, or learn from anyone else. It was a daydream I had, a curiosity about what was possible for me, and a desire to explore by my favourite means of movement.

Running the length of a mountain range seemed like the ultimate challenge to me. Doing it would mean getting to know an entire geographical feature, from start to end, and meeting the people who lived there. Doing it solo and unsupported would force me to rely on those people and interact with them as much as possible.

Without a support crew or companion, I would be totally vulnerable to the mountain range, and my experience would have a purity and integrity – the way I believe travel and exploration should be.

And what if it wasn't just a single mountain range?

In essence, what this project became was an entirely individualized, entirely made-up set of challenges in mountain ranges around the world. Completed solo – with every decision made along the way mine alone.

No one else had done it before, and I doubt anyone would attempt to repeat it. I didn't know where this journey would take me, or if it was even possible. I was always an unlikely candidate to complete any world-first athletic expedition. But I had a dream and a tunnel-vision focus.

Armed with little else, I booked a flight to Kyrgyzstan.

CHAPTER ONE

Starting Out:
The Tien Shan

The crammed, concerningly outdated plane landed with a few bumps and wiggles in the wee hours of the morning on the empty Bishkek runway. With only one other aircraft on the entire tarmac, the taxi to the arrivals lounge was a short journey, and soon they opened the doors, letting fresh Kyrgyz air enter the stuffy cabin after our uncomfortable redeye flight. I stepped out onto the metal ladder, squinting at the harsh Central Asian sun, and looked south: there, somewhat hazy in the distance, were the white peaks of the Tien Shan.

It was only 6am by the time I left the airport, and already turning into a hot July day. I managed to cram my overloaded expedition bag into a Lada almost as old as its elderly driver, and we bounced our way down a potholed highway into Bishkek. Despite the long flight, watching this mysterious city come to life gave me a course of energy. Adventure awaited.

K-Y-R-G-Y-Z-S-T-A-N. Only a few months previously, I had known nothing of this place, least of all how to pronounce it. I have a bad habit – I wonder if you do this too? – of daydreaming while looking at maps. I can sit on the couch for ages with my laptop, just zooming in on places and wondering what journeys may exist, making promises to myself to go there one day. In one of these sessions, I stumbled upon the Tien Shan Mountains, and my heart stopped. They were perhaps the most beautiful, perfect mountains I had ever seen. Images of clear blue sky and pristine white snow gave a heavenly aura to jagged and dense tall peaks. This was the land of snow leopards, wild horses, nomadic herders, and a step back in time to the Silk Road. *Tien Shan* literally translates as 'mountains of heaven', and they are aptly named.

I had a couple of days in Bishkek to start adjusting, settling in and working my way up to altitude. I also had to find some gas for my small stove, as that was the only item I couldn't fly with. I had learned that the Mountaineering Association sold some, and spent hours combing the city to find the office. Communist-style streets of perfect right angles and identical buildings, one after the other as far as you could imagine, made it a surprisingly difficult place to navigate.

'What are your plans for your holiday in Kyrgyzstan?' the young officer asked as I fumbled for some *som* to buy the canisters with.

'I'm going to run across Kyrgyzstan! From Karakol to Osh,' I beamed back.

The man stared. He had the look of someone waiting for the punchline.

'Umm . . . No.'

'No?'

'No. You can't run across Kyrgyzstan. It's too big. The mountains are very tall. Outside of the city there are no hotels or shops for you. It can't be done. No.'

I had worked so hard on this project. For once in my life, I actually felt really confident that this would work. So I dug my heels in and showed him, tracing my finger along a map of the country he had pinned to the wall, describing the passes and valleys I would navigate, the towns where I could resupply, and explaining my ultra-light equipment setup ('I won't need a hotel, I have a tent!').

'. . . and then finish in Osh. About a thousand kilometres. Hard, but doable.' I pointed my finger at the city that marked

3

the southwest edge of the country, directly opposite the northwest corner I intended to start from. By no means the most efficient 'across' route that one would follow if being the first – or fastest – person to run across the country was of high importance. It was nearly double the length it needed to be, and took a few meanders to see highlights and avoid a large mining region in the middle.

'Okay,' he slowly nodded, one finger over his lips as he thought through the presentation I had just delivered, 'this is actually a good route.'

(A sigh of relief.)

'. . . I think it is possible, actually. Someone definitely could run across Kyrgyzstan. But . . .' he cocked his head a little as he took me in. Denim short-shorts and flip-flops, big reflective sunglasses pushing back messy light brown hair. Painted nails I still needed to remove before starting (for this exact reason). Not overweight, but certainly not the form you would expect for an ultra runner. And, most criminally, young and female.

'. . . but not you.'

I felt like I had been punched in the face.

My eyes glazed over and ears shut partially while he gently showed me on the map more suitable 'holiday' activities I could take part in while in Kyrgyzstan, all under the watchful management of a tour guide and with appropriately comfortable hotels to sleep in. Places more suited to a lady. I did what we ladies always do in these situations: I screamed inside. On the outside, I smiled meekly and said, 'Okay, great, thanks!' Then I turned on my heels and walked away as quickly as I could.

It always seems impossible until it is done.

I branded that man a misogynist with bad manners – to doubt me so clearly and overtly based on my gender and appearance. But it wasn't just that. *Nobody had done this before.* Man or woman. If something has never been done, it is generally assumed it is because it *can't be done.* The four-minute mile. Commercial flight. Commercial flights with female pilots.

For two days I had wandered around Bishkek, learning about the new country I found myself in, feeling the bubbling courage in my belly that I would soon depart on The Hardest Thing I Had Ever Done. I only worried about my own personal trials ahead. My own low self-esteem and fear of failure. I had not, ever, accounted for the negative reaction from external parties. That as an unlikely candidate to come to K-Y-R-G-Y-Z-S-T-A-N and complete a world-first expedition, I would face a helluva lot of doubt, and even barriers outside of my own abilities, my own mind. I would need to build resilience not just against what *I* thought of myself, but what everyone else thought – and would be willing to say to my face.

A SINGLE STEP

I lay in my small guesthouse bed in the northeastern mountain town of Karakol, my head swimming from vodka that I hadn't truly wanted to drink. My host family had insisted on me joining the revelry of a family wedding (which had happened last week and in a different city – but celebrations apparently continue for a while), despite my not understanding the mix of Kyrgyz and Russian spoken at the large dinner banquet. Thunder shook the metal roof and lightning snapped bright in the sky. I've never made my mind up whether I believe in

5

omens, but if I did, I'm not sure an epic thunderstorm the night before The Hardest Thing I Had Ever Done would be a good one. I couldn't stop going over how it would feel when such storms hit while I was high up in the mountains with nothing but a flimsy nylon tent to keep me safe and dry. Would I get scared? Would all my stuff get soaked, leaving me with hypothermia and needing a rescue? There aren't actually any rescue teams in Kyrgyzstan, so, then what??

Eventually, sleep came, and in the morning a beautiful clear dawn greeted me with a smile that suggested the thunderstorm had been nothing but a dream. I gorged myself on an extra-large breakfast, more out of hoping to soak up the vodka than actual carb-loading, and then I spent several minutes pleading with every member of the family to believe that I would be all right, and not to worry about me. The grim, concerned looks on their faces as I departed with nothing but a compact 32-litre backpack gave me little comfort. It was overwhelming to be welcomed into the hearts of the family so quickly, but their loving concern was an extra load to bear as I hoisted my pack onto my shoulders. I flagged down a rickety taxi, an even older Lada and even older driver than my first ride, and attempted to communicate that I wanted to travel as far east as we could before reaching the border zone. Toylek, the gold-toothed driver, eventually resigned himself to the fact that I was insane, and seemed to assume that once I saw what he was talking about – that there was truly nothing out there – I would get back in the Lada and return to Karakol, and my safe guesthouse, and he would have made a good day's wage from the trip.

Near midday, Toylek helped me into my backpack (at only 10kg I didn't really need the help, but it was chivalrous) and waved as I began trotting up an old dirt track, directly towards the steep wall of the Tien Shan Mountains. He was still laughing heartily that I had insisted on being let out of the taxi 'in the middle of nowhere', and I'll always wonder how long he waited there for me to come to my senses and return.

And so I began the first steps of The Hardest Thing I Had Ever Done. Then a few steps later, I stopped and remembered to turn my tracker on. It would be my safety blanket for the weeks to come, letting my friends and family know where I was, receiving messages from them in even the most remote areas and – most importantly to me – recording my route for posterity.

DAY 1

It was instantly encouraging to discover that I could actually manage to *run* with my backpack full of five days' worth of supplies and three litres of water. It was crammed to bursting, but I quickly settled into the rhythm and felt completely at ease. I had practised running with a large pack and trekking poles a little bit over the summer, but admittedly no more than a couple of times. I had already learned that the 'ski racer' technique of pole use works better when running, whereas walking is more of a 'left–right–left' scenario. Digging the poles into the ground with the strength of my arms just took that little bit of extra pressure off of my legs and, with 1,000km ahead of them, they needed all the help they could get.

7

But after an enthusiastic start, less than an hour in and with the wall of mountain still looming ahead of me, I had to stop and gasp for air. I walked a minute, then began jogging again. *Stop and gasp. Walk. Run. Gasp.* This wasn't good.

I wrote it off as stiff legs and lungs from a week of travel, logistics and the recent vodka addition. I hadn't been able to make any time for fitness in the week or so leading up to this day. Eventually I climbed out of the dusty valley and into the alpine wilderness. Deep green fir trees welcomed me into the shelter of their shade. Squirrels scuttled among the branches, and the path became softer out of the dry sun.

I followed the fast-flowing river up the valley, and in the early afternoon a gentle rain set in. When I reached the bridge – or three logs strapped together, really – to cross the river and turn west into an adjoining valley, I decided not to bother getting my phone wet and took the junction without consulting my map. I had studied this route for so long now, and I knew it by heart.

Leaving the jeep track behind, I soon found myself reduced to a slow and careful walk up a very steep and very muddy trail, sometimes paddling through the ice-cold mountain stream when the sides of the valley were too steep or too overgrown to walk on. It was hard work, my feet were freezing and I was struggling to breathe, even at the slower pace. I leaned hard on my trekking poles and often stopped to catch my breath before taking a few more steps and stopping again. I became increasingly worried about how I was coping – I had only ascended to 2,600m elevation, and I was aiming for a 3,800m pass that day.

As I began to emerge from the treeline, the sun came back out and I found a large boulder to lizard on. Absorbing the returning warmth of the sun, I took a break, then wrung out my wet socks, ate a granola bar and checked my progress on my GPS.

'Idiot!' My voice echoed through the valley. The wrong valley. I had gone the wrong way.

I looked up, ahead of me, the direction I had been earnestly climbing towards, and saw a beautiful blue sky over an attractive mountain range. I wanted to run towards it with open arms. I looked down, the way I had just come, and saw a muddy, slippery, messy trail under a grey sky. I toyed with any possible reroutes to avoid going back that way.

This was the moment when I finally was able to admit to myself that I was suffering from altitude sickness and making mistakes. I was a hazard to myself – but I was also alone with myself. The knowledge sank in that all of the decisions I needed to make on this expedition would go unchecked by any third party – I had to rely entirely on myself to make this thing work. I couldn't be nonchalant about anything, especially navigation.

I felt my face burning, sitting so high up in the sky, so I layered on some sunscreen and took some photos on my phone while I tried to make my mind up about what to do next. I finally decided to go back exactly the way I had come, and get back to my route. Being perfectly honest with myself, it wasn't an easy choice in that moment. I had lost several hours out of my first day pointlessly climbing the wrong mountain, getting dizzy from altitude and having to return to where I had started with hardly any progress made in my overall mileage.

My mojo took an early hit that afternoon.

The narrow stream led the way, and soon I was back under the treeline. The rain came back, this time accompanied by booming thunder and sheet lightning. The storm came so close that some of the lightning strikes made me jump. As I tiptoed my way towards the valley floor, the grade became increasingly steep and the combination of wet, slippery grass and tired legs made the descent incredibly difficult. More than a few times I slipped and slid further down the mountain on my bottom, trying to cheer myself up by joking that at least I was getting there faster. A few times I fell awkwardly, and became petrified that I would break an ankle on the first day. What an unimaginable personal disaster it would be if I had to go home after only half a day of travelling in the wrong direction.

Finally, I hit the valley floor and the three-log bridge where I had made my original error. Almost ceremoniously, as I crossed the Wrong Bridge, the hail stopped, the clouds parted and I stepped onto the solid ground of the track from earlier, putting weight on my feet with confidence and picking up speed.

I began running again – part gratefully, because the terrain was run-able, and part hurriedly, because the sun was indeed disappearing and I had wasted almost the entire day. After about 5km of this steady run, I crossed a mountain spring and stopped for a drink. I took my head torch out, finally realizing that dusk was now well upon the land.

By the time I decided on a place to pitch my tent for the very first time on this adventure, it was completely dark. I found a clearing next to the river, and pitched my tent under the protection of a large tree. It was a perfect spot: flat, soft ground, access to clear water and shelter from the weather. Ticked every box . . . My only regret was that I couldn't see it in the darkness.

I first collected water, as the tablets I was using needed an hour to purify it, and then under the light of my tiny head torch I began setting up the tent that I had only slept in once before, having recently replaced my beloved and well-worn tent with the lightest one-person tent available. I knew I would eventually get so good at setting it up that I could do it blindfolded using only my left hand, but I wasn't there quite yet. I fumbled awkwardly and the rain started again. Although only a few minutes ago I had been running in just shorts and a t-shirt, as soon as I stopped I became aware of the cold mountain night, and rushed to pull out my layers and gloves so I could manage with the tent.

I boiled my dinner, ate enthusiastically, then washed my bowl, spork, socks and underwear in the river, hung the latter up on my big protective tree and crawled into bed. It was only 9pm, but remarkably cold. I checked my GPS device, which I had paused now that I was stopped for the day, for any messages.

I texted with my boyfriend, who was at home in the flat we had just moved into together in Edinburgh, explaining my erroneous day. I felt slightly better after speaking to him, but once I closed my eyes and tried to sleep, thoughts began churning in my head. *What on earth am I doing*?? Here I was, mucking around and doing everything wrong, while he was on the other side of the world in our warm, comfortable bed, well inside the comfort zone. *Why did I think an entire month was necessary?* Couldn't I just have planned a weekend hiking holiday like a normal person? Tears flooded my eyes and I felt incredibly selfish and foolish. I was way out of my league, and I had proven that in the first hours of the journey.

Sleep didn't come easily that night. The beautiful river I had pitched next to was roaring to the point that I began to believe I might soon be engulfed and swept away with it. My brain was filled with anxiety and irrational thoughts now that I had been well reminded of the risks posed by my planned adventure. *Was I really up for this?* I covered again and again the potential dangers and the precautions I needed to be taking in order to avoid them. I had been reckless that day, making an easy mistake because I was too lazy to check my route. I needed to make sure I didn't do that again. Going solo comes with many dangers. Being alone with yourself is the biggest one.

Next morning, I woke with the dawn and lazily rolled over in my tent, reaching my arms out to light my stove and get coffee and breakfast going. I boiled a little too much water, which I took as an excellent excuse to make a second cup of coffee. From the warmth of my sleeping bag, I sat in my tent watching the river go past and the forest waking up. What in the night had sounded like a torrent, ready to break its banks and drown my tent, appeared in the daylight as a glittering waterway, hastily delivering yesterday's snow from the mountain peaks to the large lake systems below. The sweeping tree branches that played shadows on my tent walls greeted the morning sunlight with outstretched verdant arms. Birds chirped in the woods around me, and all was well in the world. I resolved to forget the woes of yesterday, and look forward to a successful adventure ahead. The sky was clear and my coffee was hot – what better place in the world could there be? I breathed a deep, mountain-air breath, and felt grateful to be in the beautiful outdoors. I was back in the mountains, exactly where I feel most comfortable. I'd never been here before, but I was home.

I stumbled out of my tent, startling some grazing horses nearby. I always feel terrible when I startle animals, and felt a longing pang of guilt as the troop of horses scuttled away from me. I did a few stretches, shaking my cold legs awake to prepare for the climb ahead. I had nearly 2,000m to ascend after falling behind schedule. I collected my almost-dried socks and underwear from the big tree, washed my cup, brushed my teeth, packed the tent and set off for a new day.

SHIT GETS REAL

As I neared the Big Pass, my most significant mark for the day, wheezing and panting in the thin air, a sight made me pick up my pace: a patch of snow. I had planned the run for the end of summer in order to reach the mountains after the snow had melted and cleared my path, but climbing high enough to reach the lingering snow still excited me. As I neared the patch, practically glowing next to the high-altitude landscape of grey boulders and shale, snow somehow began falling. Before stepping into the soft snowbank, I stopped to pile on my waterproofs and an extra wool layer. The gain in elevation had brought about a drop in mercury, and my hands were already purple and numb. Coming into contact with snow that went up to my knees as my feet rapidly sank through had an instant effect on my body temperature, and I was climbing higher and getting colder with every step. I was now at the foot of the Big Pass (I rarely found the names of back-country features, so I preferred to use the map in a way that was more memorable and meaningful to me, such as Big Pass, Questionable River, Long Slog, Spiky Mountain, etc.). The top was now out of view and I began my climb from directly underneath it. The rocks were loose and my shoes sank ankle deep into the fine alpine soil, pebbles pouring in over the tops of my shoes, wedging themselves between my socks and skin. I shortened my trekking poles to their smallest height and began climbing.

On and on and on and on, up and up and up I went. Right foot, left foot, right pole, left pole, stop. Breathe. Wheeze. Right foot, left foot, right pole, left foot, stop. Cough. Curse. Wheeze. And so on and so forth.

I blinked hard and my pink and yellow and green and black running shoes came in and out of focus. I turned back to see if I had actually climbed at all, and then suddenly with a sharp intake of breath clenched my poles tighter as my knees buckled – below my feet was only air. I became acutely aware of the steepness of the climb, and as my feet slowly drifted downwards in the dry scree I reminded myself to try to keep going. Stopping, faltering or, heaven forbid, tripping would lead to a swift return back down the slope to the snow patch that I had started from. *Wheeze, cough, keep going.* I grew so dizzy I forgot why I was climbing – I only knew that I had to go up. The only way to end the struggle was up. Eventually I accepted that I would never see the top. There was no top. The route to Osh disappeared, my real life at home disappeared, all grip on reality disappeared. Up I climbed, although there was no visible improvement in my elevation. I would be stuck on that scree climb for ever. And that was just the way things would be from now on.

Right foot, left foot, right pole, left pole, cough, wheeze, curse, cough, gasp, shake head. On and on.

When the view of sky began to enter my peripheral, I nearly cried. For what seemed like days, ahead of my face I could only see grey scree that I had to climb up. Slowly, the top of the pass crested and the bright sky above came into view. Only another 12 or so steps and I would be standing at the top.

Right foot, left foot, right pole.

Gasping for air, I dragged my way to the top of the pass, and weakly flicked my trekking poles skyward for a feeble, breathless *whoop!* Using the very last of my energy reserves on the celebration, I doubled over and took a seat on a well-placed flat rock to take in the view. It was phenomenal. Before my eyes, starting from the top and working the way down, were a cloudy, big sky, a snowy range of spiny mountains, and grey, treeless slopes leading to the most stunning turquoise lake – Ala Köl, in the valley directly below me. The intense turquoise colour reminded me of Canada's Lake Louise, where I have many childhood memories. I may have lost my breath on the climb and the 3,900m of elevation, but the lake below me took the second wind. A dumb grin spread across my face, and all I could think of was the usual trail-running mantra of 'work for your views'. I soon forgot the work, but I'll never forget that view.

It was at this moment that I realized it was snowing again. *How long has it been snowing for?* I wondered as I smiled upwards. It was a hard, icy snow – a very close cousin of hail – and then the thunder boomed through the valley, rumbling deeply and crashing loudly. Given that I was sitting so close to the sky and was the tallest thing on the ridge, the thunder had an alarming effect. In less than five seconds, sheet lightning encapsulated the sky, far more alarming than the boom. I decided to stop wasting time trying to breathe on my mountain perch, and get going with the scree run down towards the lake shore. There was now just an hour of sunlight left in the day, and it would simply be a matter of finding the first acceptable tent pitch and setting up camp. I lengthened my poles, taking them from the shortest height which had been necessary going up and switching them to the longest, offering me the best hope of steadying myself on what would be a very quick descent down the steep, loose scree towards Ala Köl.

I took a zigzagged approach to prevent myself from stumbling with flailing limbs, and let my sore and knackered legs unwind and spin down the scree slope. Rocks poured in over the tops of my shoes, adding weights to my feet, but stopping was not an option – I was spinning out of control and could only hope that I would be able to pull the brakes before running straight into the glacial lake. After a few extremely gleeful minutes, I had reached the shore.

By now the thunder and lightning were so near that I almost jumped out of my skin at the latest *boom* and *flash*. I scrambled along the damp, grassy edges of the lake, searching for a dry and flat tent pitch. I literally searched high and low, trying desperately to find a patch of grass where my shoes didn't instantly sink into dampness, but utterly failed. The valley was drenched from the past few days of stormy weather, and as the thunder boomed and the sun sank, I knew I needed to suck it up and pitch anyway in the squishy ground, imagining the wet saturating my tent and my sleeping bag throughout the night, drowning me and my belongings inside. I returned to the bottom of the descent I had clambered down, and rolled out my tent on the only patch of grass big enough to fit my tiny red home.

I chucked everything under the vestibule or inside the tent and began setting up my cocoon. I stripped off my wet layers and piled on the cosy, woolly clothes that were packed in tight with my sleeping bag. Once I was snuggled cosily inside my wool liner and sleeping bag, I vowed that I would not, under any circumstances, head outside that night. If I had to pee inside my bottle, I would. It was simply too cold and wet out there. The only thing left to do was to boil my dinner along with a hot-water bottle to keep my sleeping bag warm.

Remaining within the goose-down comfort of my sleeping bag, I unzipped my tent to reach out towards my ultra-light stove, which I had already filled with water from the alpine lake. I dug out my bright pink lighter, purchased at a convenience store a few days ago, and pressed the lever to ignite the gas. With a pathetic cracking noise, cheap plastic mangled under my thumb and, in a devastating instant, the lighter was useless. The lever fell off into my hand. Whispering *no, no, no,* I desperately tried to position it back onto the flint that I needed it to ignite. Attempt after attempt and with frozen hands that now resembled prunes, I struggled to make it work again. It was hopeless. *No, no, no, no, no,* I cried into the abyss.

I remembered then the storm-proof matches that I had bought on a nervous impulse at an outdoor shop in Scotland. I dug them out and lit the first. A short fizzle and it died. *Damn.* Light another. *Fizzle, damn.* Light another. *Fizzle* again. Four more times, and I knew I faced a real problem.* A night without food would be unfortunate. A night without the ability to get warm would be uncomfortable. Perhaps a little too uncomfortable. My exhausted mind began to swim with fear, imagining how cold the temperature would drop over the next eight hours as the snow/hail continued to pelt my thin tent, with me already shivering inside. I was up against a very serious problem.

Then I recalled that while sitting atop the pass earlier I had spotted a cluster of expedition tents that were probably only a kilometre or two away. I decided I would have to find them now.

I pulled on my wet track pants and jacket over my cosy layers, and forced my feet back into my shoes, which were already starting to freeze. With my headlamp on the highest beam, I made a dash for it.

I ran with surprising lightness of foot over the slippery rocks and boulders that populated the bottom of the valley, climbing up a steep slope that eventually led me to the path

---

*It turns out they don't work at altitude.

18

towards the tents. In the darkness, the beam from my light only lit up the flurries falling in front of me, and I had to keep wiping the snowflakes from my lashes so I could see. In only a few minutes I was at the little camp, panting and out of breath.

'Hello?' I tentatively called out, standing in the middle of three tents that were pitched in a cluster. It was only 8pm, but given the weather everyone had shut their doors and gone inside. Thankfully, a German accent answered back.

Grateful that the only other residents of the valley that night spoke English, I explained my sad situation and within minutes had a lighter on loan, and an offer of biscuits, which I declined, while offering my profuse thanks.

'You have literally just saved my life!' – that may have been an exaggeration, but it didn't feel like it at the time.

I dashed back to my campsite, this time acknowledging just how treacherous the rocky path was in the snowy night. My tent was already covered in about an inch of snow, and I wondered how much the small structure could take. I brushed it off, hoping I wouldn't have to get outside again later. I dove inside, trying not to take too much snow in with me, and renewed my vow to definitely not go out of the tent *again*: it really was not a night to be messing around outside.

With a working lighter, I had boiling water in a few minutes. I poured half of it into my instant chilli, which I had brought from home as a 'treat' before the diet of noodles took over, and half into my 500ml Nalgene bottle which I placed between my frozen feet. I had gone from desperation to heaven in just a few minutes, thanks to the German mountaineers. I will be thankful for them for the rest of my life, but I'll also never forget that I was incredibly lucky that anyone was there at all.

With a warm tent and full belly, I lay down to try to sleep. It was still early, but I had hoped that I would be tired enough from the day's exertions. The silence of the night was occasionally broken by the thunderous roll of landslides on the other side of the lake, less than 100m away from me. The noise of the rocks avalanching down the slope and then crashing into the lake was impressive, and I became irrationally nervous at the sound of each one. Although the slopes were much steeper on the side where the landslides were happening, I still felt that it wasn't impossible that one would happen on my side. And my tent was pitched right next to the water – at the bottom of any potential avalanche. I tried to remember what the mountainside looked like directly behind my tent, and assess in my mind the potential hazard.

At this point my internal dialogue was going something like this:

So the storm-proof matches don't work, and now I'm going to be buried in a landslide and never found. I've already been lost once, and I'll most likely be lost again. I am remarkably incapable.

I have no business being here.

This. Is. Absurd.

Despite the heavy exhaustion, I had a very restless night between my anxious brain and the incredible cold. Every couple of hours I would wake shivering, and once again boil the water in my Nalgene to warm me up, tapping the sides of my tent to throw off the snow while I waited. The fresh warm bottle at my feet would calm me down again, and I would buy another hour or so of sleep.

By the third time I leaned out of the tent to light my stove, the snow had stopped falling, and to my pure delight the sky had cleared to reveal dazzling stars. Far away from any big cities that could cause light pollution, and at a high altitude that made me feel like I could reach out and grab them, the bright display of the galaxy above wiped the slate clean on the awful night I was having. I gazed up smiling at the stars for a few brief moments, before acknowledging the frigid cold and diving back into my sleeping bag to wait for the water to boil.

MANAGEABLE BITES

Plodding along the lake shore of Issyk-Kul, a change in route I had made after a combination of a scary weather system and my undeniable altitude struggles, the idea had sprung into my mind to set the dates for my milestones – knowing when I expected to celebrate the halfway mark in Naryn, and estimating the time of my finish in Osh, would help me assess if I was on track or not. I had knocked off 30km during the morning's run, so I took a swimming break for lunch. Issyk-Kul is perhaps the best lake I have ever swum in, the water cool and clear, the saline element helping a weakened runner to float a little – so I needed no convincing to take frequent bathing breaks. After a cool-down in the lake, I sat on the rocky beach and took out my notepad where I had already scribbled notes about each stage, including approximate distances and speculative difficulty levels. I now wrote estimated dates on the top of each stage, guessing when I expected to be in each town I would pass. I went through the dates on the calendar, noting the passing of events – birthdays and dinners with friends that I had always known I would miss – but now felt that longing. The guilt at missing these people sank my heart a little lower in my chest. I was writing dates that were in late September – a whole flip of the calendar away. I could hardly imagine that a month from now I might *still* be wearing this same sweaty t-shirt, stretching out these stiffening hips and eating cereal bars that got smooshed and melted in my backpack. The idea of running through to mid-September suddenly overwhelmed me. I felt anxious, and doubts clouded my mind – *could I really sustain this for that long?* I missed home more than ever at realizing how long it would be before I saw anyone I knew again. This was all such a foolish idea!

I stayed on the beach for a while feeling terrible about everything, and then eventually decided that I might spend the rest of my life lying there and crying about how hard my self-inflicted challenge was going to be if I didn't suck it up and get moving. Every kilometre I could get out of the way was a kilometre closer to home, and that was a very encouraging thought. I put my running kit back on, and started running again with a fresh determination.

Never again have I looked so far into the future when it comes to Hard Things. Whether it's running across Kyrgyzstan, coping through a pandemic, finishing a project or whatever you're going through: the key is always to take manageable bites. Don't think about the next bit until you're there. From then on, I only ever focused on the 'stage' of the run I was on – marked by resupply towns. I had eight stages planned out, and I was only on the second one. After that, I thought of nothing but arriving at the end of Stage 2. When and if I finished the stage, I would recover, reflect and reset. Then, and only then, would I even begin to acknowledge Stage 3.

That's how you eat an elephant, or something like that.

INTO THE INTERIOR

My lungs began to open and adapt to the altitude; my legs were settling into the routine of running all day with the extra weight of a pack, and I finally turned south towards the interior, deep into the Tien Shan. I was glad to leave behind the relatively populated world of the lake shore, but heading away from the welcoming waters of Issyk-Kul and the endless summer heat, up towards the imposing white-capped mountains and their stormy weather, took a moment of courage. I completed that leg of the journey in Bokonbaevo, where a small tourism office helped me to find a 'home stay', a clever system that allows women to earn some money by renting out their spare rooms and cooking for guests who come through town. These visits were great insights into life for rural Kyrgyz women, and I preferred the time in real homes over hotel stays whenever I had these chances.

I only stayed one night, not feeling the need to delay any more – the memory of how far I still had to travel was heavy on my shoulders, and I knew I wouldn't really feel better until I got more mileage behind me. In the morning, I returned to the tourism office to fill them in on my plans, as I had promised the day before. Ulvik, the manager, had suggested he could call ahead to the next town and help me out.

'I reckon three or four days, so let's say three to be safe,' I told Ulvik. He tried unsuccessfully to suppress a giggle. Looking me up and down in a slow, judgemental way, he shook his head and responded, 'Umm . . . no. It takes five – well, actually, for *you*, I would say six days to reach Kochkor.'

Smiling sweetly, suppressing my instinctive rage, I assured Ulvik that I was fast, and I would be there in three to four days. He laughed harder now.

'It's really hard. You will see. It will take you six days. You will see!'

I was beginning to see a pattern in these reactions, and over the course of the journey, I simply stopped telling many people what my real plans were, just for the sake of avoiding this repetitive conversation.

By now my feet were in excruciating pain. I had never run so far in the space of a week, and I felt the added weight of my backpack, not to mention the harder tarmac miles on the lake shore, more in the soles of my feet than anywhere else. As I ran out of town on the brief stretch of tarmac, already hot from the morning sun, I whimpered and hoped that I would be on a soft mountain trail soon. I felt my feet swell and throb inside my trail shoes, and spent most of the day keeping an eye open for any stream that I could briefly take my shoes off and soak my feet in. The clear alpine water was like an ice bath for swollen feet, and usually bought me 30 minutes with minimal pain before they began to throb again.

Soon I was climbing steeply into the mountains, following

a very rough track of loose rocks. My feet rolled backwards over large pebbles, sometimes forcing me to treadmill, running in place and not managing to propel forwards, thanks to the loose ground. It felt a lot like running in sand. My quads screamed; I was slowed to a walk, and even then taking plenty of breaks. The loose surface was also a nightmare for my feet, and by the end of the day the clusters of small blisters already there had converged into mega blisters. Eventually, thankfully, I reached the top of the climb and the terrain – for the most part – levelled out: I had made it up to a *jailoo*.

Jailoos are high summer pastures, where hardy shepherds move with their herds for the limited summer months to benefit from boundless grazing before snow blocks the mountains off once more. They are open, green and totally free, in every sense of the word. As I crested the climb and caught my first glimpse of one, I marvelled at what lay before me: a heavenly land of short grass, glittering streams and undulating gradients. Essentially, trail-running paradise. Although the long day had me running tired, the sight of the jailoo uplifted me with a second wind.

As I ran straight through the middle of the jailoo, I felt spectacularly alone, yet comfortable in that solitude. Somehow, though, shepherds had spotted me, and as I passed through the extensive domain of one and then the next, a horse-mounted herdsman would appear to wave hello and ensure that I was okay – they had been alarmed to see me running, and wanted to ensure it wasn't *from* anything.

I set up my tent in the open grassy plain, next to a small spring which I cooled my throbbing red feet in. In this time, I was paid two separate visits by shepherds who were both so far away that I couldn't see their yurts, yet they each saw me. I got the impression that they had been aware of my presence all day, but had seen no reason to bother me until now. Seeing that I intended to camp, they came over to voice their concerns about me sleeping alone – exposed to the wolves. They were also very curious about my tiny tent, perplexed that I could sleep in such a flimsy structure, and had a proverbial kick of the tyres around my kit. I asked each of them if it was okay for me to camp where I was, not wanting to intrude on anyone's territory. They were both enthusiastically positive that I could camp and roam wherever I wished, but remained extremely worried about the wolves as well as the cold, and offered their hospitality. With my camp already set up and their respective yurts about 5km away, I wasn't able to move, but promised I would visit in the morning, which I did.

Of course, these conversations, like most I had been having in the country, were had through a hilarious combination of charades and Russian – the latter of which I knew about eight words in.

Not wanting to insult, but equally not wanting to climb up the sides of the mountains to his yurt, I invited the second shepherd, Oshkar, for coffee, as it was all I really had to offer (mental note: buy tea in the next village!). I boiled him some sweet Nescafe, but he still asked for more sugar, which I sadly did not have. We sat by the tent and managed with surprising success to communicate about his family and lifestyle and my adventure. Nearly 60 years old, Oshkar was spending this summer at the jailoo working with only his wife, as all of his kids were now in Bishkek, nearly a day's drive away. It was clear that although he was sad that they wouldn't be with him this year to help, he was proud of them for getting an education and starting jobs in the big city. Oshkar was enthusiastic about my adventure when I showed him the map, and although he knew of all the places (and helped me to pronounce them better), he had not visited anywhere outside of his small region. He had spent every summer since he was a baby at the same spot on the jailoo where his family herded their livestock, and every winter in the village of Bokonbaevo at lower elevation.

As the sun lowered, Oshkar returned to his yurt and left me to bundle up as the temperature plummeted. The wind was picking up as well, and I worried that there would be another big storm in the night. I piled up my backpack and spare items on the left side of the tent to keep it upright against the battering wind that was coming from that direction. The storm didn't die down until nearly dawn, yet I managed to have the best sleep I had had so far inside my tiny red and grey home. Perhaps it was the beauty of the jailoo, or the comfort of knowing that the friendly shepherds were nearby, or simply the pure exhaustion of over a week on the road, but I slept soundly and comfortably through the cold, raining and windy night.

My morning run along the middle of the jailoo would go down as one of my favourite running memories of all time. It was the perfect combination of a pleasant morning with clear skies, the beauty and silence of nature, and easy running thanks to the naturally short grass and simple navigation: the spiny ridges of mountains on either side of me pointed me straight onwards, following the path of least resistance as if through a funnel. Overhead, hunting golden eagles swirled, their cries providing the only other sound to remind me that the place was real, and not a dream.

By mid-morning, and far too soon, I reached the end of the jailoo and the beginning of the downhill run. From the top of the descent I could just see Kochkor, my next supply stop, in the distance. It seemed entirely feasible that I would make it before nightfall, finishing this stage in just three days – more than a day faster than I had planned.

The steep descent took me towards the dusty valley floor. My heels skidded down the powdery, red-dirt trail, loose rocks occasionally flying up and bouncing uncomfortably off my ankles. The vegetation had changed completely from alpine to a drier, sparser, almost desert-like ecosystem. Crickets flew over the path and were teeming in the bushes next to it, often colliding with my legs as I continued my fast descent. It seemed odd to be so dry after being so close to the snow-capped mountains in a heavy storm only hours earlier.

My trail widened into a dirt double track and, as the temperature rose with every drop in elevation, I really did feel like I was running into a desert. From the hilltops looking across the dry valleys, I could always spot villages by the sudden and remarkable presence of greenery where trees were planted around houses and irrigation channels. I was learning this as a navigational tactic in order to spot towns and, most importantly, running water from afar. As a larger town in Kyrgyzstan, the view of Kochkor from more than 10km away was of a great patch of green in the middle of a red dust bowl, nestled low inside the Tien Shan.

When I hit the bottom of my downhill run and the track flattened out, I was startled out of my skin at the roar of an engine behind me – I hadn't seen a car in three tranquil days. I leaped off the path to let the rusty farm vehicle lumber past me, waving at the family inside and trying to disguise my startle. In fairness, they were probably feeling the same at the sight of me on their remote commute.

It was early afternoon when I strolled into the small but lively town of Kochkor. It had a bit of a Central Asia meets Wild West feel to it, and the relative bustle was alarming after my jailoo holiday. The main central street was abuzz with *marshrutkas* – shared taxis – shouting destinations and numbers of seats left in the cars, vans coming and going, and street vendors selling back-to-school supplies. I wasted no time in heading straight for the most available-looking restaurant, regaining humanity bite by bite. I also managed to access wifi, but then sat staring at my phone wondering what to do with it. As the various apps on my screen lit up with red dots indicating the number of messages and notifications needing my attention, my eyes glazed over and I put my phone back away, not acknowledging any of them.

STAGE 4

After taking a full rest day in Kochkor, I packed a hefty bag, prepared for the fourth and longest stage of the run. I dropped in to say goodbye to the friendly young woman working in the

Kochkor tourism office, who in a lowered tone asked again about my plans.

'I'm worried about you. You have to be careful . . . there are some bad people out there.'

The fear painted on her face was familiar to me – I've seen it on many faces in all parts of the world – but it sank in regardless. As I jogged along the dusty road out of town, I reflected on what truly bothered me about it. Was I worried about my safety? Not really. Kyrgyzstan was a safe and welcoming place. Sure, there are bad people everywhere, and no country is exempt from the worst aspects of humanity, but as a female runner, that is a burden I carry with me on every run I ever go on, regardless of how safe and welcoming the place is. I think what bothered me about her warning was how affected *she* was. A recent grad, she was just a young woman who was held back in all the choices she made in her daily life due to the 'bad people out there', as she put it. No doubt an echo of what her family, teachers and even local police had drilled into her throughout her life. It saddens me to know that even in a country where, as a woman, I felt more safe than usual, the local girls carry the same burden. They are still held back by this universal truth. The truth that the world is not a totally safe place – and it's a woman's responsibility and burden to keep herself protected from it.

I had merrily blasted through my late teens and early twenties travelling far and wide, backpacking and bike touring through as many countries as I could get to. I was aware of the 'danger' as much as I had ever been, but the gender factor was something I just *accepted*. I hadn't dwelled on it yet. But, year on year, I've become more aware of the different lives my male peers are living. The further we get from childhood, the more apparent it is to me that we have grown up to different realities – two versions of the experience of freedom on this planet, one for each gender.

I felt helpless receiving a warning from a younger generation, knowing that the cycle was far from being broken.

I spent most of the day stuck running on the side of the road, due to the sprawling farmland and communities around Kochkor. The occupants of many of the passing vehicles – open farm trucks carrying a handful of labourers, marshrutkas filled to the roof with passengers well beyond their seatbelt capacity, and of course more grumbling Ladas with entire families crammed in – would stare, open mouthed, at the spectacle of me. I hated being looked at, and after a few hours lost my resilience to it, pulling my hat down over my eyes and trying not to receive the glances. I knew they weren't sinister, but there was nothing comfortable about being gaped at so much. The only passing vehicles whose occupants weren't blatantly staring at me pulled over to offer me a lift, which turned out to be worse: I was in a very quitting mood. Something about my time in Kochkor and the resounding *no-it-can't-be-done* that I heard from everyone I engaged with, in addition to a day of being stared at (I really like my privacy), had bothered me, and the offers of a free ride up the road became far more tempting than I had ever expected them to be.

In the afternoon it started to rain, and I pulled my hood tight over my face, leaving only my eyes and nose exposed; I put a podcast on through my headphones, effectively shutting the road out. I decided that what I needed now was to just *get this section done* and get myself off the Road of Negativity, as I had now dubbed it.

The time finally came, late in the afternoon, when I had passed all of the sprawling Kochkor farms and could turn off the road and head once more into the wilderness. I had refused seven offers of a free ride in an array of rickety vehicles, especially once the afternoon thunderstorm started and passing motorists expressed deep concern and pity for me, not to mention many reminders that what I was doing *could not be done*.

I dove off the unpaved road, running excitedly downhill towards a small river that I would have to cross in order to make it to the great wide open. Behind me was the road, with plumes of black engine exhaust and the occasional speeding lorry; ahead of me loomed new mountains. In the rain I couldn't see very far ahead, but all that I could see was green. Clean, natural, peaceful green. I was happy again.

In the morning I woke to a battered body. Tight hips, fatigued calves, a twitched hamstring and an aching shoulder. I lay staring at the roof of my tent, willing the pain to disappear. The long day on the pavement heading out of Kochkor had clearly taken its toll. I went through my morning routine of porridge, coffee, stretching, reviewing my route for the day and then packing more slowly than usual, moving so stiffly it was like my muscles had been mixed with glue.

I followed the contours of the foothills to make an easy run around the rolling green hills that stood between me and my next big climb. I planned to start the climb by midday, assuming I would have an easy morning. The sky was clear blue and the mountains beyond the foothills beckoned. It was a beautiful place, and I felt at incredible ease.

After crossing the jailoo with its short grass and hitting the edge of the hills, I joined a goat track that led in the direction I wanted to go. Planning this trip from Scotland, I had been worried about finding trails and routes, as there was almost no information available online, and I was delighted to learn each day that route planning was relatively easy – there was almost always a goat or horse track to follow. I had been progressively getting more confident at navigating, and most days I found great trails stamped out by hooves.

I twisted through small valleys between the lumpy green hills, and then turned briefly downhill towards a small river, the river that led to the larger river that would be my main navigation source to take me to the afternoon's planned mountain pass.

Gradually, so gradually it was almost imperceptible, the path began to vanish under overgrowth. Now and then I would rediscover my goat track, only for it to be swallowed by dense and prickly vegetation again. I had now been walking for a while, not finding any ground accessible enough to run. I used my poles to push thistles out of my way so my bare legs could pass without bloodshed. The track wound along the side of a steep crag, bringing me finally down to the swift-flowing river.

Fuck.

The goat track continued, but it wasn't a great route. I dug out my GPS and discovered that I had less than 2km to travel like this, so decided to stick to my guns and get through the thistly path. To turn around now would mean a few hours of uphill on the awful path that I had just come down, and I would probably lose most of the day. I could persevere, so I decided to.

The goat track then led to a landslide of loose shale rocks. The path was swept away, beneath, but the landslide was only about 10m across. Again, I didn't have far to go, so I decided to go for it.

Daintily, I picked my way along the landslide. Rocks thundered down to the river behind me, and the entire slide loosened. I thought about what would happen if I broke an ankle now. I would have to call for rescue, and I was not in an easily accessible place – again remembering that there wasn't a local rescue team to start with.

Slowly and painfully I dragged my way through thistly brush. The grass was waist height, and my shins were constantly ripped by thorns. I was not enjoying it *at all*.

Again, I checked my GPS and confirmed that I did not have far to go before the river below me merged with the main river, where the terrain opened up and it would be smooth sailing.

Just get this over with.

Another landslide. This time with great big rocks, unlike the loose shale one previously. This wasn't just a place to break an ankle, this was good enough for a femur. Once I slipped and my entire left leg dangled in a hole between rocks – if any of the rocks had moved at that moment, I might well have been trapped beneath them. This was no longer just 'not fun'; this was bad. As I picked my way across the bigger landslide, I whimpered each time I heard the grumbling of shifting boulders. I was careful not to scream, however, noting the fragility of the landslide and the serious potential for danger. Looking upwards, I knew I couldn't waste time standing underneath this precarious slide.

When I made it to the other side, jumping off a car-sized boulder into the thorny grass, I realized I had reached The Point of No Return.

Double fuck.

The Point of No Return is a serious marker. It means that you *know with absolute certainty that going back will be unsafe.* A bone-chilling low rumble of falling rocks confirmed it: the landslides could not be traversed again today. The risk far outweighed anything. Once you declare that this is The Point of No Return, you have to stick to it.

So on I trudged through the thorny grass. I had to whack my way through some dry trees with low branches, crawling under some and climbing over others. It was hard going, but I refused to stop for a rest: I could not imagine feeling calm until I joined the big river. I hated this valley, and I wanted out now.

Another small landslide. This time I decided to walk around it by jumping into the river, where I hoped I wouldn't set off more falls. Even staying close to the edge I was still thigh deep in frigid rapids, and the water was rushing fast in the middle. I held onto the bank with my left hand, while balancing with a pole in my right. There was no room for error with a landslide above me and a rapid below.

The next curve of the valley, painfully close to the big river, revealed my true enemy: it was now a canyon.

Triple fuck.

The sides of the valley became perfectly vertical on either side of the rushing water, which became narrower and even more rapid between the sheer rock faces. I could not continue forwards.

But I had already promised that I would not go back.

Can't go forwards; can't go back. That leaves only up or down.

Down would be the rushing river. I considered this option logically: I had learned how to float downstream safely before, and it was a possibility. I would simply need to waterproof anything that wasn't (and most things were), unstrap my bag and let the river take me. I looked at the rapids. I looked at the rocks jutting out in opportune locations. I decided that the risk of death was fairly high, but not certain. Call it Option A.

Option B was up. Just climb upwards and then walk along the ridge above to reach the big river. All I had to do was climb. I looked around for the least steep ascent, which was only slightly behind where I was standing. I decided that the risk of death was much less if I climbed, so that's what I picked. No time to lose – wanting to get in motion before my bubbling fear took over my body completely, I set to it.

Using my poles and jabbing my toes into the loose rocky ground, I made fast progress up nearly half of the climb. But that is when things got far more vertical than I had assessed from the valley floor. Vegetation was scarce and the soil was bone dry – it was essentially a steep slope of loose gravel. To stand still meant to slowly drift back down the hill, miniature slides of scree pooling around my shoes and burying me to the ankles, so there was no place to stop and catch my breath – or plan my next moves. I just had to keep going. I zigzagged on the hill, going from rare bush to tree or, even better, a boulder – places that I could get a comfortable hold and climb upwards from, knowing that the tree or bush would catch my fall and hopefully prevent me from tumbling the entire way down to the small river, which was now *very* small below me. *Don't look down* . . . I repeated to myself, trying to keep from getting nervous. I am afflicted with very shaky legs when I get nervous, and shaky legs are not surviving legs when one is facing a last-option rock climb. I crawled with my hands to a bush, where I found that it was indeed a thorn bush. Still, thorns hurt less than a 400m free-fall, and I had no choice but to grab the branches with my hands and pull myself up and into the bush, where I could get more footing than on the loose slope. Just so you know, being stabbed by hundreds of thorns at once when you're pumping with adrenaline still feels exactly like being stabbed by hundreds of thorns at once. I used the respite to fold away my poles, and hang my GPS with its SOS button around my neck.

My next destination was a tree, just three body lengths above me. I crawled, keeping the thorn bush directly below me in case I fell. With every step my feet sank backwards, and my hands did little more than offer balance with nothing to grip onto. Scree shifted loudly as I scrambled, and I had to move fast but extremely precisely to stay on the hill and continue moving upwards. The only sounds I could hear were the cascades of small rocks with every step I took. When the tree was within reach, I launched for a branch. In a moment my heart stopped: the entire trunk, the size of my leg, lifted effortlessly out of the ground. The tree was long since dead and dried up, and I now held most of it in my hand, while barely hanging on to the hill with my other hand and feet. About to lose my balance, I put the branch to one side and dropped it, then waited an eternity for the splash in the river at the bottom – the length of time it would take to free-fall from my current height. *I am going to die.*

Quickly and breathlessly I scrambled onwards, determined to get the climb over with. I considered briefly dropping my pack, then decided we weren't quite there yet, but might be soon. I reached the large boulder overhang, and stopped finally for a moment. And then the boulder shuddered. I leaped forwards, with the last push of my foot loosening the large rock completely. There was no safe ground to trust. I was now climbing with my hands, gripping the vertical rock face and pulling myself up. I slipped, and my backpack wedged me between two rocks, stopping my fall.

I am going to die.

They say your life flashes before your eyes. That's not what happened to me. My *future* played out in my mind. I thought about my family and my friends. People I wanted to spend more time with. People I wanted to get to know better. Future expeditions I had dreamed of. Places I had yet to see. I would never get married. I would never be old. I would never own that boat I already have the name for. I would lose all those things – and it would be my fault.

Here I stopped my mind from descending into the process of digesting all of *my* mistakes that had led me to this ledge. This place where any mistake would literally end my life. There would be a time when I would have to face my mistakes, but while I was literally dangling in the air and fighting for my life was not the time.

Tears rushed down my face as I dug my fingernails into the rock, repeating out loud *I can't die today* and, inch by inch, kept pulling myself upwards.

It's one of those moments when time stands still. To this day, I have no idea how long I was on that climb for. It felt like one or two hours, but for all I know it might have been 20 minutes. Images swirled in front of my eyes of the future I never knew I dreamed of. It's incredible how your future starts to look when you *really* think you could lose the chance any second. I have never before, and never since, experienced these aspirations so vividly.

Breathe, breathe, breathe, I can't die today, breathe . . .

I crawled and clawed at the earth and somehow, eventually, when all hope truly felt lost, I pulled myself over the ledge and stood on level ground.

I was safe.

What happened next was unexpected. In an instant, the adrenaline that had just allowed me to pull my body and pack up that climb disappeared, and suddenly I was on the ground crying harder than I'm sure I ever have in my adult life (to date). Full-on, can't-breathe, ugly crying. The pure drama of the event flooded out of my eyes, and I heard myself apologizing repeatedly to my mother.

How could I have let things go this wrong?

Eventually, my tears were cried, and although I had absolutely decided only minutes ago that if I survived I was going back to the road and finding a lift to the nearest hotel and cold beer – and then a taxi to the airport – I somehow stood up, dusted myself off, fixed my ponytail and followed a gentle slope down to the big river. Within minutes, I was crossing it.

The cold but clear water washed away the dirt from the Death Slope that was clinging to my shallow cuts from the Thorn Valley. After crossing the river, I pulled myself up the opposite bank and decided I should definitely have a proper break. I hadn't eaten all day and had run out of water a long time ago. I filled my water bladder from the clear stream and enjoyed some melted cereal bars. In Kochkor I had taken the bars I purchased out of their individual wrappers in advance, and placed them in a single sandwich bag, where they had now melted into one oaty glob of carbohydrate. I broke off a chunk and lay on the grass by the river's edge, letting my feet dangle in the water.

I breathed deeply. I looked up at the clear blue sky, wondering at the severity of my recent situation on such a perfect day. Wild horses grazed nearby, entirely indifferent to my presence or my emotional state. By the glittering river on the edge of the gentle green jailoo, my near-death experience was already a world away. I decided against the trip back to the road to find a hotel and a beer. I had been told too many times that I couldn't do this expedition, and I wasn't willing to let them be right about it just yet. I was still breathing.

I could see the clear route ahead to the mountain pass that I was aiming for, and although I was now several hours behind my plan for the day, I decided I might as well go for it, even if it meant camping partway up. It was important to keep moving. My body was still visibly shaking, and I was prone to spontaneous bursts of tears at flashbacks to the terror of the ledge I had just dangled from.

So I picked myself up, put the experiences of the day inside a bottle, closed the lid tight and got back to the business of running across Kyrgyzstan.

TRAIL MAGIC

Partway through my climb, two young nomad boys ran from their yurt to greet me. They decided to run up the hill with me, and I was grateful for the company. The boys were interested in everything I had, asking, '*Shto eto?*' – 'What's that?' – and pointing at every item. One of them had a small whistle, which he blasted happily. I replied with a blow of my whistle, part of my chest strap on my buckle. We were all three alarmed at its sheer noise. I found it interesting that I had not once remembered that whistle was there when I was having a near-death encounter. The bigger of the boys shouted, 'Coca Cola!', pointing at the bottle in my side strap that I had kept as a spare water collector. I explained that there was no Coke to be had, only water mixed with electrolytes. I had just mixed it, feeling deep dehydration after my traumatizing rock climb. I then watched the two boys guzzle it all down, knowing I had nowhere to collect water for a few more hours.

After demolishing my rehydration, the boys smiled and waved, returning to their yurt downhill.

Onwards and upwards, I climbed closer and closer to the sky until I reached the top of the pass, just under 4,000m above the sea. I stopped to enjoy the moment, and only briefly reflect on the day that had passed. I cried again, and decided I

41

was not ready to digest the catastrophe just yet. The sun was lowering and I had a long way down to run to find a flat place to sleep.

I tumbled easily down the pass, heading towards the magnificent Song Kol, a high-altitude lake only accessible in the height of summer. It is famous not just for its altitude and isolation, but for the shepherds who populate its nearly 80km of shoreline for the summer. I had been looking forward to my arrival at Song Kol for months, although it hardly felt like a celebratory evening.

As I strolled up to the lake shores to dip my toes, dusk was set and I had little time to find my camping spot. At the sound of a whistle, I turned to find a shepherd across the jailoo waving his arms and beckoning me over. Who was I to argue? It was probably best that I stop making my own decisions, considering how that was going so far. So I jogged over to meet Bakytbek, who quickly ushered me into his family yurt. It was getting cold fast, and I clearly needed to be inside.

Bakytbek's wife, Ruslan, instructed me to sit down at the low table in the middle of the round yurt. I took my shoes off, pointing at the mud I had picked up, and also pulled on my tuque and puffy jacket for warmth. I was immediately given bread with a thick, delicious cream to dip it in. Ruslan put the kettle on, pointing at my blue lips, and offered me sweet tea along with *kymus* – the local fermented milk, sour and frothy. I was grateful that I was offered sugar to stir into it, which helped me to maintain a thankful face as I sipped it.

It was now completely dark outside, and the family members trickled in from a day with the horses and sheep they

42

brought to the lake every summer to graze freely. I helped Bakytbek prepare dinner, peeling vegetables and stirring the huge wok-shaped pan suspended over a dung-fuelled fire. The fire warmed the yurt and the family's welcome warmed my soul. I couldn't have asked for a better way to spend an evening after a traumatic day, although there were some grumbling complaints about my potato-peeling skills with the small dull knife. Bakytbek pulled a pillowcase out of the corner of the yurt where the family's very minimal 'stuff' was kept, and from the pillowcase selected a leg of sheep that had been salted and dried, as they had no electricity and ate only the meat of animals that they killed themselves.

When our dish of *lagman* – a stew of meat, vegetables and noodles – was ready, the family of six-plus-Jenny sat cross-legged around the small table, where Bakytbek took control of serving. Ruslan and I were given plates, which he loaded with food, while the rest of the men just ate from the communal dish directly with their forks. Ruslan constantly topped up the tea, and the family attempted to keep me in the loop of the cheerful chat through Bakytbek's Russian language skills.

At the end of the meal, Bakytbek led us in the *omin,* where simultaneously all diners hold their hands up, palms covering the face, and then lower the hands in a sort of 'shutting down' motion, giving thanks to God. It was the first time I had participated genuinely in a prayer after dinner.

I helped Ruslan to clean up, which was fairly easy given the limited amount of dishes used by the one-pan meal. Meanwhile the men put the table on its side in the back of the yurt and replaced it with sleeping mats for all six in a row. I was given one on the end, next to Ruslan, and great fuss was taken to ensure that I would be warm enough under layers of wool-embroidered blankets. That night, I have never felt so utterly cosy, safe in the companionship of this family with whom I could hardly exchange a single word in their native tongue, nor them in mine. Within half an hour of our *omin*, the family was fast asleep, and soon enough so was I.

I'm not a hugely spiritual person, but I am a great believer that the universe provides in the moments when you need it the most. That night, I definitely would have spent the evening crying in my tiny tent, reliving the terror of nearly falling to my death and recounting the mistakes that I had made to put myself in that position. I probably would have gone down such a spiral of poor self-esteem and low confidence that I could have talked myself out of finishing the trip. And I most certainly would have been incredibly cold – with the lingering dung stove still lit when we fell asleep, and the shared warmth of six bodies, I never noticed until I emerged in the morning that the temperature had been below freezing that night.

Thanks to the pure kindness of strangers, I never went through that emotional crisis and I never shivered once. Instead I slept like a log, and woke ready to continue a journey that now felt far more important to me – more important now that I knew the heart of the peoples whose land I was crossing. It was an honour to be there as a guest of the Kyrgyz nomads and, no matter what the cities brought, I knew I would always be in good hands in the mountains.

I had picked Kyrgyzstan because I wanted to get to know a mountain range different from those I had already visited, and to find out if I would still get that feeling of being home that I always get in any alpine environment. The nomads of the Tien Shen, on every interaction I had with them, showed me that it is indeed a universal truth that mountain people look out for one another.

HALFWAY

I needed to make an early start for the ambitious mileage I had planned for the day, but not without Bakytbek practically force-feeding me two more brimming mugs of *kymus*. Ruslan couldn't get up to see me go, due a headache that she often seemed to suffer from during the weather changes – it was the first frost of the fall. I left her with my supply of paracetamol, in addition to my profuse thanks for their hospitality. I gave Bakytbek some *som* to cover them feeding a very, very hungry traveller and help them get through the season. The communist regime did everything it could to change Kyrgyzstan's economy away from nomadic herding, and the devastation is still palpable 20 years later. I continue to be impressed by Bakytbek's perseverance to support his family through a way of life that he both loves and believes in, and I continue to feel frustrated that I couldn't do more for them than offer some of the cash I had. They will never know just how much they did for me – it was so much more than giving me a meal and a warm, safe place to sleep.

I waved goodbye to my new family, ruffled the ears of the dogs, who had changed their minds overnight to decide that they both trusted me and liked me, and I set off at a run once more. The colours of the lake changed as clouds moved over the sun, oozing from sapphire blue to emerald green to pale jade in seconds. It was an almost mystical place: sitting at such a high altitude, one could imagine it was a lake built in heaven.

I followed the lake shore closely, using goat tracks and keeping up a surprisingly efficient run throughout the morning. I ran as if I had a new lease on life and fresh air in my lungs. I saw a large falcon take off from a perch just metres away from me, literally feeling the rush of the wind from her massive wings. I embraced the uphill climbs and exhilarated at the short blasts downwards.

But most importantly, I had a significant heart-to-heart with myself. I decided that I didn't need this to be the maddest and baddest adventure. I didn't need to take the wildest routes available. I was *running across Kyrgyzstan,* for goodness' sake. There was a time not too long ago when I thought I couldn't possibly run 10km. There was equally a time when I thought women travelling solo in the developing world was some sort of problem. And here I was. I don't need to risk anything, I said to myself. I just need to cross the country safely. I just need to complete the expedition I set out to do. I just need to make it. I just need to *chill.*

The adventure world worships heroes who complete first or fastest journeys, a hangover from a colonial past of global discovery, when European men pushed into the most (deemed) inhospitable corners of the globe, expanding human potential as they went. Today, most of the world has been thoroughly discovered, but we still look to adventurers who can break records. I'll admit I was excited that I had a crack at one – I would be the first known person to ever run across Kyrgyzstan.

It had never been my motivation, but when I realized that I might claim that title, my ego shone to it. But that morning, the 'adventure industry', located a world away from where I was, seemed utterly silly. Hundreds of people could run solo across Kyrgyzstan, and they would come home with hundreds of different stories, experiences and lessons. That entire scene stopped mattering to me that morning, and I'm happy to say I still feel the same way about it.

Adventure does not need to be measured. It just needs to be experienced.

Filled up on gratitude for life, limbs and liberty, I ran in a practically dancing fashion around the lake shore, enjoying myself immensely. It was definitely the most positive I had felt at any point on the trip so far, and probably the most positive I have *ever* felt while running. At one point I caught myself smiling, like a lunatic.

I rallied to put in a large day of running, determined to keep my legs moving and my mind silent. The following morning, I woke early thanks to the extreme cold, a rough reminder that summer was ending, and unzipped my tent to reveal *home.* I looked outside to the alpine environment and felt almost certain that I had awoken in the Rockies. Dark fir trees carpeted the grey mountainside, and the clear mountain spring I had pitched my tent next to danced loudly over the rocks as it descended to the valley. As I sat in my tent eating my porridge and drinking my coffee, I thought of my first camping experiences near Banff in Canada, and how many mornings I had woken shivering in a sleeping bag to a view like this. After packing up I continued the downhill run I had begun the previous afternoon, still convinced that I was going to be in Banff village any minute. I even planned out what to order from my favourite cafe – grilled vegetable pita and a chai latte, which I would enjoy in the seat by the window. Although I hadn't been back to the place I grew up in a few years, it was so vivid in that moment.

It was nearly midday before an old army jeep came tumbling towards me and broke the illusion. I was definitely still in Central Asia. In a flash I was homesick, but as the cheerful young men in the front seat waved enthusiastically, in another flash I was glad to be in Kyrgyzstan again.

Shortly after, I stopped to check my GPS tracker, whose accuracy I wasn't quite sure of, but I didn't care: the screen read 500.1km. I had reached my halfway point. In just over two weeks, I had *finally* run the first 500km. All alone in the wilderness, I danced a little jig.

Finally, *finally*, I was over that hill. I was on my way to the finish. I wasn't just starting out – I had made it *halfway*. I had proved myself (although it had come pretty close!) and I was going to make it. For the first time, I breathed in deeply and filled my lungs with confidence.

For the rest of the day, I ran happily downhill towards the Naryn River, which cuts through the middle of the country. After hours of downhill, I hit that river like a ton of bricks, the flat ground sending a jolt through my system. I crossed the bridge that took me across the water and onto the main road that followed it, leading to the city of Naryn. Completing that stage felt like a huge weight had been lifted. For the first time, I began to really believe in myself.

I followed the Naryn Valley, which seemed to harbour the heat of the sun in its low corridor between the tall peaks. Dragging my feet under the intense sun, I had already managed to drink all of my water by the time I passed through a tiny and remote village. I looked around and saw no obvious shop, but that was no surprise – they're often just run out of the side of someone's home, and with villages of fewer than 50 people and almost no outsiders coming through, there's no need to advertise. A group of children came running towards me, shouting, 'Hello!'; I asked, '*G-dya magasine?*' – where shop? – and to my delight I discovered that I had asked the boy who possessed the keys to the small cupboard on the side of a house that stood as the local store. They had only large bottles of sugary drinks and a few waters, so I bought one and thanked him for opening up just for my sake.

As I passed through the village, more swarms of children came out to run with me. They all stopped when we reached the imaginary outer perimeter and commenced my favourite game played in every village, called Last Hello. The rules are basically that the children will keep shouting 'Hello', and if I respond they will shout 'Hello' again. So the victor is she who says 'Hello' last. I always lose, but it's worth a giggle. The charm of the Kyrgyz children was one of the most dependable mood-boosters on the journey.

Throughout the afternoon, I battled an intense headwind that felt like going straight into a hair dryer in the summer heat. Many riverbeds were dry, and I had to begin rationing my water. I had felt I had an unquenchable thirst – the moment I got the chance to fill up, I would empty again. When late

afternoon set in, I was out of water once more. My map showed
a stream only 7km away, but a mountain pass stood between
me and it. Feeling I had no choice, and the pass looking small
from where I stood, I went for it. It turned out to have a few
false summits and, by the time I reached the freezing cold top,
the sun was nearly gone. I was cold, exhausted, but above all
wild with thirst. I needed water badly, not to mention I couldn't
boil my dinner without it, so soon I would be starving as well.

At the top of the pass, I stopped briefly to pull out my head
torch and gloves, the blasting wind freezing my bones. I
wasted no time getting to my descent, almost drooling with
excitement at reaching the river, which couldn't be too far now.
I soon met a winding gravel road, although passing vehicles
were very few and far between. While the road used
switchbacks down the mountainside, some horse trails B-
lining it straight down the middle were visible. I love downhill
running, so I adjusted the beam of my head torch to be able to
see a couple of steps in front, and went for it.

That night was the fastest average speed I recorded on the
whole trip. Unable to see very far, I just let my legs spin and
pick up the pace. The stars were beautiful and the night was
calm. I smiled as I ran, the childlike joy of sprinting downhill
in the dark distracting me from the anxiety of my intense thirst
and rumbling stomach. Soon I turned my headlamp off in
order to fully appreciate the light of the stars and the sliver of
moon that was visible. Nights in the mountains are truly
something spectacular.

Eventually the night was lit up by the headlights of a
transport truck, which slowed when the driver noticed my

bouncing reflective backpack in the bushes and pulled over with the offer of a lift. I explained that I couldn't take a lift, but was desperate for water. The three men in the truck rummaged frantically, eventually producing the last dredges of a very warm bottle of Coke. I immediately ignored all the rules girls are taught about accepting drinks from strangers in trucks in the middle of the night. The small remnants of warm, washback Coke were honestly the most disgusting thing I had ever drunk, but it bought me a little more time before I finally lost my mind to thirst.

When I hit the bottom of the mountain pass, now very late into the night, I raced towards the river. Ahead, I could see a sign marking it and a bridge. Surely, a full sign (there are never signs in Kyrgyzstan!) and a real bridge meant that this must be a big river! There must be so much water in it! Imagine all of that water! I surged forwards with my excitement to finally have some water, after running *over an entire mountain* without any.

I crossed the bridge and stared down at a bone-dry riverbed. I felt my heart drop all the way down to my shoes. I was completely and utterly screwed. With no ounce of energy left, I pitched my tent on the dry riverbed, as some sort of passive-aggressive and self-depriving protest to the promised water.

Inside my tent, I dug out the bread that I had purchased in Naryn and intended as a running snack; I tried to chew it with a dry mouth. It wasn't a real dinner, especially after a mega headwind and mountain-pass run, but it was just slightly better than nothing at all.

That night I had a difficult sleep. I was paranoid at the noises in the bushes, and dying for a drink of water. My head throbbed from dehydration, in rhythm with my feet that were still always in pain. I tossed and turned on my air mattress, the dry rocks of the riverbed rolling beneath me when I did. It was a long night.

A NEW LEAF

I woke early, finished with feeling sorry for myself and determined that I would solve my water problem. While packing my tent in the usual order that I now had down to a perfect system, I found a spider the size of my thumb (not including the legs) on the door of my tent. I'm not afraid of spiders, but I am respectful of small things that can kill big things, so I pretty much threw my tent into the bush hoping that it would shake off this uninvited guest.

Eventually, after a few dramatic tosses, it worked. Thank goodness, because Plan B was to abandon my tent for good.

In only 4km, I found water. Real, rushing, clear, perfect water. I jumped down the steep bank and ran towards the saviour, first inhaling unknown quantities through my filter. Once my initial thirst was quenched, I could go about filling my 3-litre bladder to be purified and boiling some water for my extra-large breakfast. I washed myself and my socks from the previous day, laying both out to dry on rocks next to the gurgling stream where I continued drinking bottomless water through the filter. It was going to take a lot to overcome the dehydration and get back to a stable level.

The dehydration affected me over the coming days, but

largely thanks to the long midnight run in search of water, I arrived at the next resupply point, a small village called Kazarman, a day earlier than expected. The mountains were starting to look a little smaller, and the running was therefore going a little faster on rolling grassy hills.

When I left my guesthouse in Kazarman, the owner – who was the village's English teacher, despite not really speaking the language – offered to show me to the bus station after I told her my next stop was Jalal-Abad.

'No, I'm running to Jalal-Abad. No buses.'

'No, no, no . . . You don't understand! It's very far to Jalal-Abad and there are *mountains* in the way!'

'Yes, I do understand, I ran here all the way from Karakol!'

(Shakes head.) 'You need the bus.'

'Okay. Bye then!'

I was starting to fantasize about reaching the end of the journey and not having to argue my case anymore. I had assumed that by this point, people would believe me – I was well over halfway and had come through the hardest terrain. After Jalal-Abad, the rest of the route was pretty much flat and populated, merely a victory lap into the city of Osh. That I was still doubted was a frustration more than anything, but I kept telling myself that *after this next stage* I wouldn't have these conversations any more.

As usual, leaving a resupply point meant some hours running on a road. Traffic was very limited, and almost exclusively large transport trucks, all of whom stopped to offer me a lift, some very persistently. The most memorable, however, was a solo man in a giant 16-wheeler (how they get by on those roads, I can't understand), who was so insistent that I couldn't go by foot that he resorted to driving next to me, apparently waiting until I agreed that my plan was mad and got in the truck. Going at my pace for nearly 15 minutes, he stalled his truck several times. I felt desperate for an escape – to just *disappear from sight* – and wished that he and all of the well-meaning drivers would just let me get on with it. It can be such a helpless feeling to be constantly encouraged to quit and get in the front seat of a stranger's car. Giving a ride out of kindness is one thing, and it was always lovely and reassuring to know that help was on hand if I needed it. But constantly being told that I *couldn't* make it, and *must* get in the stranger's front seat was an entirely other thing. It was wearing on my morale.

SICK

I had enjoyed some of the most incredible camping pitches throughout my journey across Kyrgyzstan, and was already feeling sad knowing that these nights would soon come to an end. Vast, open starry skies, rolling jailoo greens, hemmed in by snow-capped peaks and lulled to sleep by moving water or temperamental weather. I had found total bliss in my small, one-person, ultra-light home. The night after leaving Kazarman, I found another stunning pitch on a rocky island in the middle of a shallow river. I took my shoes off before wading out to the dry sandbar, where I set up for the night under the protection of the final mountains of the Tien Shan that I needed to cross. On the other side of them was the city sprawl that would be my final days of crossing the country, where I knew I would likely be sleeping in hotels thereafter. I sat outside my tent, the lower altitude warm enough to permit it, watching the stars arrive in the sky above and breathing the clean mountain air.

At 2am, I woke up from sharp stomach pains. *What is this?* I rolled over onto my side, clutching my stomach and trying to assess the problem. It wasn't long before the pain worsened considerably, and I knew I had seconds to move before I redecorated my tent.

Leaning out the door, I puked until I could puke no more and then, still confused and sleepy, wandered down to the water to clean myself up and splash my face with some cold water. *What the actual fuck was that all about?* I never get sick. I have drunk the tap water in every poor country I have been to, and never suffered the consequences of outdoor markets or fresh produce. I had begun to believe that I truly had a stomach of steel. In fact, until that night, my record of never getting a travel illness had stood since I was 11 in the Dominican Republic. At least when that happened, my mom was there to hold my hair back, and nobody made me run anywhere in the morning.

I fumbled my way back to the tent, not having been fast enough to put my head torch on, and after a drink of water and brushing my teeth went back to bed, hoping that it was one of those 'get it out of you' sicknesses where everything is better now that you've puked.

At 4am, I determined that it wasn't.

At 6am, my alarm went off. I told it to shut up and leave me alone.

By 10am, the sun's heat was turning my tent into a personal

sauna, and I couldn't bear to stay inside it any longer. It was time to try to move.

Slowly, I assembled all of my things in their delicate order into my backpack. I was nauseated and miserable, and my muscles all over were shaking terribly. In short, I was in a very bad way. I tried to keep drinking water, using electrolyte tablets in an effort to restore all that I had lost in the night.

It was a hot, clear day, the wind of the previous night having died completely, and I felt absolutely wretched under the baking sun. I decided I would walk, completely unable to contemplate moving any faster, but also unwilling to spend the day sitting by the river feeling terrible and not actually moving any closer to Osh. I would have to at least *try*.

By noon, trying officially sucked. I was still shaking all over, but unable to take on food. Reluctantly, I found my way down to the dusty road that crossed the mountains between Kazarman and Jalal-Abad, and decided to wait for a vehicle to pass. At least by now I knew that in Kyrgyzstan any passing vehicles are beyond willing to offer a ride.

It took a little while before a farm truck approached but, sure enough, I didn't even have to stick my thumb out for them to stop and check on me.

'Jalal-Abad?' the cheery man driving called out, leaning over his sons in the front seat next to him.

'*Da! Privyet!*' – Yes, please! – I answered back, my spirits lifting. His wife and smaller children were in the back seat, and made room to welcome me into their truck.

I managed some polite conversation while the bright green truck laboured up the rocky mountain road, averaging about

10kph. Near the top, we approached some yurts, where the family indicated they would be stopping, but in typical Kyrgyz fashion they flagged down the next approaching vehicle, an old minivan that had had its suspension lifted, and arranged for me to be transferred to it, as it was headed for Jalal-Abad.

In a moment where I had 3G signal I had already booked an air-conditioned hotel room in Jalal-Abad, and my entire focus was on holding myself together until I got to my own private, clean, flushing toilet to put my head inside until it was all over. I was particularly lucky on this occasion – Jalal-Abad was just over 100km away, which was about as close as I had been to a hotel the entire journey. It was a luxury to be able to retire to a real city with real hotels, and perhaps even pharmacies, if things got truly bad.

My new minivan was already overfilled with a group of ten adults, but without any seatbelts in the back, the population didn't really matter. I filled the back row with three older Kyrgyz women dressed in traditional national costume; three middle-aged women in more modern attire sat on the middle bench; and three men, presumably the husbands of some of the women, sat in the front, minding their own business. It was a party in the back, and I soon realized that the women were all smashed on vodka, and my arrival presented an excuse to open the second bottle.

Our ride across the bumpy, rocky, twisting and turning mountain road was truly one to remember. At times the van leaned so hard around corners I was sure some wheels had left the ground, and then I would look over the side of the road and see nothing but sky below, hoping desperately that the vodka had at no point visited the front seat. It was a treacherous mountain road to say the very least, and the van was certainly older than me.

Every 20 minutes or so, the van would stop and we would all assemble outside with filled glasses of vodka. In Kyrgyz drinking tradition, someone must make a toast for every round, and that toast must be done standing up. Every time the ladies were ready for another swig of vodka, we would stand in a circle, me wilting on weak legs and fighting my stomach to stay down. After the toast and shot of vodka, chasers, usually Coke or some sort of fruit juice, would be passed around immediately, because no one actually likes the taste of straight vodka. Then we would take pictures, especially of me, pale, gritting my teeth and pretending I didn't feel like passing out right now, and finally get back in the car until someone got thirsty again and we would repeat the whole process.

Although it was only 100km to Jalal-Abad, it took the rest of the day. It was evening by the time I collapsed into the hotel lobby, desperate for non-alcoholic water and a clean bed.

To my dismay, I stayed in that bed for three whole nights.

On my third day of living in a dressing gown which had the name for a different hotel embroidered on it (the slippers had another name, too, and the towels yet another), I managed to keep a few crackers down, and declared that 'good enough' – I couldn't stay bed bound any longer. I needed to get back out there. So, determined it couldn't be that hard, I went to the market early in the morning in search of a vehicle to take me back to the point where I had left the trail: there, I could try again to cross the last mountains. It took a few hours to find a willing driver, and then five more hours before he had found enough passengers to make the journey worth his while. It was late by the time his creaky Lada, whose trunk opened comically every time he hit a bump, wound over the mountain and back to where I had met my saviours three days earlier. When I asked to be let out of the car, the passengers were equal parts shocked and concerned, insisting I couldn't get out *here*.

It was now mid-September, and afternoons were cold. Still, I was beyond pleased to have been returned to the wilderness yet again, and began running with extra conviction.

I ran and ran, not stopping for walking breaks or any mucking about, until the moon had replaced the sun above me, and I had made my way down a long descent towards a river and lower elevation. It was now far too cold to sleep near the mountain tops at night.

I spotted some yurts and made my way over, greeting two women who appeared to be alone to ask if I could pitch my tent next to theirs. They responded an enthusiastic yes, and then returned to milking their horses – a sight I was starting to get used to – while I made my home in their small compound nestled in the fork of the river.

When work with the livestock was done for the day, my all-female hosts, a grandmother, mother and very young daughter, came over to properly introduce themselves and inspect my flimsy little tent. Satisfied that I had everything I needed, they left suggesting that if I got cold to come inside (my interpretation of Russian was getting much better by this point), and wished me goodnight.

I still felt incredibly ill, but decided against it. I had not enjoyed being sick, and made a conscious choice to be finished with it – as if that's how the body works.

I slept amazingly soundly, feeling safe to be among the nomads again, and grateful to be back in my tent.

In the morning, I savoured my coffee and porridge. The morning air had the distinct smell of autumn in the mountains, and the turning of the season told me gently that it was time to finish this run.

I rolled up my tent, unsure if it would be for the last time on Kyrgyz soil, and waved goodbye to my hosts and their dogs, who had barked quite threateningly at me all night but were now acting sad to see me go.

I crossed the river I had slept next to, which was remarkably refreshing first thing in the morning, and I was soon back on the old dirt road that I had now driven up and down each way. My stomach jostled as I ran, but I put in a solid effort throughout the day, taking advantage of the large downhill that took up the duration of the afternoon. I was almost in shock when the dusty road suddenly turned to smooth asphalt and, looking ahead of me into the valley, I realized that I was nearly back in Jalal-Abad.

Just like that, my time in the mountains had come to an end.

I turned around to view the snow-capped peaks and wave an almost tearful goodbye. It was purely bittersweet – I was unwell and needed to finish my challenge before my body completely fell apart, but I also felt that I hadn't had enough time yet. I hadn't met enough nomads, bathed in enough streams, camped under enough stars or gleefully run enough trails.

The truth is probably that I will never get enough of those things as long as I live. Looking ahead, the route was entirely within civilization to the end. Looking back was a considerably more enticing view. I felt my head and heart pull in different directions, and I reluctantly turned to face forwards in the direction my head demanded – the direction of the finish line.

FINAL STEPS

In the cool morning air and carrying a light pack, now that I was nearing the end and didn't need many supplies, I thoroughly enjoyed my morning run out of Jalal-Abad. I was making good time, for once not needing to stop for walking breaks or to check my compass – there was only one road that I could follow. With Uzbekistan on one side and farms on the other, there was nowhere I could run aside from the main road. It was a quiet, two-lane, mostly paved road, and while I prefer trail running to tarmac one hundred per cent, it was like a holiday to run on a smooth surface, especially without the added weight of a laden pack. I felt guilty that I was no longer running on technical trails and scaling dizzying mountains, living a truly rugged existence (I had showered twice in as many days!), but it just felt so good.

My run towards Osh was like my reintegration into the real world. With every hour of jogging along farm tracks, railway lines or the main highway, I moved closer to the big city and became reacquainted with all that urban life had to offer – a regular phone signal, clean(ish) hotel rooms, vegetables and speeding traffic. I lost count of how many cars I had to wave off – the kind offers of rides, followed by the *'but you can't run to*

Osh' conversations, were all well-meaning, but as my legs buckled on the flat pavement, I needed to block them out.

In addition to blocking out the insistent offers of a lift to Osh, I had to block out the highway signs indicating the mileage. The slow pace I moved at was discouraging, and I didn't want the countdown as I trudged along the roadside. When I finally decided to take a look at my map around 3.30pm, I was met with a fantastic surprise: Osh was 11km away. Which is practically a 10k, a distance I felt convinced that I could *always* handle. My heart lifted and so did my pace: I was going to make it to Osh. And I was going to make it soon!

My legs screamed and I was nearly dizzy from the heat and exhaustion. It felt exactly like that last sprint in any running race: you are spent, aching and crying for it to be over, and you start to believe it never will be, even when you can see the finish line coming into view.

I hit the only turn I had to make the entire day, when the highway bends to join the road into the centre of Osh. Only 2km later, the big Osh sign stood on the highway in front of me. I had imagined this moment for *months,* although I never knew what the 'Welcome to Osh' sign looked like, so I nearly missed the big white pillar with a modest 'Ош' (Osh) in front of me. Immediately and unexpectedly I burst out into tears.

I ran as fast as I could muster towards the city. Some typically Kyrgyz marble arches welcomed motorists into the downtown area, and I decided that was the true finish line. They had a grandiose authority to them, and I liked the idea of running underneath them. I hurried towards them, all of the emotion of the past month – and so far beyond that – caught in my throat.

I couldn't pick any words for how much I felt at that moment. I instinctively lifted my arms into the air as I ran underneath the white arches and then I let my legs spin down to a walk.

I stumbled down the sidewalk, half crying and half laughing. At this moment, at the end of a massive run, there is usually a crew of volunteers telling you that you did a really good job and putting a medal around your neck before handing you a chocolate milk and a banana. There is always a medic waiting to see if you'll throw up, and then you collect your free t-shirt and go out for brunch.

But there was none of that. No one around me knew what I had just achieved. There was no chocolate milk, no matter how badly I wanted one, and there was no t-shirt, no matter how badly I needed a new one. I simply wiped my eyes and started figuring out my way to a hotel, which I hadn't booked as I didn't think I would finish that day – it was a 65km run, the furthest single distance I had achieved in a day, ever.

I never managed to celebrate. I had dreamed how good it would feel for so long, how I would reward myself in Osh, but I felt discombobulated at the prospect of the expedition being over. I ate a simple meal, and was in bed by 8pm. I didn't even book a fancy hotel – after 25 days in the wilderness, my appetite for comfort had changed considerably, and a three-star room in an old Soviet building was more than luxurious.

I didn't know what to say or how to feel. The truth is that I hadn't been prepared for the chance that I might actually make it, so I had no idea how to react. All I know is that I couldn't wipe a smile from my face for days, and a small seed of confidence began to develop inside me.

*

Self-belief is everything that my first successful expedition boils down to. It is no one's job – no one's job but yours – to be your cheerleader. It is your job to show up for yourself every day and believe you can do it. That is how you make your dreams come true – by getting up there and doing it yourself. Don't wait for permission – some of us are never going to get that. Only you decide what you can and can't do.

Completing a grand adventure – accomplishing a dream, shipping a project, ending an epic trip – should be filled with rose-tinted glory. The entire time you spend working towards that moment, you imagine it and the life you will live afterwards as something incredible, something better.

About a month after arriving home in Edinburgh, that is not how I felt. Everything was heavy. I wasn't running more than 30 minutes at a time, due to the severe fatigue that I hadn't shaken out of the legs yet, and I felt that I was languishing through my life. I began to write for publications I respected, and I was invited to speak at events around the country. My lofty dream of making a living in the industry was suddenly closer than I had ever imagined it would be. The outside-facing image of my life was full of positivity. And yet...

My boyfriend's patience for my 'blues' had run out, so most mornings I rose early as usual and played house until he left for work, at which point I could return to bed. I knew that wasn't right in a relationship, but I lacked the drive to fix anything. Only weeks after being on the highest high, feeling so intently my full power and ability as a person, it was as if I had let all of that slip through my fingers.

It was ages before the term 'post-adventure blues' fell upon my ears. I was mostly out of it by then, and I heard it mentioned off-hand at one of the events I was speaking at from another adventurer I admired. Suddenly, I had an answer. After Kyrgyzstan wasn't the first time I'd gone through it, it was just the worst it had been.

Giving it a name – even the wrong name – made all of the difference. By that time, I had been interviewed a fair amount and frequently asked about recovery – *How long until you're back to running?* I have now changed my answer: don't worry about the running, that'll come – that's just muscles and fibres. Recovering your mind needs attention too.

To this day, I mostly hear athletes and adventurers discuss 'recovery' only in the physical sense, but I always prioritize the mental side. Recovering my legs is easy – just stay off them for a bit. Recovering the mind, however, is less obvious.

Every stage I spoke on, every journalist who interviewed me, always finished with the same question: *What's next?*

Running across a mountain range in Asia had instantly become the most legendary and thrilling experience of my life. The blues I experienced afterwards felt almost as if I were in mourning for the time spent in the mountains, being my truest, most authentic, wild self – as if my body knew I didn't belong back in my city life. Eventually, I opened a map to pick the next mountain range. Perhaps it was the wine again, but I made a long list. There needed to be a way to whittle it down – maybe just one range per continent?

There. That was thematic. That made it a thing. It's good to have a direction to follow.

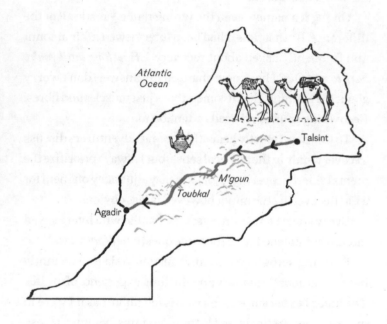

Atlantic
Ocean

Talsint

M'goun

Toubkal

Agadir

CHAPTER TWO

That Made It a Thing: The Atlas Mountains

It took two days to get by bus from Marrakesh to Talsint, the small town I'd selected as my starting point, based on its location at the eastern end of the High Atlas range and the fact that a bus did, twice a week, go to it. Looking out the dusty window, all I could see were sand and sky. The warm beige of the earth flooded my eyes, and even up to the top of the mountains nothing broke up the lifeless rock.

I arrived in Talsint after dark, stumbled towards the only hotel and set about my last-minute preparations, which of course included nothing but filling my water bottle and excessive worrying about the mountain range ahead. I hardly slept that night, endlessly listing negative thoughts about my abilities and the mountains themselves – on the bus ride across them I had not seen a single river with flowing water. The peaks looked spiky, vegetation scarce. The ground would be very difficult underfoot. The lack of water meant that survival would be questionable, at best. The unrelenting sun would punish my body undeniably. What I had thought would be a fun 20-day run across some mountains with some great campsites in between was now looking like a death march into inhospitable terrain and thirsty nights spent sleeping on rocks. Worse still, I had got out of breath climbing to the third floor of my hotel, proving that either I wasn't adjusted to the minor elevation or I simply wasn't fit enough to run up mountains with my heavy pack. I felt fat and foolish.

THE LAND OF THE BERBERS
I walked to the outskirts of Talsint and slowly twirled around to take in my surroundings. Behind me and to my left was the

magnificent, foreboding, scorched Sahara Desert. In front of me and barely rising to my immediate right were the first rocky spines of the High Atlas Mountains. It was a dramatic location, with contrasting yet equally inhospitable environments on either side. There wasn't a cloud in the sky, and although it was just after 8am and I hadn't even started running yet, I was melting in the heat.

For most of the morning I followed a completely dry riverbed that led directly towards the mountains. It was slow going underfoot, with large rocks providing a shifting platform to run on. Nonetheless, rivers provide easy navigation, and I had little to think or worry about as I ran steadily 'upstream'. I wondered how long it had been since this river saw a drop of water. I wondered how long it would be before *I* saw a drop of water.

At some point in the middle of the day I passed through a small village, where old ladies with intricate face tattoos and dressed in spectacularly colourful robes chased me down to shake my hand and say hello. This was when I learned the secret handshake of the Berbers, after getting it quite wrong the first few tries. I filled my water bottle – already emptied – and continued steadily forwards, joining a dirt double track that made for easier movement, although at the highest point of the hot day I decided to give up on running and instead walked as fast as I could without making myself dizzy from the heat. There was no relief of shade anywhere – not a single tree, rock, hut – nothing. I blinked rapidly as the largest tumbleweed ever seen began to roll into view, and it wasn't until it was a few paces in front of me that I noticed the tiny face of a donkey poking out from his incredible mound of dry sticks, and his Berber owner walking slowly behind, prodding her donkey gently as they trampled down the track. It was the only traffic I saw for hours. The region seemed so still and lifeless that I began to feel as if I'd landed on Mars, wandering alone in a vast desert.

It was 5pm when I stumbled, wild with thirst and heat, towards the sound of running water. A winding route of crazy bouldering had finally led me to the outskirts of a small village, and the irrigation channel coming out from a mountain source was flowing with clear, beautiful water. I dumped my pack and collapsed at the concrete edge of the channel, splashing my face and then drinking fast and greedily through my filter. Once I was satisfied, I filled my bottle and dropped in a purifying tablet. As I waited for the water to be safe to drink, I ate a small snack for the first time that day, and the combination of hydration and calories stopped my head spinning and muscles shaking. Almost simultaneously, the temperature was dropping rapidly into the late evening, and I felt a second wind arriving. Thank goodness – it had been an alarmingly slow day to start with.

I resaddled my pack and set off at a run again. I found a small trail that wound up my first big climb, following in the footprints of shepherds and goats. The glow of the late sun lit up the red rocks of the mountains dramatically. *I'm finally doing it,* I smiled to myself. This was what I'd wanted. A wicked fun trail, a spectacular mountain view and a rugged environment. The climb made me realize how hard I'd worked all day without the right fuel, so I stopped to do some simple stretches and enjoy the amazing view.

I reached the top of the small pass and bombed the descent into a tiny, 20-home Berber village. There was no road leading to the outside world and no telephone poles disrupting the skyline, but a small school and a mosque, the only painted buildings in a commune of homes built from the exact mud they stood on top of. The village was quiet, and the communal water fountain appeared to be dry, which I supposed wasn't really a surprise. A young man called, *'Bonjour!'*, so I asked if there was a shop in the village. *'Oui,'* he pointed at a building nearby.

I approached and discovered the shop was closed, and when I looked at the young man in confusion, he waved me into a nearby house. The entrance led into a small courtyard shaded by vines, and soon at least six people, young and old, arrived to overwhelmingly welcome me. My water bottle was filled and I was ushered into the courtyard, where after some barking at the young women of the family someone produced a plastic chair for me to sit on. Little French was spoken, but I understood I was to sit and wait a second. A table and more chairs were brought out, and soon tea arrived, along with the entire family. The woman of the house, a slender, middle-aged Berber in an orange and brown gown and turquoise headscarf, sat next to me, keeping my cup topped with sweet mint tea. Bread and marmalade were produced and I gratefully tucked in; moments later a single omelette was placed in front of me. I felt awkward that no one else was eating, and more awkward still that my first test of Berber lifestyle had already presented itself: eating without cutlery. I ripped off a piece of bread and attempted not to make an eggy mess or taint my food with my bare hands. It was harder than it looked, especially with everyone watching and asking questions via the two teenage boys who spoke a little French (or at least, a little more than I do).

My kidnappers/hosts were quite adamant that I should stay the night, but it was too early for me to stop, and I felt anxious that I had so far come nowhere near my mileage target on only the first day. After taking a few photos and exchanging phone numbers I was finally released, with my bottle filled again and some fruit somehow stuffed into my pack that I would have sworn had no extra space in it. The two boys escorted me out of town – I walked with them until we reached the limit of their territory, took a selfie on their phone and set off at a run, completely rejuvenated and delighted by both the food and the hospitality.

I was now running down a rocky double track that functioned as the only supply route to the village. I saw no cars, but evidence of donkey hoofprints suggested a more reliable transportation option on the rough track. The sun was beginning to set fast, and with the cooler temperatures my running picked up to a more familiar and respectable pace. I was still guzzling my water, making up for the long hours under the desert sun when I was rationing, so when I passed a grove of orange trees I investigated to find their water source. A small, older woman tending to her plot without a light after dark surprised me, but – to my enormous gratitude – she took my bottle to fill it from the direct spring source, rather than the dirty ground source I was preparing to filter. Again, she invited me to spend the night at hers, but I was determined to achieve some mileage now that I was finally moving at a decent clip. If I could manage some night miles at this desert end of the mountains and find shelter during the hottest part of the day, that would be better for my body and avoid the serious risk of heat exhaustion.

I continued down the track, enjoying myself magnificently as an incredibly starry sky came out. I switched off my headlamp at this point, as the stars and moon were so bright anyway and I shouldn't waste my battery so early, especially when I didn't know how long it would be before I passed a town big enough to buy new ones. The stars were brilliant, mesmerizing. The only other place on earth I'd seen so many stars was far out at sea. I was happy. Beyond happy. For the first time that day my feet sprang effortlessly in rhythm. Fresh mountain air filled my lungs. My breathing was steady. I felt good. I felt strong. But then, *oooooft*.

I landed with a crash. I had no idea what had happened. I was in so much pain it was as if the world was actually coloured in red. Screaming red. I lay, tangled, wherever I was, for a moment, waiting for the dust around me to settle (literally) before I could see where I had landed. As the dust cleared and my eyes began to focus again, I looked up and saw the ledge I had just run straight off. It was about 2 or 3m above me. I hadn't tried to move yet. Underneath me was a pile of rocks. I knew I hadn't got away with this. Something must have been broken. My legs were twisted. My backpack was still on, but had come up over my head. Some of my belongings had spilled out, but I couldn't find them in the dark. Slowly, I began to move. I methodically engaged one limb at a time, checking for damage. I was in so much pain it was hard to say where it was radiating from. I lifted my right arm and opened and closed my fist, then did the same with my left arm. I dragged myself onto my knees, then one by one engaged my legs to stand. I shook and collapsed. I sat down again. I started to breathe, rapid and stressed.

'*Oh my god, oh my god, oh my god!*' I kept repeating. I was literally stunned. Time passed and I tried to regulate my breathing. I pulled out my headlamp and switched it on, deciding to check my kit for damage as well. I tracked down my water bottle, which had rolled away – thank goodness it was bright green – and put everything back together. Nothing seemed to be damaged, just scratched a little and covered in the dust that I had disturbed with my crash landing. I ran my hand down my legs and found the hole in the upper thigh of my tights. *Dammit*. Brand-new, expensive, hot-weather-technology tights. On the first night. In the moment I was more focused on this than on the blood that was spilling out onto them. I was in a lot of pain but, deciding that I hadn't broken anything, I wasn't worried about the bleeding. It couldn't be anything bad. But a scratch, surely.

I gingerly stood up again and hoisted my backpack. Time to find my way back up onto the path. Eventually I was there and standing again, so I began staggering along the route I was taking. *Pretend nothing has happened.* I was covered in dust and blood – hardly inconspicuous.

I don't know how long I limped down the path for, relying heavily on my trekking poles and wincing with every step. I was too stunned to think about what to do. I needed to find a place to camp by a river so I could wash my cuts as well as the blood off my clothes. Instead, I heard the sound of feet running towards me. A young woman stopped when she reached me, out of breath. She explained – in perfect but rapid French that I struggled to understand in my confused state – that she had spotted me when I passed through her village earlier, and had been chasing me since. I didn't want to turn around and go back in the direction I'd come from, but decided that I was in no state to take care of myself that night, and accepted Meryam's offer of hospitality. We walked slowly back to her home, Meryam catching her breath from what sounded like her first experience in running, and me still dazed and in too much pain to move freely. The village had no streetlights, and it was too dark for her to notice my state. I didn't say anything about it.

We reached the small dwelling where she lived with her mother, her two daughters and her niece, all the girls under the age of ten. Meryam's husband had abandoned them, and she was left to care for her children alone. She was well educated and spoke excellent French and some English. She was warm but pragmatic. We became instant friends.

The walls and floors of their home were made from mud, and a couple of beautiful, tasselled Berber rugs covered the dirt floor. There was an entrance hall and three rooms, one with a TV and two beds pushed against the wall, where Meryam's young family were gathered around a low table doing homework. In the back of the house was a small hut with a pit-toilet and water tap where Meryam handed me a towel and soap to wash up. I'd been careful to keep my right side hidden from view, still in complete denial over my injury and not wanting Meryam to see. I took clean clothes out of my bag so I could wash my tights, and in the bathroom light got a first look at the damage. The cut was large and spilling blood from my upper thigh. The biggest bandaid I had didn't come close to covering it, but I slapped it on the worst of the scene and knew I'd have to find a village with a pharmacy soon. A part of my brain – the quiet voice of reason in the very back of the room – knew that the wound needed more than a thin bit of tape over the middle, but I was still partially in shock and unwilling to acknowledge what I'd done.

After hanging my clothes to dry I joined the family inside, where Meryam's mother had already made some sweet mint tea – probably the most comforting drink imaginable at a time like this. They offered food, but my stomach was flipping from the crash. I was shaking and tried to hide this by clutching the warm cup of tea.

It was lovely playing with the girls as they finished their homework and got ready for bed. Meryam gave me one of the beds – my protests were forcefully ignored – as well as a pile of blankets, again ignoring my suggestion that I could use my own sleeping bag. My bed was cosy and comfortable, but it was hard to find a way to lie down that didn't hurt. I settled on my left side, and Meryam laid out blankets on the floor below me to sleep between her two daughters, while her mother and niece settled in a similar fashion in the neighbouring room. The girls were full of giggles and joy at the surprise sleepover party, and their innocent warmth went straight to my heart.

After the lights went out the memory of my crash vividly appeared. *How could I be so stupid?* If the drop had been any more than 2 or 3m, I would have broken something. If it had been much more, I would have died. I couldn't escape the thought that under different circumstances, my stupidity could have killed me. How would my family feel if I died being so idiotic? An accident they would learn to live with; pure stupidity and falling off a ledge in the dark, probably not. My eyes flooded with tears as thoughts of more serious circumstances pressured my mind. Doubts filled my head. I started to recount *every* mistake I had *ever* made in the mountains. Times when I'd slipped. Times when I'd forgotten something. Times when I'd been lost. I thought about the Atlas and how serious any of my past catastrophes could be if I made the same mistakes. *I'm not capable of this,* I told myself. *I shouldn't be here.*

I hardly got any sleep. I didn't toss and turn, however, as the pain only allowed me to settle in one position. I felt the blood running down my leg and saturating my sweatpants.

EARLY CONSEQUENCES

In the morning the fabric was stuck to the wound, but still wet as the bleeding hadn't stopped. Still, I didn't want to upset Meryam and her daughters (I'd already learned that the Berbers were too nice, and if they knew I was wounded they'd fall over themselves to get me help), so I did my best to disguise the blood patch and get dressed in my tights once more, applying another fresh but pointless bandaid and a strip of duct tape to the wound that grazed my entire right thigh.

After a breakfast of bread and olive oil, washed down with more sweet mint tea, I said my farewells to my new adopted family as the girls headed out for school. Walking was extremely painful, so I took an ibuprofen and set off delicately down the road. There would be no running today.

I winced at every step, my right hip already incredibly swollen. When I was out of the village I could see for miles in every direction and, spotting the opportunity for solitude, walked with my shirt off for a few hours. Again, as early as 9am, the heat was almost unbearable, and I worried about rationing my water, knowing that, especially at my dreadfully slower pace, it would take most of the day before I had the chance to get more.

The morning ticked by slowly, my thoughts still constantly turning to the crash and imagining worse scenarios that could have transpired. After a few hours my hip had warmed up enough for me to walk faster, and I even dared to jog a little. It was a pleasant and silent day in the red, rocky hills, and I tried with all my might to improve my mood to match the cloudless sky.

There was an unpaved road in the valley below me and I walked/jogged on a diagonal so I eventually met this road, which ultimately led to my next destination. There was next to no traffic out there at the eastern end of Morocco, so when a truck slowly passed I was beyond grateful that the driver stopped to check that I was all right, and offered to fill my water bottle. I shouldn't have been surprised, but I was extremely glad that so far anyone I'd seen out in this hostile environment was always carrying extra supplies of insulated, cold water. The driver offered the customary three times to give me a lift into town, but I declined, again standing at an angle to ensure he didn't see the blood and ripped tights on my right side.

It was 3pm when I reached the village with shops, but sadly no pharmacy in sight. I was so thirsty that I'd forgotten to care. I bought a handful of drinks – water, pop, yogurt – and headed out of town with 3 litres on my back. The weight pushed me down, but it wasn't like I was going fast today anyway. Still, the pain in my shoulders was intense and, with the added difficulty of my new injury, I resented the weight, and worried that I wouldn't be able to run with it. It was simply too much to carry, and the worst part was limiting the amount of water I could take. I mentally scanned every item in the pack, looking for things that were unnecessary. But, of course, everything inside it *was* necessary. Limiting myself to only the belongings, plus food and water, that could fit inside a 30-litre backpack guaranteed that there were no extra comforts weighing me down.

Still, I had to find a way to lighten the load. This pain wasn't sustainable.

As sunset approached I passed a well, the third such incredible saviour I'd found today. I decided that with little light left and no guarantee of another water source for another 18km, I would have to stop here for the night. The well was about 30m away from the road, and beyond it was a small mud hut with only a tiny crawl space as an entrance; it appeared to be empty inside. I kicked around the solid, red desert ground behind the hut to pick the spot where I would lay out my bivvy for the night, using the hut as a barrier between me and the desolate road, not that any cars had passed in hours.

After laying out my things, I went to the well to pull up a bucket of water. My tights were soaked in dust and blood, and I was desperate to wash them out, along with my socks and underwear. Just before I disrobed, however, I noticed a man approaching, tipped off by his large white dog running towards me and barking angrily. I worried that the well was owned. When the man arrived he greeted me in French and had a lot of questions about what I was doing. I established that I was welcome to use the water and sleep there, although he was very persistent in his offer to let me sleep in his office, which was just across the road. From what I could understand the man was a security guard for the telecoms infrastructure that lined the road. Unfortunately for his generous offer, my rule is only to stay in the homes of families, and never single men. We were in the desert, after all.

To my frustration, the man took a seat, lit a cigarette and seemed to decide that he would be spending his evening watching me, rather than the TV back in his office. He asked questions about everything in my bag and continued to insist that I spend the night at his office, which I persistently declined. I boiled water for my dinner, feeling uncomfortable that he was still watching, having reached the limit of our language barrier and run out of things to talk about. Eventually I asked, incredibly awkwardly and made even more awkward by my broken French, to have some privacy so I could sleep. Ever so slowly, he finally left.

I washed up after my dinner, and finally washed my clothes as well as my arms and face – not a full bath like I had planned, sensing the lack of privacy was an issue – and organized my things to go to bed. I was worried about wild animals of the crawling and slithering variety, so I kept my campsite quite clean and tucked myself into my bivvy.

The stars were amazing, and I switched between reading my book and simply gazing above at the beautiful night. It's such an intense pleasure to be somewhere on this human planet that has no light pollution to come between you and the galaxy above.

Despite the heat of the day, the desert still got cold at night, and my elevation had risen slowly, and so I covered myself up in all of the layers I'd brought, scanning the nearby ground for scorpions. I recalled in vivid detail a nature documentary I'd recently watched where a scorpion was recorded piercing his target repeatedly with his venomous tail, and I imagined that happening to the only skin my bivvy left exposed: my face.

I squirmed onto my left side, my right hip now far too swollen for me to even lie flat on my back, and soon found peace from my extreme exhaustion.

Barking startled me, and I saw a light approaching. Fear rocketed through me as I realized that the man from before had returned. I checked my phone: it was after 10pm. *Why would he come back at this hour?* My heart pounded through my temples. I looked around me instinctively to check the scene: my bag was mostly packed, my shoes were near and my trekking poles, as always, were laid directly next to my right side, ready for carbon-fibre defence. Soon he arrived at my feet, and I made my disapproval clear. *'Je dors,'* I proclaimed in my terrible French. *'Je suis fatiguée,'* hoping that this would send a clear enough signal that I didn't want to socialize or anything further. To my dismay, he sat down next to me and lit a cigarette. He asked if I was married, told me that he was not, and my heart beat louder. *This is bad,* I thought, as I glanced again at my shoes. They were laid neatly next to me, ready for me to hop in and run fast. I looked at my bag, already with my camera, wallet and GPS tucked inside, so I could easily grab my valuables and make a break for it. I looked around. The desert valley was devoid of any vegetation or, apart from the hut I thought I was hiding behind, structures. If I chose to run, he could watch me for further than I had the strength to continue. It was hopeless. I stayed frozen.

After continued questioning and conversation to which I mostly replied either 'I'm tired', 'I want to sleep' or 'I have a husband', he finally finished his cigarette and made to leave. He had brought with him a heavy blanket, which he insisted on covering me with himself, tucking me in awkwardly and somewhat intimately, before slowly meandering back down the path he had come on. Whenever the man went anywhere, his dog led the way, barking ferociously, which at least meant that I felt certain he couldn't sneak up on me later. I breathed a sigh of relief.

I slept just past sunrise somehow, and woke safe and alone, as desired. I slipped on my shoes over my wool socks, my feet already tender and battered from only two days of desert running, and gently tiptoed back to the well where I had left my stove, ready to boil water for breakfast and coffee. I was sitting on the ledge of the trough leading from the well, enjoying the warming porridge, when the man's dog sauntered over to say good morning. He didn't bark this time (having spent most of the night doing so), and instead was fairly cuddly. I felt horrible for having had no trust in his master the night before – it was as if the dog had come over with his cuddles as a form of reconciliation for making me feel so scared with the uncomfortable visits.

It was nearly 8am by the time I'd finished breakfast and packed up, which made no sense to me – *how did I waste so much time?* I folded up the blanket and walked over the road with the white dog to return it, but decided only to drop it at the door of the office and tiptoe away, feeling no desire to meet my socially challenged friend ever again.

I continued walking (limping, actually) away from the road, my pack filled with water from the well, and set off up the steep hills in search of more interesting terrain. While the road would be easier and faster, I couldn't bear the boredom of it. The hills also came with the advantage of getting to hike with my shirt off again, but when I stumbled suddenly upon a nomad camp I had to quickly pull it back on. Cleverly concealed between rocky outcrops, the camp was out of sight until I was directly upon it.

The nomads lived in black, goat-hair tents, with their small flock surrounding the temporary home. I almost couldn't believe my eyes to find anyone living up here: there was no water, no vegetation, no relief from the scorching sun. Even the trails were treacherous, and I was slipping constantly on the loose scree. What kind of life could this be? How could they to support an entire flock of goats, not to mention their human family? It seemed like an incredible feat of survival.

I passed a couple of these camps in the morning, the nomads

and me looking at each other in equal bewilderment to find anyone else on the side of this rocky hill, but there was always an enthusiastic greeting after the shock wore off. When the sun reached its full height and the heat became too strong, I descended to the road again where the wells seemed to be conveniently spaced approximately 7km apart. By the side of the road I moved much faster, and felt safer with the presence of wells, but it sure was boring. In the distance I could see the green cluster that marked the next village and my goal for the day, and I was running towards that green target for hours. It never seemed to get any closer, and the hazy desert light flickered on the red earth spanning out ahead of me. I had planned much of my route through this section scanning satellite images for these green patches, easily spotted in the dry, red desert. Every community is built around a water source and tends to trees and gardens, creating the green beacons that I needed to run between in order to survive.

While the hip was supplying constant discomfort, I made a note in my diary mid-afternoon when the pain suddenly switched and became much more intense, as if it were literally on fire. This change alarmed me greatly, and increased my motivation to reach the medium-sized town up ahead. I needed to see a pharmacist. A doctor would be better, but healthcare in the Atlas Mountains is almost non-existent, and I wasn't at the point of wanting to leave the mountains for a first-aid break just yet. I took the note as a form of due diligence in the event that I had to in the future, but I was clearly still in denial about the severity of my injury.

The green dot came closer and finally I reached the first

trees leading into the town of Er-Rich. I smiled broadly and even fist-pumped the air at the sight of a moving river. It was beyond a relief to see water, and a good sign of things to come: I was heading upstream, indicating that the water was coming from where I was going, and I hoped that the next ecosystem I was moving into would be more hospitable. I waded across the deepest part of the river for the pure joy of feeling the cool water on my feet, and did this several times, splashing in the stream.

It was only mid-afternoon when I arrived into the town centre, but I was keen to stop for the day for the simple reason that I desperately wanted to shower, and it would be a few more days before the opportunity presented itself again. I found the local hotel, and almost didn't understand the receptionist telling me the price in French because I had prepared myself to listen for *cent* – a hundred – but it was only 75 dirhams: seven euros, less than eight US dollars. The shower I'd been looking forward to was just a knee-height cold-water tap next to a bucket, but with the privacy of a locking door I hardly cared. I inspected the damage inflicted by my first three days of running: my feet were swollen and sporting several blisters, each of which would need to be popped and cleaned; both my collarbones were red and puffy from the heavy backpack; and the bruising on my right leg had started to come out, running almost the entire length of my thigh down to the top of my knee. I cleaned my wound with care and washed my clothes, which were already dusty, bloody and sweaty again, before heading to the souk with my post-crash shopping list: wound dressings and a needle and thread.

Er-Rich could be described as a dusty, bus-stop town, with

a small souk and a handful of cafes around the central square. In the early evening, the square and the tables of the cafes were filled exclusively with men, and it was clear to me that public spaces were only for them. Women darted, usually in groups or with a few of their children, to their destinations, never lingering to socialize or joining their husbands. The front of my hotel was a cafe, and I was asked to use the door to a neighbouring business to exit and enter the building – for a woman to pass through the café publicly and visibly was nothing short of a scandal. I felt like a second-class citizen, and then realized that it was because *I was*. My stomach rumbled and I looked forward to a large cooked meal, but had great difficulty finding a venue that would accept me as a customer. The few small cafes and restaurants shook their heads at me, while a handful I didn't even dare try, the male patrons in plastic chairs outside making me feel too uncomfortable or blatantly harassed. On the streets I was subject to catcalling and annoyance from men of every age, and I was desperate to get some food and then go hide in my hotel room.

I finally found a small 'snack bar' that welcomed me with a smile, so I took a chair inside, tucked in a corner where I hoped that no one on the street could see me. I had noticed that during my walk through town, I had started to try to physically shrink myself. I wanted to be invisible. The food was not very good – reheated chicken, fries and some salad to go with it – but I was grateful for the kindness of the cafe owners and astonished at the cheapness of the bill. It was dark when I left and the streets had really filled up, so I walked as quickly as possible, desperately trying to block out the lewd calls coming from all directions. Back in my hotel room, which to the receptionist's relief I managed to get to without being seen by anyone but him, I breathed a sigh of relief, locked the door and climbed into bed early.

To say I was disappointed that I couldn't get a coffee at the hotel where I had been a paying guest because its cafe was public and I was a woman would be an understatement, but I knew it wouldn't be productive to flip a desk here. I lit my camp stove in my room and made instant coffee and porridge, telling myself that my mere presence on the guestbook *might just* contribute to the basic human right to caffeine, if not to real incremental change. I could only hope. I sat by my window, listening to the music from the cafe and the sounds of cups hitting saucers, turning me green with envy that I was missing out on coffee and coffee culture below me.

I duct-taped a measure of gauze to my wound, made messy by the cut applied from my proudest souk purchase: the *Samurai 2000 Pocket Knife*. For about 80p out of the expedition budget, I now had a (feeble) weapon and a means to cut sections from the roll of gauze I had bought from the pharmacy. The makeshift wound dressing stuck out visibly through my tights, but by now the swelling was so enormous that all hope was lost on that side of my body. I was taking a full dosage of ibuprofen, and wondering if I should have bought more – this looked like it was going to take a while to heal completely. I told myself that, if I could keep moving, I would. My longing to run across the Atlas Mountains far outweighed a desire to nurse an injury at home.

I walked out of town with my shades on, hat low and

headphones in, keeping my head down and doing my best to ignore the ongoing male attention, trying to keep calm and telling myself it was not the time or place to lose my cool or retaliate. So I walked, briskly and individually, pretending not to notice the calls from busy cafes or chilling looks from passing men.

Navigationally, I wanted to follow the river, so I looked for small trails running alongside it. The land beside the river was all farmed, a patchwork of small crops, tended to by hand. I enjoyed the narrow trails jutting between patches but, without any rhyme or reason to the pattern, I was constantly turning right and left; with the large fruit trees blocking my view of the river, I began to feel like I was in a lovely green labyrinth. The opportunity to run in the shade was too enjoyable for this to be worrying, although on occasion I did check that I was still heading west. The women working among their small crops waved and smiled as I passed, probably startling them as I darted out from the green and disappeared around another hidden corner, entering their lives and their workplace for just a brief moment. One of the younger women I passed chased me down, frantically asking me why I was there and where I was going. Dressed in a long, pale pink robe with a matching headscarf and plastic flip-flops, she couldn't have been older than 15. She was distressed that I was in the area, and gave me directions to the road. I asked if there was a problem with me running here – trespassing doesn't really exist in Berber territory, but she seemed upset by my presence. She replied that I was more than welcome, but that they would rather I ran on the road, as it was dangerous there.

I was confused at this, so asked, 'What kind of danger? Human danger?'

She nodded, then thought carefully about what to say next. 'Yes, dangerous people. One dangerous person.'

I must still have looked confused, so she elaborated, 'There is a man who loves the women.' The look of terror in her eyes filled in all the blanks for me, and I felt my stomach drop.

I continued along my lovely shaded path for about another 30 seconds before fear made up my mind for me, and I turned a sharp left up towards the road, where I ran for a few uneventful hours.

VULNERABLE

I reached the small village represented by the patch of green I'd been running towards all morning, and stumbled, overheated and dehydrated, to the only open door, which appeared to be a shop. Outside was a gaggle of teenage boys and, after my time on the road as well as my stay in Er-Rich, a group of young men was the last thing I wanted to see. Still, I needed water, so I went to buy some, along with some type of orange pop that looked refreshing. The men acted as predicted, so, without saying a word to them, I took my cold drinks and walked around the corner, searching for a place out of sight where I could sit down to drink my pop and fill my Nalgene with the fresh water.

Only minutes later, one of the boys approached, alone. I made no acknowledgement, but he continued, confidently, directly towards me. Keeping my gaze down, I could now see his feet beside me, pointing towards me. His shadow covered me, and for the first time I realized just how big he was. Only a teenager – a minor – but taller and broader than me, by a lot. He began by saying hello, which I ignored, so he persisted. He asked if I spoke French, to which I shook my head no, so he asked if I spoke English, to which I also shook my head no. I waved for him to go away, and tried to drink my pop faster, which wasn't very successful. Continuing in French, he asked me to go back to his room with him. His tone was more of a 'you will' than 'will you?' I was gobsmacked that a teenager – *a child* – thought it was okay to approach an adult woman and ask such a thing. I looked in all directions and saw that I'd given him the perfect opportunity – there was no one in sight. He was safe from shame or embarrassment. He persisted, his voice getting stronger as his patience with me clearly wore out. I said no forcibly this time, equalling his aggression. At this he became visibly irate, even stomping his feet and shaking his head at me, as if *I'd* been the rude one in this interaction. At the stomp of his foot, I was again reminded that he was physically stronger than me, and that despite the age difference I was in a vulnerable position. I held my breath, boring my eyes into the ground, hoping his temper would recede. With a *tisk* he finally stormed off, and I let out a breath of air. I finished my pop in a single gulp and picked up my things quickly. I didn't want to be in this village for one more second.

By this time I could no longer deny that I was extremely angry at the patriarchal society. The man who came to my campsite, my experience in Er-Rich, the women I met who worked in daily fear of a dangerous man, and that teenage boy were all building a storm of rage inside my mind. My feelings were a mix of total heartbreak and sympathy for the women of North Africa who faced this every day, and my own selfish disgust with the way I'd been treated in the last few days. I knew that I was now spiralling into a dark mood, and needed to do something fast to get out of it. Sometimes you can't fix the whole problem in one afternoon, so instead I looked for a hill to climb, away from civilization. I had extra water now, and figured that, if I rationed it, I could stay away from humans at least until tomorrow. That would do it.

At the foot of the steep climb, a shepherd hailed me and tried to persuade me to turn around and go back to the *piste*. There was nothing up there, he said. In his eyes, a mountain and a trail were *nothing*. Only shops, pavement, cafes, hotels, counted as *something*. After the climb and some wandering around on the edges of the spiny ridge, I found a narrow shepherd trail, so faint and thin that I didn't see it until it was under my feet. It was phenomenal. I ran, for the first time in days, joyfully along, springing down ripples and trudging up the other sides, dodging boulders and propelling myself forwards with my poles. It was bliss. I couldn't believe no one would understand why I came up here. I couldn't believe I had it to myself. A trail this good back home would be packed with hikers and trail enthusiasts, but out here it was seen only as a hardship left for the shepherds and their flocks; a hardship beneath anyone elevated above manual labour.

It was an attitude I'd met only in the Atlas Mountains. The mountains themselves were only formidable barriers. Dangerous and 'empty'. Nothing worthwhile was up a mountain. To climb one would only be to create a pointless difficulty. Why run on a demanding mountain trail, when new, paved pistes exist? I had yet to find anyone who saw my point of view on this. The people here lived in the mountains as a result of a problematic history that forced their ancestors to flee to this arduous place, and they hadn't learned to love it yet. I found myself feeling bad for the mountains, neither appreciated nor enjoyed by their population. That feeling didn't last, however, as I saw the great benefit to myself: pure isolation. After a difficult couple of days with humanity, I had my peace.

The stars came out, so brilliantly that I could see the Milky Way. I boiled a little more water for my evening treat of a mug of hot chocolate, and settled into my sleeping bag to watch the sky above. I switched off my headlamp and leaned on my backpack. This was sheer perfection; exactly the kind of Atlas nights I had been dreaming of. I'd gone from completely grumpy earlier this morning to total relaxation and happiness tonight. Well done, me.

My bubble was popped by the roar of a motor. At first I was confused – there were no roads anywhere nearby. I assumed that the Berber camp I had collected water from before sunset owned a vehicle, and it was only them I was hearing, the noise travelling easily across the hills without any barriers. But the roar grew louder. I pulled my bivvy up to my shoulders instinctively, somehow believing I could hide in my bright blue cocoon. Within minutes, a headlight was shining on my perfect campsite. A small motorcycle with two men on it had somehow found me, and somehow made the off-road climb on this old bike. I was equally stunned and terrified as they dismounted and approached, the headlight still flooding my campsite and blinding me.

'*Bonsoir!*' a man in jeans and a leather jacket called out.

'*Salam* . . .' I tentatively responded.

His companion, dressed traditionally in long white robes and a small matching cap, nodded a greeting. I sat up as the men continued to the edge of my bivvy. They introduced themselves, in French, as security guards for 'the region'. I asked, then, if I was allowed to camp here, to which they replied no – *too dangerous*. Too dangerous? I theatrically looked around, shrugging at the potential danger. There were no animals, no people, the weather was perfect, what could be the problem? The men shook their heads, and informed me that they'd be taking me back to Er-Rich – the last place I would like to go, not to mention my obvious objection to getting on a rickety motorbike in the middle of the night with two men who had yet to produce any evidence of their positions as security guards. I insisted that I was not budging, and – quite bravely, I dare say – asked them to go away now. Both men took out their mobiles and made a succession of phone calls in Arabic, all the while smoking cigarettes and wafting the second-hand smoke into my previously perfect, now completely destroyed, bivvy spot. I looked longingly up at the starry sky, trying to recapture the stargazing session that I wished I was still enjoying. I should have been drifting off to sleep under the silent guard of the stars now, but instead I was being pestered by a motorcycle, cigarettes and chatty men – everything I'd wanted to escape.

While killing time – for what, I wasn't sure – the two men

sat down cross-legged next to my sleeping bag, where I was still huddled for warmth and to reiterate my insistence that I was not moving. They pestered me with questions about *why* I was out here, and not in a hotel. It seemed unfathomable to them. After a long wait, the air was punctured by the sound of more motors. In no time at all, a 4WD crested the hill next to the motorcycle, followed swiftly by a second. Passengers piled out and, before I knew it, I was sitting in my bivvy looking up at a total of ten armed men. I took a deep breath. It has to be one of the most intimidating situations I can recall being in – me, alone, already in bed, looking up at ten men, guns swinging from shoulders, all eyes fixed on me, motives as yet unknown to me, but it was clear we weren't on the same side.

Almost all at once, the men were peppering me with questions, many moving in closely with aggressive and dominating body language. The problem was clear: they didn't want me camping here for fear of danger – although *what danger* I still hadn't figured out. There couldn't be a more tranquil hill on earth: at least, before they arrived it had been. As the group of them harassed me with questions, instructions and opinions, I needed to think clearly and regain control of the frightening situation. I made a quick decision to fake ignorance, and tell the group that I didn't understand any French or Arabic – I only spoke English. This had an immediate positive effect, as only two men in the group spoke English, rendering the other eight instantly silent. Big relief. All the while I maintained a positive and cooperative attitude, only too ignorant to acquiesce, so I continued to sit firmly in my bivvy, insisting that I still planned to sleep there. The guards continually motioned for me to get into one of the off-road vehicles, one of which was badly smashed in one side; and neither was decaled with the Gendarmerie logo, although they insisted they were all officers. This shortcoming I also used to my advantage, insisting that as many of them were not wearing uniforms and the cars were not marked I simply couldn't trust them and couldn't be expected to go anywhere with them. All the while I continued to make my sincere argument that there was *no way* I would be safer at this hour – now after 10pm – in Er-Rich than I was alone on this hill. No way at all. I dug my heels in deep and insisted that I wouldn't be getting in a car.

Throughout these 'negotiations', phone calls were frequently being made and there were many breaks for deliberation, during which I sat silently and watched. At length, it became clear that I wouldn't be getting any rest here and I would, ultimately, need to move. But where hadn't yet been agreed. Er-Rich, aside from having been an entirely dehumanizing experience for me, was 54km away, and I had no intention of being forced to run that distance a second time. During one consultation when all of the men were huddled and not focusing on me, I seriously considered making a dash for it, but decided against it on account of the off-road vehicles and of course the guns hanging from several shoulder straps and utility belts.

I sighed and began to pack my bag. Frustratingly, one of the officers insisted on helping – as if it was any help for two people to pack a backpack, much less when one of them had no idea what he was doing. I shooed away his hands as he tried clumsily to help me stuff my sleeping bag inside my backpack, pulling my belongings away from him, always making my disdain for their presence clear. *Don't touch my things.* I was pissed off, and it was making them uncomfortable. Perfect.

Places for me to sleep tonight were proposed. Go back to Er-Rich and get a hotel. No flipping way. Stay with this man's family. No way – I didn't know him. Go to another town that had a hotel. Nope. Finally, a proposal came forward that was going to be my best option: stay with the Berber camp that I had passed through earlier. It would still mean a loss of mileage, but at least I wouldn't have to get in a vehicle. Reluctantly, I agreed. Now the fun began – me and my army of ten set off, all eleven of us, on a hiking trip to the Berber camp where, as far as I could tell, no one was expecting us. I mean – who would expect such a party to arrive at 10:30pm? Or ever?

The men swarmed me, all falling over themselves to help me with the hike, which I took great offence at – *how do you think I got this far? I've already hiked up this trail!* They offered to carry my backpack. Several of them shone their flashlights on my path at the same time. Any obstacle – rock, step, climb, whatever – hands came out to help me like a damsel in distress. I continued to shoo them away. *I know how to walk.* When we reached the Berber camp, everyone was awoken. An envoy from the small army had arrived ahead of us to arrange everything, and I was introduced to the lady of the house. She was young and ever so polite, and I apologized to her profusely for the disturbance (in French, to the surprise and chagrin of my guards).

In a Berber household, there is usually only one sleeping room, where the entire family lays out mats and blankets each night. However, non-familial men and women cannot share a room, so it was with the deepest regret that I spotted Grandpa being roused and kicked out as a result of my arrival. The poor elderly man had to find somewhere else to sleep, and I couldn't have felt worse. I transferred that guilt towards the guards, naturally. As if this wasn't bad enough, the guards then asked me if I would like the lady of the house to cook me dinner, or at least boil some tea. I couldn't believe the extent to which they felt it their right to impose on this family, and duly refused. *All I want now is to sleep – you woke me up, remember?* I began laying out my sleeping bag and preparing for bed while officers shuffled back and forth, still making frequent phone calls and probably rousing the entire camp.

At this point, as I was already fluffing a pile of clothes to make a pillow, the lead guard came into the room to ask what time I would wake up. I gave him a look that was a mix of confusion and anger – *what business is that of yours?* I said six, but reiterated that I'd wake up when I damn well felt like waking up.

It was well beyond my bedtime when the door to the sleeping room was finally shut, now with only myself and the lady of the house inside, all males having been evicted and by the sounds of it sharing cigarettes, tea and noisy chatter outside.

What a night . . . I sighed as I tried to finally get some sleep.

CATCH AND RELEASE
In the morning my alarm went off just before 6am, as I had assured the officers I would be leaving at six precisely and did

not want to spend any longer in their company. I piled my things quickly into my bag, and tiptoed towards the door. To my horror, it had been locked from the outside by a piece of rope attached to the handle. I reached through the small gap that I could get my hand through, trying desperately to free myself when I noticed that another hurdle had been laid: three officers were sleeping across the door, outside. One of the men woke up and let me out. I didn't stop for a moment, didn't make eye contact and didn't permit him to utter a word that might wake up the rest of the camp. I just shook my head and moved out quickly.

I stopped at the well and filled my bottle and camp stove, which I carried down to the dry riverbed a couple of kilometres off to boil water for porridge and coffee, sheltered by large leafy palms. The sun wasn't up yet and it was still cold outside. I sat on a boulder and huddled over my coffee – I hadn't had anywhere near enough sleep, and the fact that I had been locked in like a prisoner had not woken me up in the best of moods. I washed my face in some well water and felt slightly better. With my wool sweater and tuque donned, I began the trudge back up the hill we had all hiked down as a party last night. I didn't even try to move fast, feeling the futility of climbing this trail for the second time.

When I got back to the patch where I had originally been camping last night, I stopped to stretch out my legs, which were now slightly warmer from the climb. The sunrise behind me was golden over the mountains opposite, igniting the whole land in a red glow; I took a moment to breathe and enjoy this, affirming an intention to quit my bad mood and have a positive day. Ahead of me was the ridge that I had been planning to run, and I was looking forward to gaining some altitude.

My route changed when I was pursued for nearly two hours by a man running after me. With nothing – and no one – around us in any direction, I made the choice to outrun him rather than meet him, and in my fear decided to run higher in the mountains than in the accessible valleys. After I was sure he had gone, I turned west once more and spotted a Berber house. If I could refill my water I definitely should, as the difficult run had made me far more dehydrated than usual. I was greeted by three colourfully dressed women who quickly ushered me inside.

It was a big house, although completely isolated in all directions. The 'driveway' was incredibly rough and several kilometres long to reach the nearest road. When I arrived, the women were tending their relatively large and abundant gardens, and yet again I marvelled that they could thrive out here all alone. I was taken into a large, cool room where I flopped down on a mat, leaning against some embroidered cushions. The room was painted blue and filled with colourful mats and cushions lining the sides. A small coffee table was produced, and I was joined by an elderly woman who sat patiently across from me while barking orders at her daughter and teenage granddaughter. The youngest quickly produced cold water for me, which I inhaled almost in one. It was promptly refilled. Items for tea were carried out and handed to the grandmother, who waited for the boiling water to be brought to her so that she could perform the important tea-pouring duties. Small plates containing marmalade, butter and oil were placed on the table, with a blanket folded around very large wheels of bread next to them. Soon the boiling kettle was brought in and, once the almost ritual ceremony of Berber tea had been performed, we could dig in. A large branch of mint was dropped in each glass of tea, which had been pre-sweetened with two fist-sized bricks of white sugar, and I was served first. The youngest girl ripped off a large corner of bread and handed it to me, indicating the dipping plates which I gratefully dived into. At the first mouthful of smothered bread I realized just how hungry I was. I tried to eat at a polite pace and also not to leave the family without any rations for the rest of the day. The mother began packing a wheel of bread for my backpack, and I assured her I couldn't accept that, but continued to eat just about that much anyway. I couldn't help myself, I was famished and, surrounded by female energy and hospitality, I had finally relaxed.

The mobile phone – an old, brick phone – on the table rang. The young daughter answered and, after a long ramble from the caller, a grave expression fell on the faces of my three hosts; they stared across at me in awe. I didn't need to ask who had called. It was only minutes before I heard the revs of the police jeep outside, and four men walked confidently and dominantly into the room, shifting the energy of our ladies' tea completely.

Handshakes were exchanged, although slightly reluctantly on my part. One officer in plain clothes took the place of the older woman and began preparing tea for everyone, making himself completely at home and leaving me confused as to whether he was, in fact, at home. Two of the men were in absolutely immaculate uniform, their small handguns swinging in white leather cases at their hips. It was immediately clear why these two had been sent to find me – they were both young English speakers. They knew me by name already, and explained that they had been looking for me all day. I stared back in silence, deciding that I wouldn't offer any input until asked a specific question – I had had a rough sleep last night, had been chased today and had now been interrupted from tea with the girls, so I was really in no mood.

The main police officer – that is to say, the one who spoke the most English – turned his cap nervously around in his hand while he struggled to explain to me the dangers of what I was attempting; meanwhile I met his doubts with aggressive independence and a contrarian stance. It was clear that he was completely distressed at the thought of the danger I was putting myself in, and wanted nothing more than to help me avoid certain death, so eventually I was worn down and became as cooperative as I could muster. I showed him my GPS tracker, highlighting the magic SOS button that would page a helicopter; at that he visibly relaxed and began to accept my assurance that I was competent in the mountains. He promised that the Gendarmerie Royale would not, at any point, stand in my way or affect my mission, but simply wanted to accompany me and 'stay in touch' to ensure my safety. I rolled my eyes and sighed theatrically, never letting my police minders forget my unwavering contempt, although it was beginning to recede a little.

Although I desperately wanted to stay with my Berber hosts, drinking more tea and avoiding the intense afternoon sun, it was time to run away from the police, so I packed my things, shook hands with the officers and set off on my way, waving off one last request that I head in the direction of the road, not the mountain. Defiantly, I pointed my feet further towards the mountains than was even necessary for my route and set off as fast as I could after my long afternoon's race. My legs buckled and lactic acid-flooded, not to mention my stiff hip holding me back, but I pushed through the pain, intent on making a good show of what a competent runner I was.

At the end of the day, it was clear to me that my encounters with the Gendarmerie simply come down to a clash of culture: their presence in my expedition could not be accused of any sinister intent. On their side, it made no sense that anyone should want to head towards *wilderness* where modern amenities were lacking and peril lurked in their place; not to mention that a woman alone was an unheard-of spectacle of guaranteed danger. Meanwhile, on my side of the table, I simply could not appreciate any infringements on my personal freedom or pursuit of adventure. Accepting this as a culture clash and determined not to let my police episode go down with any negative emotions, I ran ever forwards into the fading afternoon, willing to just 'let it go'.

After my mountain segment, my route would inevitably join the paved road once more and pass through a small town. In the strict interest of avoiding any further awkward encounters, when my phone signal returned I booked a room in the single hotel. It was remarkably inexpensive and I was in desperate need of a filling meal and a good night's rest. It rained gently on and off as I ran steadily downwards into the village. Minutes later the street was lined with young children chasing me and excitedly demanding, *'Donne-moi un stylo!'* Up until this point, I had not encountered any begging and its sudden arrival caught me off guard. I laughed off the first few kids, offering the requested high-fives, but as the pestering continued I began to feel annoyed and glared accusingly at parents who stood idly by, watching their offspring beg and harass a passing tourist with no visible awareness of my discomfort.

Finally, I arrived at my hotel, where the hosts were lounging on plastic chairs outside, smoking and checking their mobiles, but sprang to life at my arrival. They had not been expecting me, having not checked their bookings for the day, and the hotel was otherwise empty. I had not hoped to be the only guest, craving some anonymity, but the hotel inside revealed an oasis of a quiet courtyard garden, clean rooms and, best of all, hot showers. I asked my host about the evening meal, to which he scratched his head and promised to 'find something', while I set off to my room to luxuriate in a good scrub.

For dinner I was given a slightly large tagine all to myself, and took no issue with embarrassing myself by scoffing the whole thing down while my host sat next to me and chatted away politely. I wished he didn't feel the need to entertain me while I ate, but I was beginning to understand that privacy and alone time didn't exist in this culture. At any rate, I was grateful for the *franglais* conversation and learned a lot about the area from my kind, talented chef of a host.

With a full belly, shampooed hair and wifi updates complete, I crawled into the double bed in my room and was asleep within seconds, not stirring until my 7am alarm.

Part of our previous night's conversation had been about tea and coffee culture around the world, my host and I comparing notes on different attitudes, during which I had mentioned Canada's preference for quantity over quality when it comes to coffee. I had also casually complained about the coffee culture in Morocco excluding women. It was probably due to these topics that at breakfast I was given the *entire pot* for myself. Needless to say, I drank the whole thing without difficulty. It amazed me that after last night's immense tagine I was already hungry again, and devoured omelette, bread, yogurt and an apple – about three times what a normal person should need for breakfast. It was the dawn of Day 6, and I was now entering the Hunger Phase of an adventure challenge – the point where I could no longer comfortably replenish my body with enough calories to replace the number I was burning. This was when survival eating started: I had to force myself to eat whenever the opportunity presented itself. During the hot days when I was running hard, it was usually only with great difficulty and discomfort that anything got down, so it was up to the two meals at the start and end of the day to ensure I got any decent calories in.

I began my run out of town while the residents were only starting to wake up and head outside for work. It was a traditional Berber settlement, with homes cut into the jagged rocks above the river valley, leaving any farmable land for crops, rather than wasting the space on buildings. The occasional motorcycle whizzed past, but for the most part donkeys were the preferred mode of transit here. After five days of limited water, I drooled at the view of a clear, running river cutting through the deep canyon I was entering. I desperately wanted to go for a swim, but didn't feel comfortable disrobing in such a public place in such a conservative area.

After my magnificent night's sleep, I felt I had the energy to run well, but my feet betrayed me. In the Moroccan novel I was reading, men who rebelled against the system had their feet beaten with rubber hoses by the police, and so intense was the pain on my soles that I began to feel paranoid that the officers I had met the other night *had* beaten them and I had simply forgotten about it. I winced visibly putting weight on them, and found awkward and uncomfortable ways to distribute weight to relieve the worst of the pain, like walking on my tiptoes or on the outer edges of my feet. It didn't help, and after an hour of run-walk-crying, I pulled over to take an anti-inflammatory. My hip had become so large at this point, and was still bleeding constantly, that I knew my body needed the drugs anyway. I would need to restock at the next pharmacy. I took note of this tangible sign that things weren't going very well.

In addition to the insane pain in my feet and the incredible swelling on my hip, the blisters my pack had produced on my collarbones had already burst and were at the early stages of looking infected, so I decided to tape them. The muscles in my neck and upper back were suffering severely, and every time I rolled my shoulders it was accompanied by a startling crunching noise, like a wheel going over gravel. And it was only Day 6.

Nearing midday, my wishes were answered as I found myself crawling up the winding river gorge and, for the first time, with water big enough to fit my body in and total privacy.

I wasted no time running in for a splash. The water was silty, clearly the result of recent rains in a river that had been dry all summer, but it was refreshing and soothing on a sore body. After I had dried off and pulled my running clothes back on, I stopped one more time to cool my feet in the river. The sensation of the pounding swelling dissipated almost immediately when my feet were submerged, and I wished I had this opportunity more often.

I was now navigating upstream in a stunning deep canyon. The river in the middle was only a trickle, but signs of high water from years past were cut into the rocks that I was clambering over. Progress was slow as I searched for a path, knowing that communities survived in this geographical wonder, so paths must indeed exist. It was during one delay of turning back to pick a better way that I noticed I was being followed. A man stayed back at least 20 paces, making constant calls on his mobile. Unsure whether he was actually following me or just heading the same way, I decided to sit down in the shade and enjoy my lunch of bread and cheese packed by last night's auberge. The man also sat down, still 20 paces away, and waited idly. When I got up to move again, so did he.

The man continued to follow me soundlessly most of the afternoon until I made a mistake and chose the wrong path. At this point he piped up, shouting at me to turn back and follow him. The follower now became the leader, and his overbearing instructions for dealing with any obstacles such as a trickle of water or a step higher than my ankle started to annoy me. I walked on his heels, constantly asking him to speed up in both French and Arabic. I knew it was poor manners, but then following a woman you don't know into a deep and isolated canyon could also be considered quite forward. It's hard to explain, but I didn't feel remotely apologetic – in fact, I felt like a prisoner. He hadn't outright declared an allegiance to the Gendarmerie yet, but the close follow and the constant phone calls seemed like a tip-off. Slowly, I was learning how the system worked.

The final stages of the canyon hike were some of the most stunning I've encountered on this planet. It rained on and off, and my minder, now joined by another, even slower man, constantly warned me of the danger of the fast-rising water. I only replied with a request that we quicken the pace and, when the trail was finally wide enough, I overtook my guides and left them in the dust.

At the top of the canyon I entered an old kasbah, now a derelict town cut into the sides of the rock, safely perched high above the river that at this time of year was still dry, but the locals told me could rise to dangerous levels in the winter. The old kasbah was captivating, and I walked down the narrow streets, peering into empty stone structures and wondering what stories the rocks here might tell. My touristing had allowed my stalker/guides to catch up, and they were both on their phones again – we were about to meet up with a dirt road, and I thought I knew what would happen next.

Sure enough, the two men delivered me with pride to the 4WD waiting at the end of the road. I was impressed that this vehicle was considerably nicer than the beat-up Gendarmerie jeeps I'd been meeting so far, when a man in a suit stepped out of the passenger seat.

'Hello, Jennifer!'

'Uhh . . . You know my name?'

'Of course! I've been watching all of your videos today.' There is no way to deliver that sentence and not sound sinister.

The man in the suit, Mohammad, represented the regional authority, and I deciphered that I had now moved up the ranks from the officers of the Gendarmerie to the suits that controlled them. I was vaguely impressed by my swift rise to stardom, but mostly concerned that the monitoring system I'd been increasingly frustrated by was about to escalate.

Mohammad drew maps for me, showing me the three available ways to continue the next stage of my journey *en piste*, and demanded to know which one I would take and how long it would take me. I had no intention of using the pistes, but gave him a vague answer anyway. He was clear with me – for the first time since this whole police debacle started – why we needed to keep in touch: they were convinced that I was 'somebody' (his term), and if anything bad happened to me, it would make the news in Europe and they would all lose their jobs. I now understood the threat to their livelihood and why none of these men could afford to let me out of their sight, so convinced were they that the mountains were teeming with danger. I futilely tried to explain to Mohammad that a) I was capable, and b) it was not their fault if I wasn't, but he was having none of it. 'It is our job to keep you safe, not yours.' Wow.

With the day's on-and-off rain, the locals were all incredibly concerned over flooding, although it hadn't rained in so long that it seemed unlikely that a dry river would so easily break its banks. Mohammad warned me that the road would be flooded ahead, and that it would be exceedingly dangerous now that the rain had started. I found it hard to believe him, but thanked him for the information. All the time we were chatting around his car, with a growing crowd of interested local men who had presumably heard that both Mohammad and I were in town, I found myself unconsciously backing away and turning my feet forwards, twisting my poles in my hands and preparing to break out into a run. The day had been massively delayed so far, and with the rain I was getting anxious to cover ground. I finally thanked Mohammad for his concern, reminded him one last time to tell his men to leave me alone, and excused myself – I had a big run ahead, and I needed to beat the rain now.

FRIENDS AND ALLIES

Being constantly pursued by questionable men persisted throughout the day, despite Mohammad's reassurances. When darkness fell I still hadn't found an isolated place to camp, having been discovered in my last one and not getting a nice vibe from the man who found me. After nearly an hour of running through pure black, I was suddenly startled when my feet hit the uncomfortably solid pavement of the road. It was disorienting, but I remembered the map and so turned right to follow the road for a bit. I didn't want to stay on it, just in case, but I needed some guidance for navigation in the dark night. The rain clouds had completely blocked out the stars and moon and for once I truly couldn't see anything.

A motorbike approached, and predictably the driver

stopped ahead. He spoke excellent French, but I waved him off, completely disgruntled by my experiences with the men in this region to date. Sensing my distrust, he said something about his English-speaking daughter, then got out his mobile. Soon he was thrusting his phone at me, and I was speaking with his daughter, who was at university, majoring in English.

'Please, go stay at my house tonight. My father is a good man, you can trust him. Oh, and I apologize in advance for my mother – she's very weird. But you'll be safe with them tonight.'

I told her I would describe my family the exact same way if our positions were reversed, and then took directions from the man, Brahim, to his house, which was only a few kilometres further down the road. He sped off on his small motorbike, assuring me that a hot meal awaited when I got there.

I ran easily in the dark, following the road confidently now that I knew I had a host looking out for me. Soon, however, I saw Brahim once more – parked next to a jeep. Here we go again.

When I caught up, Brahim was speaking with four officers, all in uniform for a change. They greeted me by name, which no longer surprised me. The officers reprimanded me for going off-piste again, which I barely acknowledged. Standing still, it was fairly chilly and the four men from the coastal north of Morocco were all bundled up in their army-green winter coats, shuffling their feet and complaining about the cold. They explained to me that gendarmes were relocated every few years in order to be trained in all environments, and none of the exclusively Arab–Moroccan force enjoyed being in the mountains with the Berbers.

After enough phone calls had been made and Brahim's interrogation was complete, the police acknowledged that I could stay with him and bid us goodnight. The track leaving the paved road and heading up to Brahim's house was to our left, so I hopped on the back of the motorbike in order to finish the ride up. I soon wished I hadn't. Wearing a backpack and having no helmet were not the best introduction to dirt-bike riding, but Brahim's skill on his rugged trail in the black night was frankly deserving of a medal.

I stumbled off the bike when we reached his dwelling, a typically Berber house made of clay and wood, in a simple rectangle and not decorated from the outside. We entered the front door into a small foyer where I was given sandals to wear in place of my trail shoes. To the right of the foyer was the sleeping room, where I put my bag down, and to the left was the cooking/living room, where Brahim and I joined his family. I was struck by how messy the family room was, as every Berber household I'd been in so far had been immaculately clean. I met Brahim's wife, and quickly remembered how their daughter had described this woman. She spoke only Tamazight, the Berber tongue, so we communicated through Brahim and my terrible French, interspersed with occasional phone calls to their trilingual daughter.

We shared a dinner of delicious omelette, bread and a soup so terrible that I really had to dig deep to put on a brave face and get it down with a gracious smile. The traditional Berber soup includes flour for some reason, along with a host of salty vegetables, and I was almost certain she had put marmalade in this one. It was quite horrible, but I did appreciate that they had generously shared a place at their table with me. Brahim continued to push me to eat well after I was over-full, sliding plates of olives nearer me and dropping more food onto my plate.

Throughout the evening I surprisingly gained a lot from our French discussion. Brahim and his neighbour spoke of the plight of the Berbers, telling me that they are the majority people of North Africa, and not holding back their negative opinions of the government and even the king. Up until now, I'd never heard a bad word uttered about the monarch. Despite the interesting discussion, I was completely knackered and it was nearly midnight when I could finally excuse myself to sleep. The Gendarmerie showed up to check on things, but Brahim insisted that I stay put, relaxed against some pillows in the corner, while he 'dealt with them'. I felt terrible that the reward for his generous hospitality was the police showing up at his house so late at night. Brahim, at least, saw my distress and dislike for the gendarmes' presence and did his best to keep me from having to see them on this occasion. His daughter was right – he was a good man.

After going outside to the toilet with Brahim's wife and other daughter – where I discovered they never built a toilet in their house, they simply went in the barn where their two cows stayed – I collapsed into my bed. Brahim wished the women goodnight and went to find somewhere suitable to lie down, since I was in the sleeping room, meaning he could not sleep there now. I felt terrible about this as well, but in seconds I was asleep.

At first light I was ready to go. I knew that I wasn't running as far as I would like lately with all the police delays and the social tea hours I'd been keeping, and I needed to get going. Brahim asked me to stay for breakfast, but as his family was still in bed I knew it would be a while and, most importantly, I felt I couldn't take any more of their food. He walked me down the trail leading up to his house to point me towards his water source, where I filled my bottles and bade him a final farewell. Brahim was one of the golden hearts of this journey and his generosity and kindness really touched me.

I started along a trail I found heading in my direction, and turned away from the road and the valley, which offered easy navigation but too much attention. I soon found another trail winding up the side of the rocky mountain, and the route was incredibly enjoyable. From the top of the pass, I spotted camels below, and waved to their shepherd as I passed. I was back in the Atlas I had dreamed of – a fantastic trail, challenging navigation, camels and friendly Berber shepherds. I took my time winding down the steep and rocky mountain pass, losing the path a few times before realizing that the trail was, actually, that incredibly steep bit that was more of a slide than a walking route. Focusing intensely on the placement of my feet and on not losing the faint trail in the rocky terrain, I completely forgot my stress from the previous days. I was just running, and nothing else. I stopped in a Berber cave on the side of the mountain – a shelter built to provide refuge from the sun while flocks grazed – to have a snack and a break. I liked that, behind the wall of rocks built outside the natural overhang, no one could see me. I imagined the people who had taken refuge in this ancient stone cave before me. Created from nothing but the natural environment, and yet offering an ideal place to rest. I smiled at its simple perfection. I was feeling more at ease in this Atlas environment, beginning to understand how the Berbers coped with it.

Despite the improvements in my mood, the pain in my body could not be denied. My hip had now swollen to an incredible level – I hadn't seen a mirror since the incident, but when the sun was behind me I could clearly identify in my own shadow the protrusion of swelling. The cut was constantly ripping open and bleeding, and I had to clean it as often as I could – difficult when there was no running water and no privacy. My feet throbbed. My shoulders ached. I was struggling.

I reached the town of Ait Hani in the early afternoon. As seemed to always be the case, the schoolkids were outside, rather than inside the school, and the attention of the adolescent boys was far worse than that of any uniformed men with guns. I noticed a small cafe and ducked inside, timidly asking the owner if it was okay for me to have a seat. I realized how backed into a corner I had become – not having found anywhere that would serve me since leaving Talsint, I was now shyly asking a café for permission to be a customer. I was completely overjoyed when the man pointed me to a table and produced an already prepared tagine with an almost-cold Coke. Although I had picked a seat that was hidden in the corner so no one from outside could see me, the experience of ordering food in a cafe and paying for it made me feel human again.

SURVEILLANCE

Hazy morning light dawned on the giant red slabs of rock. I was nestled underneath an overhang, a natural cave site with a sand floor, a perfectly designed bivvy location. Sadly, I woke to discover I was still not alone. The night before, an older man in a long white robe had insisted that he had the authority of the local chief to 'protect me', and I was disappointed to see that he was still there. He had sat watch, chain-smoking cigarettes, all night long. I won the battle to insist he stayed a far enough distance from me to avoid second-hand smoke, but waking to discover that I was still under supervision – and had been *while I was sleeping* – stirred an awkward feeling in my stomach. I was not comfortable with this arrangement at all.

I assumed he hadn't slept, so while I found the experience a level beyond incredibly invasive, I was also slightly touched by the paternal – although misplaced – protection, and made amnesty with the offer of a cup of coffee. I asked him if he had any water of his own that I could use to boil for coffee, and he didn't, which sent me immediately back to being annoyed – how could they think that *I* was in danger out here, when *they* were the ones without the common sense to bring provisions in a desert ecosystem? It bewildered me how many men had now chased me into the hostile landscape without proper supplies, and I'd ended up having to offer them my own limited water, which was often carefully calculated to get me through to the next water source, so I didn't have any to spare. I was already surviving on a thin edge of being dehydrated.

Having used more water than budgeted, I was forced to

start my day in the wrong direction, towards a nearby village where I could get more. In the village, I was once again greeted by rude and jeering schoolboys – which made me wonder if they ever actually went to school, or just hung around outside waiting to tease passing runners. I tried to stay out of sight of a football pitch, but the boys there spotted me and abandoned their game in favour of bullying the foreigner. Edged on by testosterone and each other, they were soon sending rocks flying in my direction, and I ran frantically, realizing that they did not recognize the serious risk of injury they were posing: as they encouraged each other to be bolder, the rocks started landing bigger and faster.

I made it unscathed, although in a seriously declined mood, to the piste which now wound through the steep mountains. I was nearing Mgoun, the second highest peak in Morocco, and the scenery was changing rapidly into the big mountains I had envisaged in planning this expedition. This alone comforted me, and I fell back into a happy rhythm of mountain running.

ALTITUDE

The harsh sun was forcing its way into the small window in the room of the *gîte d'étape* (hostel) telling me I couldn't stay any longer. I'd been throwing up all night, and I felt absolutely awful. Supporting myself with my hands on the red clay walls of the ancient home, adjacent to a magnificent old kasbah, I stumbled down to the kitchen and painted a smile on my face to assure the gite's owner – another Brahim – that, despite sleeping late, I was okay. I did my best to finish my omelette and bread in order to replace all of the calories I had lost in the night, but I was seriously concerned about my health.

Brahim's granddaughter came to sit on my lap, and I took comfort in the short-lived cuddle before her mother shooed her away to get ready for school. I've always appreciated how children don't need to understand a word of your language to enjoy spending time with you, and we had been the best of pals since I arrived at the gite late the previous afternoon. When the kids left for school and the women of Brahim's house commenced their work, I knew I needed to rally and get myself moving.

The run that day started with a long, long climb, up the highest mountain pass – *tizi* in Tamazight – I'd seen so far. It was a hot day and the surrounding peaks sheltered me from any cooling wind. My head pounded and nausea came in waves as I slogged up towards the sun. It was incredibly unpleasant, and I had the shakes. I knew I needed electrolytes, or anything in my system, really, but couldn't stomach anything. I drank water greedily, thankful that I could at least handle that much. I had lost a lot the night before, and dehydration was probably my biggest worry under this baking sky.

I reached the top of the pass, where a cold wind was a welcome relief from my suffering. My muscles were still shaking, and I didn't trust my stomach. At least I knew it hadn't got much more than water to expel at this point. The piste wound down to the town of Amezri, but feeling bold, I decided to jump off it and shoot down the goat tracks that scratched the mountainside in all directions. It was incredible fun, and took my mind off my illness and overall adventure frustrations. It reminded me why I love running in the mountains, and by the time I reached my destination I had a huge grin on my face as well as dirt all over my freshly washed clothes.

Amezri was one of the bigger towns I'd visited that didn't have a paved road. I shouldn't have been surprised any more that the entire place was expecting me, and my arrival had even been alerted by a man sitting near the top of the pass, who shouted after me for not taking the piste – I guess he had been planning to meet me and walk me in. I went directly to the river, slipping off my shoes – much to the amusement of the local women, who were all gathered on the banks of the river doing their household laundry. I waded out to a little rocky island where I could sit with my feet in the stream and eat the apple I'd been given at the gite that morning. My body badly needed the sugar, and the shakes dissipated slightly. Young girls, who had accompanied their mothers to do the laundry, gathered to watch me, giggling.

As the crowd increased, I knew it was time to get moving. I crossed the river, put my shoes back on and asked some of the kids watching me where I could find a shop. There was only one answer: 'Monsieur Abrahim.' I suspected he was a shop owner, and asked to be taken in his direction. A gaggle of children took great delight and pride in showing me the way. They ran back and forth, little boys jockeying for position closest to me and all shouting for my attention as we wound through the town. The streets were narrow and dusty, and old metal doors hung from sand-coloured houses that rose up on the hillside. Many of the doors were painted, with hand-lettered Arabic or Tamazight text above them. Aside from the doors, the entire village was the colour of sand. Finally, the growing crowd of boys declared that we had reached Monsieur Abrahim: I was disappointed to discover that I had been delivered to a house, not a shop. I was greeted by a middle-aged man, who showed me inside and pointed me to a room. Slowly, I understood that Monsieur Abrahim owned a gite and expected me to stay tonight. It seemed I was the single tourist in the entire region this week, so I could appreciate that businesses would expect my custom, but it was only noon. I explained that I couldn't stay, but I had been looking for a shop. Soon, a mobile was thrust into my hand and I was speaking to Monsieur Abrahim himself – the village chief.

Abrahim told me that his job as chief was to know *everything* about *everyone*. 'Who is getting married, who is ill, who is having a disagreement – everything. That's my job. So I need to know what you're doing.' I can't overstate how glad I am that I don't live somewhere like that. I enjoy my privacy far too much – a trait that this Atlas journey was really bringing out in me.

'I'm just looking for a shop and then I'm going to keep going . . .'

'But where will you sleep tonight?'

'Monsieur Abrahim, it's the middle of the day. I have no idea where I'll sleep tonight. Somewhere approximately six to eight hours away from here, I guess.'

Finally, after meeting literally a dozen villagers all trying to push me into the gite, I was shown towards a shop where I could buy clean water and a cola, hoping the latter would sort out my queasiness.

I got far enough out of town for the crowd to disappear, but as the heat of day rose I was really not feeling well. I decided to walk, so I could continue to make some progress. Since hurting my hip I was consistently falling behind on daily targets, and couldn't afford any more setbacks if I was going to finish within my goal of 20 days across the Atlas.

I was now in a fertile valley, and the constant presence of green vegetation, shady trees and a clear-running stream felt a world apart from the hostile beginnings of this journey. With working soil, however, came population, and I was forever going through small communities, some delightful, some filled with more bullying children who demanded money, candy or *un stylo,* and threw stones when denied. One incident encouraged me to try running again, and as I sprinted from some particularly naughty young boys, I ended up running straight past the gendarmes who had been waiting, blocking the road to ensure they caught me. I sprinted on. This was where the road ended, so I disappeared down a small trail and the cops had no way of following me in their car. The feeling of being under surveillance was overwhelming me, and I craved the freedom that trail running has always supplied me. The freedom that I was now realizing I had taken for granted in my whole life until now. I looked at the small trail as a hope to feel free for a moment.

The trail took me down to the riverbed now and, following the clearly stamped outline of a track, I was crossing the river back and forth. It was refreshing but icy, and I was conscious that doing this many river crossings so late in the day would mean that my shoes probably wouldn't dry out overnight. Not such a big deal, but I was starting to get cold from the constant submersion and even wearing my gilet for warmth – a true mark that I had ascended into a new alpine ecosystem.

At the end of the working day, traffic along the river route picked up considerably as families with loaded donkeys returned from working on their plots. Berbers of all ages walked alongside their donkeys, whose baskets were filled with corn. They said hello and watched in amusement as I picked my way through the fast-flowing river in my trail shoes, using my poles for balance, while young and old dived in without apparently noticing the temperature, wearing cheap plastic flip-flops, often with their hands full already.

Dusk drew in and I was certain that I'd have no trouble finding a place to camp – there were both abundant water and plenty of trees to take shelter (and privacy) behind. As it grew darker, traffic had mostly died down as most families were back in their homes by now. I began the search for a place to spend the night.

This, of course, was when the spies that I hadn't noticed emerged from the woodwork. The second I stepped off the trail, I realized I was surrounded by men who had been tracking me, waiting for this moment to ensure that I didn't dare try to sleep outside. I was almost beginning to believe that stargazing was the highest crime I could commit, so seriously were they taking the business of stopping me from doing it.

I continued, playing oblivious, but picking up the pace. Torches began appearing on all sides, and before I knew it I had practically run straight into one. It was now entirely dark, so I couldn't see much of who had won the game of Capture the Runner, but I could make out that he was relatively young, wearing a t-shirt and the standard flip-flops. He explained that he had been asked by the Gendarmerie to come and meet me. Of course he had. I immediately made it clear that I didn't want any help and knew where I was going – *thank you, bye.*

'No, no, no, no, please!' He ran in front me. 'One of my favourite mottoes is: *fuck the police.*' I laughed harder than I think I had since starting this adventure. Of all the reactions to the police I'd had that week, I had yet to come across this one. If it were a different culture, I might have just kissed him right then and there.

Moha (short for Mohammad, and by far the most popular name for boys in Berber communities) was the first and only student in the entire valley to have gone away to university and, luckily for me, he had majored in English, so when he said that the Gendarmerie had asked him to come and meet me, the truth was that they had *told him* he had to come and meet me. It didn't matter that today was one of the busiest days for working the fields (hence all the human and donkey traffic I had passed) and he needed to help his family – the pursuit of stopping me from sleeping out was far more important than his family's livelihood. The Gendarmerie really were pulling out all of the stops.

I walked with Moha, enjoying a conversation in fluent English with a fuck-the-police sympathizer. It was a chance for me to download my thoughts from the past week to someone who finally got it, and I found myself unloading on the poor kid. Luckily, he had a great sense of humour and – unsurprisingly, considering the first words he had said to me – progressive views that sympathized with independent women. Moha shared with me his own frustrations with the small communities, saying that he even took 'holidays' to Marrakesh for a few days of being in the big city, surrounded by different types of people and ideas. Although I had told Moha that I wanted to camp that night, he joked that he would take it personally if I didn't accept his invitation to dinner at his family home. I knew it wasn't a joke.

It was a long walk, weaving in and out of the river while Moha did his gentlemanly best to help me by shifting large rocks and sticks for me to walk over, despite my constant reminders to him that I had come this far and could handle getting my feet wet. I truly enjoyed our conversation, learning so much about life in the Atlas, the plight of the Berbers in an Arab country, and the struggle of young Berber men torn between the modern world and the rigid responsibilities to their communities.

A steep climb out of the river valley led us to the small village where Moha's family home dominated. It was a village of nearly 400 people, and only ten houses. I began to understand Moha's need to escape to the big city every now and then. In his early twenties now, he would live in this house for ever, and the building would grow as sons married and children were added.

Moha's home was unlike any Berber household I'd seen before. Since he had been to university, I'd already guessed that his family was wealthier than those I had met so far, but entering his home I was suddenly aware of how grubby I was. A metal gate led us in through a garden, and even though it was completely dark I could sense I was surrounded by a lovingly tended Eden. The entranceway was decorated with traditional Berber rugs and flowerpots, and led us into a small, colourful courtyard. A large storeroom was filled with the day's maize collection, which Moha said would be left to dry there for some time, and the labour was the reason that the house was full tonight – all of the family was required to work this week, so everyone had been called in.

I was led upstairs, where a contingent of men who were part Moha's family, part Gendarmerie and part curious villagers awaited in a small room that was lined floor to ceiling in Berber rugs, with a bench covered in bright fabrics and cushions lining the wall the entire way around. I realized I'd become accustomed to sitting on the floor, and placed myself awkwardly on my seat, remembering how to use furniture. Tea was served by a younger sister, and bread and meat skewers arrived as appetizers soon after. Typically, mobile phones buzzed constantly as Moha translated my story and interested parties around Morocco – whoever they were – were filled in on my day's adventures.

One man in a brown robe, associated with the Gendarmerie but clearly unaccustomed to and uncomfortable with dining with a woman, so he never addressed me directly, muttered something and the room broke out in laughter. Moha translated.

'There is a joke going around the valley today, that Maroc Telecom is so happy that you've visited our country.'

I was almost relieved to hear that the endless phone calls

about every detail of my day were, in fact, unusual, and a little proud that I featured in the valley's new favourite joke.

Some of the men went home – long walks back to their own villages in the dark – and it was nearly 10pm when dinner arrived. I was struggling to keep my eyes open and faint from how little I'd eaten that day; I'd considered just going to bed without eating, but remembered Moha's comment that it would be an offence to him and his family if I didn't dine with them. Dinner was a large communal bowl of couscous, covered in a variety of vegetables, with chicken underneath. Me and the six men remaining were given spoons, and one knife was left on the table for someone to cut up the chicken pieces once we'd eaten through the vegetable layer. Glasses of fermented milk were passed around and we dug in. It was beyond delicious. Even in the city restaurants of Morocco, I never found a couscous as good as that one.

I was given my own large, carpeted room with a mattress in the middle, and shown where I could wash up with running water. I felt surrounded by luxury, and was so glad of Moha's friendship. I slept remarkably well, recovering from the rough illness of the previous night and relieved to be safe from pestering men, in my own private room in Moha's wonderful house.

'FUCK THE POLICE'
I had breakfast with the men of Moha's family, to whom I expressed my overwhelming gratitude before setting off on a chilly morning. The change in climate at this new altitude was incredibly welcome. My morning trail led me instantly back

down to the river, and a particularly deep crossing chilled my bones. It had been a while since I had been truly cold.

The river valley soon ended and I was returned to the piste, which cut off abruptly at the valley. The transition from pebbly and muddy riverbed to solid tarmac was stark on the legs, but the instant increase in pace was a good idea – I was *really* falling behind targets now.

With a piste came drivers, and it wasn't long before I met today's Gendarmerie. Officer of the Day was Hassan, and he was, for a change, dressed impeccably in full uniform. Perhaps my fear of plain-clothed men chasing me was the only feedback they had taken on board from my download to Moha. Lingering behind Hassan, failing to disguise their curiosity to meet the famous female runner, were about six men in varying outfits, from less grand police uniforms to business suits to shabby work clothes. The suit was the first to come forward and, through Hassan's translation, explained his important position as the village 'chief' or, the way I understood it, 'man who knows everyone's business'. I never quite wrapped my head around the concept of a guy who just seemed to go around collecting the gossip and occasionally offering counsel, but it did help me to further appreciate the level of culture clash that I was going through with these men. While it was foreign and frustrating to me to have so much nosey involvement in my journey from so many uninvited guests, it was equally foreign to them that I might want to keep any corners of my life private. They simply couldn't see how my sleeping arrangements or dietary preferences *wouldn't* be any of their business.

My route continued on the quiet road, and after about an hour I saw Hassan's police car pulled up beside it, with him and a couple of others waiting. He held his arm out to stop me, as I suppose I had now gained a reputation for blowing these guys off and, taking my headphones out, I shrugged at him, as if to say, 'What's this about?'

Hassan beamed and pointed me to a shack across the road. A wooden structure missing significant amounts of the original building, with a crooked door and no business sign, stood plainly; hiding in the shadows was a quiet girl, clearly waiting for me as she had been instructed to. Only because she was there did I allow myself to be ushered inside, where I found that, in the dilapidated shed with a dirt floor, the girl had laid out her best of a morning tea – small plates of honey, walnuts and bread, along with sweet Berber tea. While I ate, awkwardly by myself, I turned around to discover that she had already snatched my water bottle and filled it up, returning it to me along with a small red apple.

I heaved myself up from the floor, thanking the girl profusely and nodding at Hassan – I didn't want him to keep doing this, but it was clear that he was trying to smooth things over for me and ensure I had a good (and safe) time.

At the point where I met the boundary of Hassan's jurisdiction and turned off the gravel road, onto the pathless abyss of the Atlas Mountains, he and his men were waiting, almost ceremonially, at a pull-out when I arrived. The sun was lowering, applying a golden hue to the red earth and increasing the drama of the farewells we then performed. I posed for a few photos and selfies, and was surprised to receive words of genuine well-wishing and – best of all – true admiration for my expedition. It was a nice boost to hear positivity and respect from these men, and I was grateful for their brief involvement – invited or not – in my project.

I tucked my headphones away and sprinted down the thin path that led away from civilization once more. With no vegetation or living soil to bear the marks of erosion, the 'path' was hard to spot, but I was determined not to make any errors while the gendarmes could still see me. I kept my pace, gleefully running towards wilderness and isolation.

My first climb of this segment was a glorious experience of sweating and labouring. I took my shirt off, relishing the freedom of being truly alone in a part of the world where women can so seldom feel free like this. In fairness, I wouldn't normally take my shirt off to run in any nation, no matter what their culture for women, so it was a liberating experience in its own right. The late-afternoon sun baked the trail and my head, but the whisper of a breeze near the top of the climb felt amazing on bare skin.

Then the descent happened. Suddenly, the earth fell away from under my feet and I was left with a sheer rocky slope to calculate. The path was so faint it was rendered useless, and the dry slope slid away too easily with the impact of a footstrike. As I started making my way down, I discovered that my legs had gone 'Bambi' again. My quads consistently gave way when I tried to plant confident footstrikes, and I found that I couldn't trust my legs anymore to take me safely down the mountainside. As I shook with both muscular exhaustion and the onset of fear, my movement became increasingly awkward until it stopped altogether. I stood frozen on the flank of scree, the valley still an impossible distance beneath me.

Please, I whispered to my legs, *just get to the bottom of this and I promise I'll stop. I'll even stretch tonight.* I was attempting to negotiate with my own pins. They did not answer. Only continued to shake. They shook so hard I wondered if my knees would literally knock against each other soon. I could not will either foot to pick itself up from its planted spot and try to advance. I looked at my position, and reasoned that I couldn't even sit down, so precarious was my place on the sliding, precipitous rocky slope; the fear that any movement would send me tumbling down the mountain took hold of my brain and my muscles.

Breathe, I commanded myself. *Please breathe.*

I took small, sharp breaths. I started trying to count. I couldn't go for five, so I counted inhales of three, two, one . . . and then exhales of three, two, one.

You can do this. I was now speaking out loud, although not very convincingly. Even my voice was shaking, in conjunction with my legs.

What should have taken a healthy body *minutes* to descend took me until well after the sun disappeared. Negotiating the steep descent in the dark of course only worsened my nerves, and when I reached the bottom I was a mixture of grateful and annoyed at myself. My legs still shook from both exhaustion and fear. The floor of the valley was marked by a concrete irrigation channel which had just over an inch of running water moving down it. My bottle slowly filled, and I found a flat patch of ground not far from the water source and began laying out my bivvy. Finally, peace and quiet. I was actually getting to camp outside, alone with the starry sky above. My recent episode disappeared from my mind quickly, and I was back to smiling. The liberation of getting to remove my clothes and 'bathe' with a wet cloth, taking my time and stretching aching muscles as I tended to my body, was a pure pleasure. I pulled on clean underwear, my baggy sweatpants and wool sweater, and laid out my inflated mattress and sleeping bag. I did more slow stretching while waiting for my stove to boil, and watched the stars arrive as I ate my couscous in total solitude. I lay back, using my backpack as a pillow, and fell asleep with a smug grin on my face: I had evaded the Gendarmerie for one night, and here I was, doing the thing I love most, sleeping under the stars in a mountain wilderness. It was total bliss.

TWO WEEKS IN

I surprised myself by being awake and feeling good before dawn, and had even managed to have my coffee and porridge and splash my face in the shallow channel before the sun arrived. I was packed up and moving under a head torch, my tender feet beginning to warm up on the rocky riverbed as I located the next route up. The long climb was one of my biggest of the journey, at 3,200m, and near the top I realized that I was now two weeks in. I was elated at this discovery, partly because I had covered so much ground, but largely because I was marking two full weeks of living my dream. The Atlas had not gone remotely to plan so far, with my hip injury now showing clear signs of infection and my dramas with the Gendarmerie affecting my emotional health, but, all things told, the difficulties only made me more proud to be able to continue and to be in this magical place that had required so much grit to eke out even just two weeks. At the top of the climb, I paused to celebrate.

From a high point in the Atlas Mountains, on a day that isn't too hazy, you can see the Sahara to your south and the plains of Morocco to your north. East and west are more rocky mountains. I've never found a place on earth with such startling views. To be able to stand, at altitude, and cast my eyes out over the great sands of the Sahara was a feeling like no other. I was entranced.

I bounced down the trail in the sun, running again without my sweaty top on, relishing the cool wind on my bare skin. Two weeks of sweating heavily with a backpack rubbing up and down had left raw sores on my shoulders and collarbones, and I tried to hold my backpack straps off my skin to give these sores a chance at fresh air. Being wrapped up in dress-code running clothes that aren't being washed often enough wasn't proving healthy for broken skin all over my body.

I didn't get enough time to rectify my clothing violation – at the bottom of the descent, a man was heading straight towards me on a mule. I fumbled to toss my backpack down and get my shirt on, but he didn't hesitate. Instead, he came storming towards me, watching me quickly pull my shirt down over my exposed bra. I was horrified that he had seen what he did, and that he hadn't given me any show of modesty.

'Jennifer?'

Oh, good. Here we go again.

'I'm Mohammad. I'm here to get you. Get on the mule.'

'No, thanks, I'm good.'

'Well, I've been given orders to bring you back to the village . . .'

'No, thanks, I'm good.' I had breathed in the sheer taste of *freedom* at the top of that pass, and I wasn't in the headspace to let it go just yet.

This obviously didn't work. I tried to maintain my running pace, but Mohammad's slow mule blocked my path and I frequently tried to run past him. Mohammad spoke excellent English and I had explained the situation to him: I was just out for a run and really didn't want an escort. I got the impression that the Gendarmerie must have told him to come back with me or not come back at all, such was his conviction that we needed to remain together. Mohammad ran a gite in the next village and probably expected me to be a willing customer. It was early in the afternoon when we arrived, and I had to break it to him that I was not going to stop this early, and further that what time I stopped and where were entirely my own decision.

In the foyer of Mohammad's grand gite was a congregation of officers awaiting my arrival. Apparently me staying out last night where no one knew where I was hadn't gone down very well. I secretly smiled at that.

I was provided with tea while we went through the standard rigmarole of looking at my passport, talking about my route, asking why I wouldn't run on the pistes or just accept a lift in a car to my next destination. I was tired of it, and these men were really irking me. Why couldn't they just send one or two? Why did it always have to be half of the police force? I looked out the window, aching to be back running. The morning had gone so well, and my body had felt good. I wanted to keep going. I hated being held up by these meetings, which always went the same way. I already knew how it would end, and I grew impatient.

'Enough. I'm leaving.'

I attempted to stand up, but the gaggle of men really kicked off then. My bag was strongly held by at least three hands, and I was pushed back into my seat. Mohammad stood in the doorway, visibly offended that I wasn't booking a room for the night – even though it was only 2pm.

All the men were talking loudly at once, in at least three languages to try and get the point home – *we are concerned for your safety.*

Like a broken record, I repeated the same plea again: *I want freedom and privacy. Please stop following me. Please stop sending people out to look for me. Please stop ignoring everything I say.*

An ember of rage was glowing hot in my belly, and I seriously wondered if I was about to cry. If I wanted to be treated like a human adult, not a lowly *woman,* I really needed to keep control of my emotions.

This time I snatched my bag faster than it could be grabbed by anyone else, took my passport and rushed out the door. I couldn't keep wasting the hours of the days in offices with patronizing officers. I couldn't keep having the same enraging conversation every day.

I bit my lip and pulled my sunglasses down, hoping to disguise my emotions and hold them in until I was out of sight.

I ran in a minor rage away from Mohammad's small village, tracing the edge of the dirt road to the next one. But before long the police truck pulled up in front of me, at an angle that deliberately blocked my route. It was Hassan, the local chief (my third Chief Hassan, by my count).

'Jennifer,' he held a hand up in a stopping gesture, 'I understand you want to do this little run, and I do respect that, but I need you to get in the jeep. The next fifteen kilometres are too dangerous for you to go alone, so I'll drive you and then drop you off after fifteen kilometres. All right?'

I struggled to imagine what could be so much worse than anything I had already overcome.

'What's so dangerous, Hassan?'

'There will be no mobile phone service for fifteen kilometres. Please, it's not worth the risk, get in the jeep.'

Most mountain enthusiasts rejoice at a lack of phone signal. I couldn't help but laugh.

'Bye, Hassan.'

EVASION

Early in the morning, I was jogging slowly along a paved road as the cluster of villages near the highway came to life. Behind me, I noticed something completely out of place: another runner. A young man wearing sweatpants and sleeveless shirt, exposing his large muscles, was running at pretty much my exact pace. It's a situation that would be unnerving anywhere in the world. I told myself he might just be out for a jog – he was certainly dressed for it – but it didn't seem at all likely that a strong young man without a backpack or two weeks of marathons in his legs would only be doing *my* pace. Knowing I couldn't outrun him, I pulled off the road and waited. When he caught up, he shook my hand and assured me he wasn't following me.

We jogged together for a while, and I learned that my new pal was, indeed, in the Gendarmerie, and of course was out to catch me. At least this one came prepared to run, even with his own water bottle.

As we neared the highway that intersects the Atlas, I came up with a fantastic plan. When we reached the crossing point, Hassan was predictably there with his jeep and crew. I informed him that I was heading back to Marrakesh today, and had had a wonderful time in the Atlas. From this intersection, it was only two hours to Marrakesh, where I could spend the night to regroup and come back by the next afternoon, not losing too much valuable time from my expedition. Within minutes Hassan flagged down a bus for me, the driver of which refused to take payment, and I was off to the city, leaving Hassan and all of his colleagues satisfied that I had finally come to my senses.

After two weeks of Atlas bliss, Marrakesh was overwhelming to the senses. It was nothing like the city I had been to when I first arrived at the start of my journey. I felt as though someone had turned up the dial on the sounds, smells, heat and bustle. I rushed to the riad that I had stayed in at the start of my trip and left a few clean belongings in. I had texted Said, the manager, from the bus to tell him I would be staying for one night, and he was waiting for me with a pot of tea already in my room.

I tossed all of my dusty and sweaty clothes into the sink, and had my first real shower in perhaps too long. It was also the first time I saw the full damage to my hip in a mirror, and I was horrified. A scar tissue clump the size of a small apple was protruding from the side of my body, and the bruising extended all the way from my hip to the middle of my thigh. The cut itself was festering slightly, but I was far more worried about the protrusion. I began to wonder if I had made a good decision to run over 500km on this injury (so far).

Bustling Marrakesh nightlife held no interest for me, so after washing everything thoroughly and repacking with new supplies, I went to bed early, feeling totally at peace that I was alone in my locked, clean room, in a bed. No police officers, no midnight visitors, no beetles crawling on my face. It was perhaps one of the longest and best sleeps of my life.

A NEW LEAF

I left my camping equipment – stove and sleeping bag – with Said and went to find a ride back to the Atlas, this time with a considerably lighter backpack and a cunning plan to improve my journey. I was over halfway through the distance now and, given that there were more villages in the western Atlas Mountains, there would be no requirement for my heavy camping gear. As bivvying outside had been the crux of the issue with the Gendarmerie supporting my expedition, I resigned myself to staying in gites or with Berbers for the rest of the journey. I knew that the Gendarmerie now believed my expedition to be over – enough of the Hassans had texted me in the last 24 hours to confirm this. I also knew the next segment took me to Imlil and Mount Toubkal, by far the most touristed place in the entire mountain range. I wouldn't stand out, so the chances of my police detail picking me up once more seemed slim. It was so clever that I giggled to myself as I stepped out of my shared taxi two hours later, tightening the straps on my backpack and heading west, on my own.

The gain in elevation as I neared North Africa's tallest mountain brought with it a beautiful change of scenery. My route for the afternoon was a canyon that was, for the first time, flowing with clear, clean water. Most of the time, I was up to thigh deep in the refreshing river, moving gradually uphill by boulders and rocks smoothed over by the water. It was deliciously soothing to stay in the water all afternoon, but the pace was very limited. I knew I had lost some time on my Marrakesh field trip, but hoped that the lighter backpack would help me pick things back up.

I met my first *gîte d'étape* at the base of the final climb to take me into Imlil at 4pm. It was an awkward hour to arrive at such a spot – the few remaining hours of sunlight wouldn't be enough for me to get over the pass, but stopping early would make me feel antsy. My decision was made by the owner endlessly mansplaining the concept of outdoor recreation to me, as if I had just fallen out of the sky and had no idea how to use a trail. I didn't want to spend the rest of the afternoon with him, and the mountains were calling. Only one night in the city had had a profound effect on me and I needed some wilderness.

I wrote in my diary that night: '*Made it to the 3,290m col* (tizi) *just at sunset and nearly cried at the beauty as I saw the oranges and purples going down on the other side of the pass. Insane mountain moment. Will never forget it.'*

Sometimes, moving in the mountains can be a spiritual experience, and that night was a profound one for me. It felt like I had started a new chapter in my mission across the Atlas and things were about to change. Things were about to get really good.

I picked my way down the pass in total darkness, made much easier with the light pack, but the vision of my hip injury stayed strong in my mind and held me back from sprinting down the slope. The trail zigzagged steeply, and falling off the side in the dark would have serious consequences. The stars were out by now, and although I was tired and no longer had the option of camping, I was in no rush to make this wonderful night come to an end. I knew that another gite was stationed at the bottom of this side of the col and, thankfully, the owner – another Brahim – turned out to be incredibly welcoming. He laughed when I told him I had just come down the pass in the dark, and I knew I had found someone who was going to react differently to my lifestyle. He shrugged off his brother's complaints that I had shown up so late, and barked him back into the kitchen to make me something anyway. I was starving and incredibly grateful when an omelette showed up minutes later, followed by a *sort of* warm half-shower. I sat in the living room drinking tea and looking at Brahim's skiing photos. Being an avid skier in the Atlas Mountains seemed like a heart-breaking hobby – he and his friends had to hike considerable distances to find a patch of snow big enough to slide down, and in many seasons he didn't even get out once.

I went to bed that night completely pleased with this new chapter. I had spent an entire day without surveillance, and it had been an amazing day in the mountains at that. I was brimming with excitement for the next few days, which involved the biggest mountains of the range and the places I had looked forward to seeing the most.

THE HEART OF THE ATLAS

As I left Brahim's gite, my morning was greeted with a delightful downhill run to the village of Imlil. With my lightened pack and equally lightened mood, the fresh air of dew and smoke rising from the kitchens of Imlil smelled like the start of a good day.

Imlil is the hub town for active tourism in Morocco, with Mount Toubkal nearby as the main attraction. I had held a vision of this town in my mind for weeks, and as the Atlas had got harder and harder – especially culturally – over the past few days, I kept retaining hope for Imlil, where I could relax for a bit. As I neared the town, I began to see tourists for the first time in the Atlas. I was shocked to see white skin flashing from short sleeves and shorts – far more of the human body than I'd seen on anyone lately, including myself.

Imlil was much smaller than I imagined, with only one real intersection, still managing to have something of a traffic jam between three *grands taxis* and a couple of camels. One of the taxis was stuck in the rocky climb, the steepness and the loose gravel a pretty ambitious route for an old sedan, and the other two sat behind honking endlessly, which did nothing to help that I could see.

It was about time for second breakfast, and I went straight for a cafe with a rooftop patio. My excitement brimmed when the waiter didn't bat an eye at this lone woman taking a seat in his establishment, and he passed me a laminated menu. I ordered my first *cafe nous nous* – a milky Moroccan espresso – and an omelette. When the omelette and accompanying bread arrived, the waiter then took his turn to disapprove of me, nodding at the fork he had laid on the table.

'You eat like a Berber,' he observed, and it didn't sound like a compliment. Blushing, I picked up the fork, slightly horrified at myself that on my first chance to eat in a real cafe I had still managed to disgrace myself. *Must blend in better.* I took a second coffee and watched the life of Imlil from the balcony, smiling down at tourists bartering for Berber crafts from the small shops lining the streets while cars perpetually got stuck in the same spot the taxi had been earlier. I wondered how long that hole had been there. (Side-note: I returned two years later, and it was still a source of chaos.)

Imlil mainly served tourists, and the attraction of comfortable hotels, welcoming restaurants (as in, welcoming even to solo foreign women) and the people of the town's nonchalant acceptance of me was a tempting prospect. I could have stayed for days, relaxing with the comforts and relishing my anonymity, if I let myself, so I knew I had to get moving. The longer I stayed, the more likely I would lose my resolve to keep going, so I promised myself that I would come back as soon as I had dipped my toes in the Atlantic, which felt much closer now – if Toubkal was the highest point on the range, surely it was all downhill from here.

Following the trail out of Imlil over my next pass, it was odd to see the treads of European hiking boots in the dirt, rather than Berber sandals or, more usually, no human prints at all. At the top of the climb I met a hiker from Namibia, lounging under the shade with his shirt off and the tattoos of his pale skin on display for all. We chatted briefly, and he told me that he had come to Imlil to hike every winter for 25 years. I was glad to have the confirmation that the place *was* as spectacular as I thought it was, but also surprised that in such a long period of time he had never considered how culturally inappropriate it was for him to be here with his shirt off. In hindsight, it doesn't seem that bad – but after more than two weeks of moving through some of the most conservative communities in the country, Western behaviour was providing a real reverse culture shock, and I felt embarrassed by his bare skin.

I wondered if that was how the locals had felt around me, with my bare head and neck. I had covered my arms and legs, but I had admittedly compromised to assemble an outfit I felt I could still run in. It had been incredibly uncomfortable, at first, to dress in a way that *wasn't me*. I always ran in shorts, no matter what the weather, and I felt awkward in the long leggings. Complying with the dress code and constantly being conscious of something as innocuous as my knees seeing daylight had been a big stress for me coming to Morocco, but by now I had accepted this part of the culture. Humans are incredibly adaptable and, almost anywhere you go, people will ultimately blend into the local ways. In only two weeks, it was no longer something I thought about, and I actually felt most comfortable in the evenings when I could stand to wear my baggy sweatpants and sweater, covering myself up more when the temperatures dropped. The Western tourists in Imlil seemed as foreign to me now as the concept of covering my knees had been only a couple of weeks ago.

Leaving the shirtless guy from the top of the pass, I happily descended the switchbacked dirt track, weaving on a dusty path between sparse trees. I had seen so few trees in the past two weeks that their presence was a sheer delight to me. I filled my nostrils with the fresh scent they provided, and marvelled at their life in the otherwise dry and harsh Atlas. I could have greeted each one individually, but settled for keeping my pace up and just smiling at the mountainside as a whole, appreciating its vitality.

A slog along a riverbed slowed down the rest of my afternoon, but I pushed forwards with the newfound optimism that came from my return to freedom and solitude. Evening arrived as a sudden surprise, after I'd spent too much time chilling in Imlil, and I found myself in a village with an auberge, so made my way there for the night. It was a fairly run-down establishment, and it felt strange to be back in the anonymity of being just another tourist at a Moroccan backpacker joint. I was shown a room with a broken shower and sagging bed, with a football game blasting in the main room just outside my door. I couldn't really argue with the price, nor the opportunity to sleep alone behind a locked door, and after a filling meal of Berber omelette (which I ate with a fork) and a difficult cold shower, I was soon sound asleep on the thin sheets.

DESCENT

I stopped to sit on a boulder by the river and apply duct tape to the worn blisters on my feet and ankles, and I wondered how many more days my feet could really take inside these shoes. When I left my bivvy in Marrakesh, I filled up the empty space in my bag with a pair of sandals I haggled for in the souk, and was diligently switching my sweaty socks for the air of sandals any time I stopped running, but the damage to my soles couldn't be fixed with an hour here or there – it would take weeks of painful healing. I knew this from Kyrgyzstan, which had left me with cracked heels so painful I couldn't stand to walk for many days following, and hardened skin and blisters, not to mention the fragmented or bruised toenails. A piece of duct tape that I had just torn off from the roll I made around my water bottle stuck to my thumb as I searched for the place to put it, but reflected that the entire foot really needed saving. My skin was puffy and sensitive, fluid pooling underneath. The ankles of my shoes were dark with many days' worth of blood from the small but constant ankle cuts I received on the harsh rocky landscape.

And that was just my feet. Working my way up, my legs were depleted. At the start of the expedition, my thighs had been perhaps the largest I'd ever seen them, thanks to a summer of intensive cycling. Now, in less than three weeks, they were nearing the thinnest I had seen them, all of that muscle mass gone with the sirocco winds. To see my body visibly weaker in just a couple of weeks was an alarm bell that I really needed to finish this thing off – and in the meantime,

I really needed to eat more. My injured hip was still swollen, and the wound raw and open, now oozing as it tried to heal from underneath my sweaty tights. I did my best to keep it clean, even throughout the day passing a sanitary wet wipe over it, but that would also need weeks of healing that it couldn't get while I was still out here running all day. My torso felt worn and depleted like my thighs, and my shoulders, rubbed raw and bruised from my backpack, were forming a hunch as my posture caved in. I could hardly recognize my body. It had come to Morocco as strong as I could make it, and now, with still over 200km of running ahead of me, I had nearly totally destroyed it.

Nearly.

I still had plenty left, I told myself. I continued padding my worn feet along the hard surface until I saw something by the side of the road to give me new enthusiasm: the first mileage post for Agadir. A small rectangular rock, painted white with a red stripe on top, written first in Arabic and then in Roman, displaying 236km to go. Of course, I wasn't following this road the whole way, so the distance wasn't accurate for me, but it was literally a sign that Agadir was within reaching distance. A smile cracked across my face and a spring entered my step. For the rest of the morning, I couldn't help myself running calculations in my mind about when I might be able to reach the ocean – with my lighter backpack and the new abundance of hotels, maybe I could run a lot further every day? Could I be there by Wednesday? Tuesday? Should I book a hotel now? I allowed my mind to drift to the finish, imagining how it would feel, fantasizing about the cool Atlantic water I intended to dive into. I played out the entire scene – taking my shoes and pack off, running into the sea, lying down on the sand, turning my tracker off. I imagined how good this one was going to feel, after all I had pushed through to get there.

I let this fantasy swim in my thoughts for a while before finally stamping out the temptation and forcing myself back to the present – it was still a fair distance to cover, after all, and it's not done until it's done. I would need to keep working for it. I knew that.

EVERYTHING YOU NEED

Sitting underneath the sparse shade of a tree, pulling apart a pomegranate, I was spotted by a young man in a rickety blue car. Smiling, he came over to shake my hand, speaking in Arabic that I couldn't understand a word of. Noticing my dim-witted expression, he raised his finger with that 'I have an idea' sign language that works wherever you go. He typed rapidly into Google Translate, then handed me his phone.

'Everything you need is at my brother's house.'

WTF.

'Yallah!' he beckoned, with an impossibly warm smile. *Let's go.* I shrugged. I've always trusted my gut instinct – and he seemed genuine.

'Okay. *Yallah,'* and I followed him to his brother's home.

The warmth of a family home within the otherwise chaotic urban sprawl was a welcome sanctuary. The smiling man (Mohammad, again) introduced me to his mother and his seven-year-old niece, who both made a great fuss over me. I was seated at the dining table where Mohammad and

I shared a pot of tea while his female family members went about assembling far too many plates of food. Within minutes an entire tagine, a basket of bread, a bowl of limes and even a birthday cake were covering the table. I knew I needed calories, but my ability to ingest any was wobbly at best in this heat and, besides, I felt like I was denying the rest of the family their lunch. That tagine must have been prepared early this morning, before they could possibly have known that I was going to arrive, so the food was not intended for me. Still, remembering my lesson from another Mohammad, I knew that the most polite thing to do was to eat the food – mine or not – and complimenting the mouth-watering homemade tagine gave visible pride to Mohammad's lovely mother.

That family lunch, conducted entirely through (mostly faulty, but hilariously so) Google Translate along with smiles and giggles, had restored my love for this country – and gave new energy to my run. The kindness of strangers truly was the greatest gift of the Atlas Mountains, despite the abundance of safety warnings of the exact opposite.

My desert riad that evening was embarrassingly comfortable, and I tried my best to allow myself to enjoy it. I stopped early enough to enjoy the pool, letting the cold water – they don't have any need to install heated pools in this region – do its best to heal my aching muscles and counter the building heat exhaustion in my head. I went to bed earlier than Mohammad's little niece probably did, after a shower with rassoul clay and another replenishing meal of Berber omelette. I had become a connoisseur of the meal, knowing that it was almost always the fastest food that a Berber kitchen could offer; other Moroccan food like tagines or couscous often required more than an hour to cook, but eggs were almost always available and omelettes could be produced immediately. I didn't mind having the same meal sometimes twice a day – every cook did them slightly differently, depending what vegetables and herbs they had on hand, and by this point I was too tired to really mind what I was fed anyway.

TOWARDS THE ATLANTIC

I figured I had a day and a half left to go as I staggered through the rolling hills of the end of the Atlas Mountain chain. I had climbed away from the overheated and over-busy valley roads, and was once more on gravel pistes or goat tracks, often shaded by large leafy trees. Small goats leaped up impressively high into the branches to reach the best greens, and I often didn't notice them until an alarming *'blaaaaah'* screamed out as I passed underneath.

My legs stumbled constantly, the power now completely gone, and my sides cramped intensely, so I slowed to a walk for almost an hour, stopping at every opportunity to get hydration from small shops along the way, hoping to repair my body just enough to make it through the final hours to Agadir.

Tomorrow. I kept repeating to myself. *This will all be over tomorrow.*

I have only parcels of memories of that day. I didn't take any photos or write in my diary, mostly because I no longer had the energy to, but also because I couldn't stop moving. My legs failed regularly, tripping on the smallest of rocks. I relied entirely on my trekking poles if I needed to get over anything as tall as a step, and more than a few times I caught myself falling over as they simply gave out underneath me.

What I do remember vividly is the first moment the sea air reached my lungs. After more than three weeks in the desert, the scent of the sea and the humidity it carried were intoxicating. My ponytail, which had swung pencil-straight down my back in the dry heat, quickly curled into a spiral with the rise in humidity, and that was how I knew I was close. From the weather vane that is my own hair.

I dug out my phone and checked my location. Just over 20km to the coast – a mere half marathon. Somehow, that didn't sound far in that moment. If I convinced my legs to put in one last effort, I could be done in two hours.

Not tomorrow, tonight!

The long shadows of the late-afternoon sun spread across the quiet, single-lane gravel road, and I pushed hard on my trekking poles to continue a steady jog. The pain shooting through my legs grew in intensity, but I fiercely ignored it – it was the last night. If I could just keep going, it wouldn't matter how much they hurt tomorrow. I could spend the whole day in bed!

The sun set before I reached the final pass, where down below me I saw Agadir for the first time. The city lights clustered around the shoreline, where the Atlantic spanned towards the horizon. The Atlantic. At last.

Tears welled in my eyes as I inhaled that sea air, and then

lifted my arms to the night sky in some sort of exhausted battle cry: this was it.

I ran and ran into the night. First steeply downhill, and then just slightly slanted along the city streets. The first traffic light I had encountered in three weeks made me burst out laughing – the concept of orderly traffic between pedestrians and cars hadn't existed in the mountains, and my exhausted brain found it wildly amusing. I kept running down the pedestrian lanes of Agadir's lush green parks, where teenagers and families promenaded in the warm night air. I ignored their confused glances as I ran, haggardly but steadily, towards the beach. I didn't check where I was going – it was obvious where the Atlantic was, and I didn't really care *where* I entered the sea: all that mattered was that I would. What happened afterwards was of no concern to me.

Just before midnight, I stumbled onto the sand. I pulled off my running shoes one last time, overwhelmed by emotion as I set my things down, just as I had pictured, and began wading out into the crashing waves. In the image I held of this moment, I hadn't accounted for the touts, still searching for tourists to sell necklaces and surf lessons to even at this hour, so I didn't go far into the sea before returning to collect my things and find a hotel, where I planned to stay in bed for at least two days.

*

I came home immediately to speak on the main stage at the UK's largest outdoor-industry festival. The sharp turn from solitude and mountains to a full-on festival atmosphere jolted me back to reality. I loved re-integrating into a culture where I was one of many, and my successful completion of two world-first expeditions opened new opportunities that even two years ago I couldn't have imagined having. Armed with the confidence of a success, and with fire in my belly from my recent experiences as a woman on this planet, I gave all of my energy to developing a career in this industry. I figured you can either complain about something or put your hand up and do something about it.

Finally heading back home, as the train drew nearer the centre of Edinburgh, the green outside the window turned to grey, and the bustle of city life slowly turned up the volume. An anxiety that I had never met before clutched my chest.

Within the week, I bought a van. Cheap, rusty, old, but a vessel for freedom. My new campervan would let me live in two worlds: I could still exist in my city life, where work and friends also lived; but I could escape at any moment and stay out in the wilderness of Scotland. I loved that van, and the anxiety in my chest loosened just knowing it was there, parked outside.

I knew I wanted to keep going with the project, but as I had self-funded the first two, I would need to come up with a better financial strategy to see the goal through. Over the months I worked, learned and committed myself to a goal that had become my *raison d'être*. To finish what I started and run across a mountain range on every continent. Come hell or high water, this was happening.

CHAPTER THREE

Aren't You Afraid?
The Bolivian Andes

The bright blue bus with the biggest wheels I have ever seen on public transit bounced along the winding, potholed dirt road that twisted deep into the Andes. At small outposts, one or two passengers would disembark, until there were only a few of us left, staying on until the frontier. A few short miles away from the Peruvian border, although at a remote outpost where no one would cross, the bus came to a final halt. I had been clutching my stuffed backpack, with my knees tucked up as the seats were too close together, for ten hours straight. I was impressed with myself that I held my breakfast in for the incredibly bumpy ride, but I had mainly been concentrating on my bag: as we both went airborne so many times I thought it best to try and stay together.

Pelechuco is a small cluster of tin-roofed homes and workshops, mainly inhabited by miners and their families, but also serving as a central location for the even smaller *pueblos* in the mountains beyond. It was late, the only bus – which came twice a week – had dropped off its passengers, and that was about all that was going on. The driver left his bus in the middle of the plaza, from where he would take outbound passengers to La Paz in the morning. I smiled my thanks to him, but glowered at the visible springs of the bus coiled behind the giant wheels. They had been far too lively for me over the course of the day.

After a full week in the bustle of La Paz, I was glad to breathe the clean mountain air and hear little but a few kids playing. A vibrant, densely populated city of incredible colour, La Paz was a cool place to acclimatize to the dizzying altitude of the Bolivian Andes. Most of my acclimatization involved simply staying in my hotel room or going for short exploration walks – at first, I couldn't go very far without running out of oxygen and needing a rest. I rode the contrastingly futuristic coloured gondolas all over town, buying day passes each day so I could take unlimited rides on this most genius solution to big-city public transportation. From above, I could look down on the bustle of the city and pick *barrios* to explore.

Despite the 'main bus stop', Pelechuco didn't receive enough visitors to justify a hotel, so after a bit of asking passers-by, I found a home willing to rent me a bedroom for the night, and then found the one cafe serving *sopa di mani* and *papas fritas* – peanut soup and fries. With a nervous stomach, I forced as much food in as I could, knowing that I didn't really have enough to make it comfortably through the first segment of my run. I was mostly ignored by the locals, and that suited me fine. My mind was spinning with anxiety for what was to come, and second-guessing all of my intentions. I knew that if I spoke to a local, they would agree with my worst-case ideas and only add to my pile of fears. After eating what I could, I strolled around the small pueblo to explore a little. It had been raining all afternoon, the sound amplified by the tin roofs of the buildings. The dirt streets were now a sticky mud, and all of the locals had already shuttered their doors and windows against the incoming evening storm.

When my alarm sounded at 5am, I curled up in a ball, squeezing my eyes shut and refusing to get out. I couldn't go back to sleep, but I pulled my sleeping bag up tight around my face, and wrapped my arms around my knees. My heart rate steadily rose as my mind went through the stages ahead, until it was pounding in my ears and I had to pull my sleeping bag down to lessen the noise.

I reached for my phone to look at the weather. I could hear the rain pounding the tin roof that was just a few feet above my bed, and wanted to know if it was going to stop soon enough to justify a late start. Or, perhaps even hopefully, it was going to be too great a storm, and I would get back on the bumpy blue bus. It would have to be pretty bad to convince me to take that ride again, but my fear was desperate enough to make me consider it.

I had no phone signal, but kept scrolling, flicking through apps, wasting time. Desperate. Searching for any viable reason to high-tail it back to La Paz right now. Perhaps I could do something else? Run some different mountains that weren't these big scary ones, shrouded in a week of thunderstorm forecasts? I knew there was no other option. I knew I had to get my bag packed and head into the dark, wet mountains looming above Pelechuco. But I would have taken any available excuse in that moment.

Finally on my way, I wheezed as I climbed up the steep, muddy path towards the first mountain pass. It wasn't long after leaving Pelechuco that the gravel track deteriorated considerably, and as the clouds covered the town below me, I felt completely isolated. A fog settled and I couldn't see more than a few metres in front of me. The earth was a faded green, with only short grass surviving at these altitudes. Herds of alpacas and llamas wandered, many of their ears decorated with vibrant tassels to denote their owner. The llamas were all shaggy, their coats in a change of the season, and tangled in mud and branches around their haunches. Many were too shy to be photographed, but it never stopped me from working on my Spanish conversational skills with them. I weighed heavily onto my carbon poles, determined not to stop and take a break on only my first day – especially considering that I started two hours later than intended.

When I made my first pass of 4,800m, I barely lingered at the top before bombing down the other side. It would be a short descent before starting again, climbing to 4,900m for the second punishment of the day. I had no choice but to make it down the other side of that second pass, where I could descend as low as 4,500m – the lowest altitude I could possibly get to in order to sleep that night. With another storm rolling in, I needed to make it as low as possible, even if it was still a dizzying 4,500m. My legs and lungs complained loudly as I pushed up the second pass. Snow had begun falling, so rapidly that in almost no time the dirt road was completely covered, and ice poured into my thin trail shoes, biting cold at my ankles. When I finally reached the top, I was gasping for breath and my legs were screaming, but the snow continued falling at a rapid pace and the daylight was fading. Shrouded in a whiteout, I cautiously looked for the path down the steep mountain.

At the very bottom of the descent, before the next climb started on the other side, lay the tiny pueblo of Sunchulli. I had been warned, fiercely, that it was not a pueblo for a *gringa* – foreign woman – to enter. All of the residents were miners, and it was a rough place. *Peligroso* – dangerous – I had been advised. My mind wandered through everything I had learned about this region while researching from back home: illegal mines, illegal coca trade, mostly male residents, high incidence of violence against women, higher incidence of violence against foreigners. No paved road access, and so no police presence. I knew I needed to find a sheltered place to bivvy before reaching the pueblo, so my presence wouldn't be noticed. Before I made it down, the sun had set completely and I was wandering by the light of my head torch, the thin beam reflecting off the falling snowflakes. I found no shelter. The flank of the mountain was wide and exposed, with nothing but soggy grass and freezing streams. Well above the treeline, there was no chance that nature would provide a sanctuary, and without committing to any patch of wet ground to call home, I soon neared the village that I had been forewarned not to enter – especially at night.

A cluster of mud-brick houses with colourful doors and shuttered windows marked the entrance to the pueblo. A narrow city street led to the plaza, where a single yellow lamp illuminated one corner of the public area. The *tienda* was serving a few customers with dry goods, but for anything more substantial they would need to travel for a day and half to reach the start of the nearest paved road. Most of the people living here grew their own food, with what they could manage in the bare soil. The three locals – two women and one man – huddled by the tienda window stopped as I approached and waved me over.

'*No tienes miedo, gringa?*' Aren't you afraid?

I took a deep breath. I was cold and wet, and visibly exhausted from my double-mountain-pass day at altitude.

I had been practising the conversation in my mind before arriving, my Spanish not quite confident enough yet. Slowly, and making probably every possible mistake in grammar and pronunciation, I explained my situation: *I have everything that I need, and I don't need anything from you, but if there is a roof you can point me to that I can sleep under, I would be very grateful.* I imagined a llama stable, hopeful they could offer me one that didn't already have a llama in it.

The group turned to each other and began speaking rapidly in Aymara, the only word I could understand being *gringa*. Finally, the deliberation reached a conclusion, and they turned back to me and continued in Spanish.

'You can sleep in the school, it's Saturday anyways. We just can't remember who has the keys to the front door . . . I'll be right back.' And with that, the man disappeared around a corner for a few minutes, while the two women watched me fill my water bottle from the central tap. The man soon returned and whistled for me to follow him. Silently, he led me around the clustered buildings. If there was a planned layout for Sunchulli, I could not understand it. Narrow lanes dimly lit by my head torch and his mobile phone snaked around the small homes, each seemingly dropped at a random angle and location to its neighbour. We walked across the wet football field, and reached a dilapidated concrete building. Some of the windows were broken, and piles of bricks crumbled around the outside.

'This is the school, no one will bother you tonight, you are safe here.' With that, he held the door open for me and then disappeared. As promised, no one bothered me in the night.

At first light, I felt completely fresh. The fear that I had carried all the way from Pelechuco to Sunchulli had weighed on me heavily, but with the first glimpse of blue sky I'd seen since landing in Bolivia, my spirits were lifted. The people of Sunchulli had been incredibly accommodating – I had just forgotten one of the basic rules of world travel: all neighbours fear the next pueblo over. Call it feudal history, call it human nature. It is a global truth that the city nearest is always the worst place. At home, it's the rival hockey team. Out here, it's rumours of criminals and murderers.

While I packed up my bag, a group of men from the village approached together.

'*Buenos dias!*' They each offered a big smile and handshake.

I tried my best to keep up with the rapid Spanish of the conversation. The men had obvious questions: *What on earth is a gringa doing out here all alone?* I explained my trip to them as best I could, but the desire to be so uncomfortable and travel in the mountains when I could clearly afford to take the bus was a lost concept. Bamboozled, they changed the conversation topic to learn more about my gringa life, and somehow immediately turned to politics – they were big fans of 'Brother Evo (Morales)', the current president, and wondered if I liked Justin Trudeau, too. I couldn't believe that name had made it as far as all the way out here, where no internet connection existed.

At last, my bag was packed and I couldn't linger any longer, wasting the precious few hours of daylight and potentially sunny running. As I made my farewells, one of the group stopped me – 'But gringa, where are you going now?' I explained my route ahead. Their faces fell in unison. 'No, it is very dangerous that way. Criminals and murderers, that pueblo isn't safe!'

The sensation of sun on my bare legs was incredible. I could feel the warmth of the sun, along with the generous people I had just met, run through my blood, lifting my spirits and my feet. I jogged lightly along the muddy path, frequently pausing to twirl a 360 and take in the views. Snow-capped peaks, shining with their fresh dusting that last night had brought, so close I could touch them, against a bright blue sky. Not a single cloud, and at nearly 5,000m above sea level, the sun felt incredibly close.

When I reached the next pueblo – the place I had been warned about – I was hesitant. It was quiet in the middle of the day, and with no vehicle traffic hardly a sound pierced the sky, aside from the *clink clink* of my trekking poles on the gravel track. But as I approached, people emerged. Even from a distance, I could see locals spilling out of their colourful concrete houses to watch me run towards the pueblo. The sense of being watched in this way would make me nervous in any country. It wasn't necessarily sinister, but I've never been a fan of being looked at, preferring to stay out of the way, in general. But on a wide-open grassy slope, in these mountains that have no trees, I had nowhere to hide. I imagined my pale legs reflecting the sun brightly, letting the locals spot me easily.

As I neared, I slowed down my pace, unsure how to approach the situation. By now, nearly a dozen men were standing, staring, waiting for me to arrive. I attempted a wave. It was reciprocated by a few enthusiastic waves and an encouraging welcome. I was just being silly, once again.

I picked my pace back up and trotted into the small pueblo, where once again each delegate came forward to shake my hand and pepper me with questions – mainly *What are you doing?* and *But aren't you afraid?*

Once again, when the subject of my departure and which way I was going came up, the response was negative – *It's too dangerous that way.*

I left the pueblo, hiking up a steep ancient stone path. Not far from the village, I noticed some old stone circles, and it dawned on me that I was using an old Incan route. I had read that the Incan transport network consisted of runners, typically young men or boys who would carry messages for a short relay, before passing the message on to the next person. I had been excited to run in the Andes, knowing I would be, at times, tracing their footsteps. That the original transport network had been made by long-distance runners thrilled me no end, and as I climbed up a steep pass on the thin rocky trail, I couldn't believe my discovery. The last pueblo had pointed me in this direction, saying it would be safer as no trucks could go this way. I was beyond grateful that they had made the suggestion – the route didn't appear on any maps I had come across, a reminder that local knowledge is still always the best way to research, even if they continued to insist that the neighbours were trouble.

Local knowledge with a grain of salt, I guess.

The Incan trail zigzagged up a steep climb: at points I was reaching out with my hands on the rocks in front of me and basically crawling to the top. I wheezed hard, stopping constantly to catch my breath while my head spun. The rain had returned, and I was at least grateful that it wasn't snow yet.

When I reached the bottom of the other side, I stumbled upon a beautiful waterfall. The clouds had cleared at the perfect moment to reveal the series of cascades, secluded here in the Andean wilderness – and I could have it all to myself. A series of falls carried snowmelt all down the mountain in front of me, culminating in a grand fall at least three times my height, plunging into a gentle pool. Deep green grass pillowed on the sides of the fall, and I found a comfortable spot to drop my bag and start taking everything out – a coffee made by a waterfall was exactly what I needed to sort out my spinning head.

I kicked my shoes off, giving my soggy feet a brief respite. Blisters were already forming and I would need to apply duct tape again – the most effective blister solution I've ever found. I sat on the wet grass, drinking my Bolivian Waterfall Coffee, inhaling the beautiful nature I was surrounded by. It was a respite for body and soul – after only a day and a half of running, I needed a break.

I took a scan of my body. *I shouldn't be feeling this exhausted, this soon.* It was normal for my feet to be in such rough shape early on – they usually needed about four or five days to harden up, each day progressively worse until one day they magically adapted. But my legs were knackered. My lungs felt constricted. And I felt *stressed.* The emotional weight of all that fear I had started with, and the suspended state of anxiety I was existing in, was coursing through my body. When I finished my coffee, I tried a few minutes of breathing exercises to calm my mind, but the shuddering in my lungs when I tried to inhale fully left me worried.

It's probably just that freezing pass from yesterday. Running in a snowstorm does tend to linger for a day or two. There was no need to worry yet – surely?

It was late when I stumbled into the larger pueblo of Curva. The Juan Potosi valley was quite different from the last one – it was lush, with brilliant shades of green and all sorts of plants, instead of just the singular alpine grass. As I dropped lower in altitude, there was even a variety of trees surrounding Curva. Rain pelted the hood of my jacket, and frequent lightning strikes lit up the sky. I was eager to find a place to sleep and hang my wet clothes to dry.

Unfortunately, no such place existed. Curva was a ghost town in the storm, and I was told that the only guest rooms had closed years ago, on account of no one ever visiting. I continued to the next pueblo down the road, struggling not to trip over my own feet that dragged across the ground. I couldn't find the energy to pick them up any more. My legs screamed in pain as lactic acid flooded my thighs, and I feared that if I stopped moving even just for one moment, I literally wouldn't be able to start again.

Like Curva, Lagunillas was silent. I strolled to the window of the sole tienda, and inquired about the guest room. I was told it had also shut years ago. A nearby Cholita – one of the local women, characterized by the stunning clothes that they wear with pride – overheard my conversation, and ran up alongside me while I walked away, dejected, cold, wet and without a place to stay.

Marina was young, perhaps younger than me, but dressed in the complete Cholita attire: a bright red velvet skirt that hung just below her ankles, the ruffles swaying as she walked; a multi-coloured hand-knitted jumper, and a smart bowler hat on top of her long braids which reached down to her hips. She was short – about shoulder height to me – and I felt completely odd next to her, our body shapes couldn't have been more different. Marina offered me a place in her guest room for the night, as was common practice in pueblos without hotels, and we agreed on a price for dinner and a room. She assured me that her home was warm and had running water – I was sold.

Marina's small house was a new build, completely out of place among the older, concrete and tin-roofed pueblos I had seen so far. She beamed when she told me, 'Evo built this house.' Morales's campaign to make life better for the indigenous people of Bolivia made him unanimously popular in the Andes. I played with Marina's daughter while helping cut potatoes for our dinner. Children ran in and out, three of them belonging to Marina, but the neighbourhood childcare being more of a collective situation. There was no sign of a father, and I didn't ask. I liked that we were just women for the night, and Marina was also clearly proud of her independence. I hate being asked why I'm alone and why I'm not married – so I wasn't keen to do the same to her. In fact, she returned the favour. For an entire evening together, two adult women never spoke about men or defined themselves by their relationship status. How revolutionary.

LEGS AND LUNGS

Lying in bed, I reviewed the map. Charazani, a pueblo I had hoped to stay in as it had a natural thermal bath, was only a short distance away. I assessed my exhausted body, and decided that a half day finishing with a hot spring was exactly what I needed to reinvigorate myself. The best part was there was no need for the 5am alarm – I decided to wake up whenever Marina did, which turned out to be relatively late.

Knowing that I didn't have far to go let me enjoy the running more. Normally, I would focus on running sustainably, continuing perpetual forward motion. But a short day meant running the way I enjoyed it – springing over bumps in the earth, trying to clear puddles (even if there was a route around – it's far more fun to see how far you can jump), bounding down the descents and challenging myself to push harder on the climbs. I had my first thigh-deep river crossing, and the freezing water on my bare legs relieved the dull ache in my muscles temporarily. My head was still spinning, lungs still aching, but knowing that I had a resupply coming up, I decided to take some ibuprofen and see if that would abate the symptoms a little. The air was heavy with fog, and I felt isolated in the small bubble of the world which I could see, never more than a few metres ahead of me. When the afternoon thunderstorm came – a daily event I had now learned to expect – I was rapidly winding my way down a nearly vertical donkey track. I continued to lose altitude, which was marked by an increase in green vegetation, and soon a real forest sprang up, suddenly dropping me out of the rocky mountainous trail and into a jungle. The trees broke the fog a little, and I breathed a little easier.

At the bottom of this descent was the thermal pool of Charazani. An old concrete building, painted coral and yellow, with a chain-link fence surrounding it was like a swimming pool anywhere else, just a little bit lacking in upkeep. It was empty, aside from the one employee, monitoring another quiet day. The pool used to be a social centre for the local population, but since plumbing improved – and working hours increased – most locals did not need to/did not have time to come to the local bathing house. Good news for me, on this occasion.

The smell of sulphur permeated the air; steam rising off the pool and the deck mingled with the low fog. I eased my sore body into the water, and let the healing properties do their thing. I inhaled the steam into my aching lungs, while slowly stretching my limbs. It would have been perfectly relaxing, if the employee hadn't moved his plastic chair to the pool deck to sit and watch me the entire time. It was an uncomfortable one-on-one experience, and I tried turning my back to him and even swimming to the far end, hoping to get a basic level of privacy without explicitly asking for it.

Climbing up the steep concrete steps that led from the public pool to the pueblo of Charazani, I couldn't believe how much better my legs felt already. If I could have had a hot spring after every day of the expedition, it would probably have been a lot easier.

Unfortunately, my lungs hadn't achieved the same level of improvement, and when I arrived at the local guesthouse with a dry cough, the owner made me a manzanilla tea with leaves plucked from his garden, and told me to rest. In my small room next to his lovingly tended garden, I spent the rest of the evening drinking tea and coughing fiercely.

I slept terribly, partly because breathing was so difficult and partly because I was worried about how difficult my breathing was.

While I had been racing my bike in Kyrgyzstan just two months earlier, competing in – and winning – the gruelling Silk Road Mountain Race, I had developed a new mantra: *fix your own problems.*

In the wilderness, on an unsupported expedition or race, and in life, 'fix your own problems' is an essential attitude to success. Don't wait for someone to come along and rescue you. Don't ignore your problems and let them fester. No wishing or hoping. Action. Your problems are yours, and taking action on them and ownership for them is more than just survival – it's integrity. I had developed the mantra to succeed in an unsupported bike race, where I had to take responsibility for tactile things like fixing my bike or finding enough water, but while I pedalled through the nights and days of the Tien Shan, I ruminated on how important this advice was for every area of my life. That's how it grew from a race strategy into a mantra, one that I still favour to this day.

Fix your own problems. My lungs were aching. I could barely breathe. Walking from my small room to the kitchen where more manzanilla tea boiled for me left me out of breath. I *wanted* to continue running – follow the plan. But I had a problem that needed fixing, not ignoring.

Mid-morning, I boarded another rustic bus to take me back to La Paz. I leaned my head on the window, watching the mountains go by and desperately longing to be running in them, but I knew I had made the only choice. I was gutted.

FIXING MY PROBLEMS

The doctors at the American clinic were young and attractive, many of them from wealthier Latin countries. The Argentinian doctor assigned to me was empathetic and thorough, and it was probably the most productive medical appointment of my life. She took my blood, ran chest x-rays, and conducted a physical examination. After less than two hours of waiting in the air-conditioned centre, she had results back and a diagnosis: HAPE, or high-altitude pulmonary edema. Fluid had begun to pool in my lungs, meaning I was already in the hardcore stages of altitude sickness. If I continued, I could drown from the inside.

She recommended at least five days of rest. I felt my heart hit the floor. I went back to my La Paz hotel, where I had left a duffel bag, including my laptop, which I had wanted in order to do some work during the week I had already spent acclimatizing before starting. I opened maps, weather reports and a calendar, and reviewed my plans.

I didn't have time. Unless after ten days of recovering I returned as a superhuman runner, I would not be able to complete. I looked at my flights, and knew that I had to be on the plane scheduled – the biggest work weekend of my year was immediately upon my return, and I couldn't let anyone down. I had a hard deadline.

I lay in bed, fretting day and night, despairing that my body had failed me on this occasion.

I simply couldn't understand it. Two months ago I had been in Kyrgyzstan, literally racing my bike over >4,000m passes, pushing myself through the nights and only sleeping three hours per night throughout the two-week long race. I had triumphed – my first real win, and I had walked away with more confidence in my body than I'd ever had before. Which is to say any at all, truth be told. I had had no struggles, and that had been only weeks ago. I knew Bolivia was a higher altitude, so I had taken things far more seriously. I flew into Lima, Peru, giving myself a day and a half of bus travel to slowly arrive at altitude, skipping the infamous La Paz airport where oxygen tanks reportedly line the arrival lounge. I had taken the drugs this time, dutifully. I waited in La Paz for a week, doing nothing but breathing thin oxygen and letting my body adapt.

And still, it had backfired.

The hours I wasted despairing over this injustice were futile, but I couldn't pull my head out of the negative trap. As someone who rarely falls ill or gets injured, I've always known that I don't handle it well on the few occasions that my body does retaliate. But this was terrible timing. I had flown to the other side of the world. I had secured funding for an expedition. I had left my home, work and social life – a life I had barely seen in over eight months of back-to-back adventures, races and work trips – to be here. It had to be a success. I had no Plan B. Failure would mean coming back next year – flying across the world again. I already struggled internally about the amount of flying my lifestyle relied on, and the sheer distance to Latin America meant that, for me, this could not be part of my regular commute. I had resolved that every time I did fly, I had to make it worth it. I couldn't waste it.

Guilt over the flight, the funding I had received from

sponsorship, and my self-focused determination to be away so often compounded my rage against my lungs. In many ways, this was so far turning out to be the best year of my life. My career as an adventurer had finally taken off, and I was busy doing work that I truly loved. I had succeeded in two bike races, one in Ireland where I came second, and the one in Kyrgyzstan where I came first. I had been on funded trips as well as adventure projects with other creatives. My public-speaking schedule and writing demands were paying the bills. I was receiving emails through my website on a weekly basis from adventurers around the world, letting me know that I had inspired them in some way. I had also barely spent two nights back to back at home since April. Most of my friends understood, but I knew my role in their lives was diminishing. My relationship also suffered greatly, and my partner repeatedly retaliated to the point that it was hard to tell him about my success – good things for me were instantly greeted by him making me feel guilty. He wanted me home more, but I wanted to grow. The life of my dreams was finally coming to fruition, and to stop now would be a huge disservice to my own ambitions and the hard work I had already put in. I felt betrayed by his attitude to my achievements, which only led to me wanting to be home even less. While I tried applying *fix your own problems* to the rest of my life, our relationship was left to fester while I spent most of the year away from it.

I wasn't willing to let the good year end badly. I couldn't face a failure. *Just let me have this good roll, please!* I begged of my body.

After a replenishing breakfast, making the most of my return to the city by including fresh fruits in my diet – something I couldn't find in the Andes – I climbed the hotel stairs to the rooftop for a yoga session. After only ten minutes, I was sweating and panting on the mat, destroyed as if I had just completed hours of hill reps. I couldn't believe how weak I had become in such a short space of time.

I returned to my laptop, and sat there for most of the day with endless cups of herbal tea, planning and re-planning my route, taking out exciting detours and flattening the line as much as possible – this would no longer be a dream run, wiggling my way across the Bolivian Andes. This would now be all about ensuring success. I couldn't have any hiccups – every day would need to be at least 40km strong, or I would risk missing my flight.

Not only did I have to re-plan my route, but I had to reset my expectations. I had to let go of the confidence I had so briefly held after the bike race, and decrease my self-assessment to a much lower level. My heart felt heavy as I watched my plans and aspirations slip through my fingers.

I spent restless days lying in my hotel bed. I had taken to watching Spanish-language Netflix programmes to improve my vocabulary, but all of the Latino shows were on drug violence – not the vocabulary I hoped would come up in any of the Aymara communities. I picked up a lot of swear words.

Between nerve-racking episodes of extreme Mexican violence, I would wander the side streets to buy fresh produce from Cholitas who squatted next to plastic baskets of avocados, tomatoes, peppers, eggs and bread rolls. I would buy enough to make a couple of sandwiches on every outing and, when my legs felt up for it, walk a little further astray to peruse the markets. Depending on the time of day, different stall owners would pop up with their wares, and I learned which streets in my district were for what. There was the household cleaning product street, with the overpowering scent of lemon and laundry detergent knocking the aromas of La Paz out of your system for a moment. There was the street of knock-off clothing, slightly mimicking designer labels from Europe and America. School supplies, electronics, hardware, ladies' accessories, fabrics – you name it. I never understood why each stretch of market stalls would only host sellers of the same type, rather than dispersing around the city more evenly, but I enjoyed people-watching as busy locals rushing past always knew exactly which of the eight identical stalls selling coca leaves was the one they purchased from.

DON'T CALL IT A COMEBACK

After two nights of going crazy in my hotel room, I boarded a microbus to Sorata, where the next segment of my journey began. A verdant town, Sorata had something of a tourism industry where the Andes meet the Amazon, and I decided mountain air was better than city air. I told myself I would wait in Sorata until I felt better, but I knew I was only lying to myself. As the micro wound through the Andes on sharp corners and precipitous ledges, my eyes stayed fixed on the mountain flanks we passed, looking for thin llama trails and picking out lines, imagining myself running strong and powerful around the rocky slopes.

With virtually no tourists in the Andes, on account of the awful run of weather they were having, I found my guesthouse deserted. The owner had called to tell me to just 'look after myself', and so I played with the house dog and kept the kettle going with bottomless coca tea. I took myself out to the one restaurant in town that was open, serving Mexican and fusion South American fare. While I waited for my quesadillas, which I just knew would be much better than anything I could get in Europe, I was reading my book on my phone and minding my own, when a Frenchman entered and loudly set about ordering in terrible Spanish, without looking at the menu. He sat at the table next to me, and I made an extra effort to look engrossed in my novel. He didn't take the hint. Without permission, he was soon sitting at my table, asking me what I was doing here all alone.

There are two types of gringos – those who attempt, often quite poorly, to be chameleons in the culture, and those who proudly cling to their own culture and assume all other gringos will be just like them. All I'm saying is that he could have invited himself to sit with any of the other diners – but I was the only white one and he sat with me.

Jair Bolsanaro had just won the Brazilian election, much to the horror of anyone who has any common sense. The Frenchman was a supporter. I thought I had misheard, until his opinions turned to me.

'You really can't come to a place like this alone.'

'Well, I disagree, and this is my second time coming to Latin

America alone. It's not my first rodeo, but thanks . . .' I sipped my beer, keeping the screen on my phone lit so he might take the hint that I was not engaged, and did not wish him to stay.

'That's stupid. People here will rape you. Everyone here is like that. This isn't like Europe, you can't understand what it's like. It's totally different. You need protection.'

Sometimes, you've got to choose your battles. I couldn't have been more enraged by his comments, but as we had already established his love for Trump and Bolsanaro, I had no hope for his soul. With my head propped up on my hand, tilted to the side in equal boredom and disdain, I listened to the man talk, never agreeing, but never biting. Finally, he reached the end of his sermon on *what people are like here* with a grand finale on how women should never go anywhere alone, and I couldn't suppress a patronizing laugh.

'I don't think keeping us locked up changes anything – I've still got a life to live. I'm not oblivious to the dangers, but I can't just give up and lock myself in my room until I get old and die.'

Mercifully, my quesadilla arrived. I picked up my book and signalled that we were done here; thankfully, he went back to his own table. I could have sworn the owner of the restaurant turned the TV up, too.

In the morning, a succession of micros took me back north to where I had left my route, so I could begin running towards Sorata according to the original plan. This time, I made my best attempt to *not* look out the window, wanting to ensure that when I ran through the region, I would be experiencing it for the first time.

The sun embraced me back into the Andes, but I knew that

I should have waited. Mentally, I was raring to go. In the three days of idling, I had found myself missing the mountains, desperate to return. The more time I spend in them, the more alien I feel in cities. My skin itches and I feel timid and awkward. In the mountains, I roll my shoulders back and stand tall, I feel good and I know who I am and what I'm about. The only overwhelm I experience is that of the majestic beauty or the grandiose scale of the terrain before me. In cities, my overwhelm is an assault on the senses and the jostle of too many people trying to exist in a cramped space together.

My body was, on the other hand, not ready to return. I knew this. I couldn't pretend otherwise. But my head and heart won over my legs and lungs, and by mid-morning, I found myself unfolding my carbon trekking poles and preparing to run. And I intended to run very well – my head and heart needed to roam.

Left, right, left, cough.

Right, left, pause.

Right, left, right, gasp for air.

Left, right, double over.

I could barely maintain a walk. My poles arced as I leaned all of my body weight into them, trying to take the extra pressure of my full backpack off my crumbling legs. They had the strength of a stalk of straws, and the pain of a sea of acid. Knowing that my lungs were on limited capacity on account of the pool of fluid sitting in them only seemed to contribute to the discomfort as I wheezed, desperately sucking in air that already had too little oxygen in it at this altitude to fill my disabled lungs. My head spun fiercely, and I grabbed a boulder to ensure I wouldn't fall over. I was winding up a steep, zigzagged trail, and a fall to the side could easily be the last mistake I made.

CAN'T GET A BREAK

When the routine negative shift in weather occurred in the mid-afternoon, the clouds dropped low, enveloping me entirely. I had never in my life experienced such an intense loss of visibility, and I walked gingerly with my compass in hand, trying not to be entirely freaked out by the inability to see anything – or anyone – around me. It was an eerie feeling, and I begged the sky to just give me a break – anything. One of the most mentally disturbing challenges in wilderness expeditions is the lack of an option to take a break. You can't go sit inside and wait for things to pass. You can't get comfortable for a little while. You generally don't have the option of waiting. You can close your eyes, for a bit, if you really want to, but you'll still have to deal with the problems in front of you. My GPS tracker confirmed later that I spent most of an hour going in actual circles, completely incapable of finding my way without sight. The whole time, I became increasingly conscious of trying to move silently, imagining in my exhausted mind that I might not be alone in the cloud. I could never see more than a couple of metres away from me.

Finally, I broke above the cloud. Without a thought, I unclipped my waist and chest straps, dropped my bag with a thud, and simply stood there, face tilted towards the blue sky. The blisters that had formed on the second day were niggling at me, so I took the excuse to sit down and have a faff. I slipped off my trail shoes and damp socks, revealing the mushy white skin of my feet – the body part that always takes it the worst on these things. I used the duct tape that was rolled around the top section of one of my trekking poles to protect the blister, then I leaned back on a boulder, stretching my tired legs out, for a moment of respite. With the sky miraculously clear, I could see the snowy peaks ahead of me, and watched in wonder at the intricacies of their glaciers, imagining the first mountaineering teams that were called by the mountains to attempt to scale them. Far in the distance, a condor circled, her impressive wingspan apparent even from such a distance. The intensity of the physical discomfort and the simmering anxiety I had been going through since the start gave way to a brief moment of jubilation as I drank in the best of the Andean beauty. *This is what I came for*, I smiled to myself as I looked out. Then, as I followed my gaze down along the valley floor, back up the slope of the mountain I had just climbed blindly, and finally to the tips of my knackered feet and exhausted legs, I could only laugh. Of course, a place this incredible will need to take a large payment, and I was certain that I was giving these mountains all that I had. I wrung out the socks that I had left drying on a rock, and reluctantly pulled them back on, gingerly hauling myself to my feet to continue climbing. This pass was going to be one of the highest on the entire journey, and I consciously shut out the fear of what ascending to that height could do to my body at this stage, focusing solely on the relief I would feel later that evening as I descended from that lofty height.

What could have taken minutes for a healthy body took

hours. I clawed my way up the pass, slipping on its dry scree slope. This far into the wilderness, there were no longer any tracks to follow, but navigating the mountains was fairly intuitive (without the disorienting cloud cover) – if you could see the 'saddle' between peaks, you knew where you were aiming for, and simply looked ahead to pick the best route. So far above the altitude that any vegetation could grow on, my only obstacles were impassable crags, which I would need to navigate around by going either above or below. Looking ahead, the pass was the kind of climb that (my) dreams are made of. There were infinite options to reach the top, and as the scree floor moved with every step, my prints were instantly erased – just like any wanderers who may have come here before me. It was like writing in invisible ink – I could pass by in my own, creative approach, and the mountain would almost instantly forget, leaving a blank canvas for the next explorer.

At the top, my watch read just over 5,200m, the highest I had ever been on this earth. It was a brilliant feeling, but I knew I had to keep moving and get below that altitude as quickly as possible. I placed a rock on top of the cairn, and pulled on my jacket and tuque for the descent. The cloud had returned, removing any temptation to linger at the top – a relief for my lungs, which felt shrivelled in my chest, working their hardest to bring in oxygen but never getting anywhere near enough to support my body. My head swimming, legs aching, but emotionally triumphant at the height, I raced down the scree slope of the opposite side, and kept going until I hit the valley floor just before sunset.

I had chilled considerably as I descended, and by the time

I found my next source of running water I was already wearing most of my layers, genuinely concerned that another frozen night was ahead of me, and I had no choice but to endure it. At this thought, Pachamama, the Incan goddess Mother Earth, gave me a gift: the valley floor was made of fine sand, and a fissure created a sheltered dugout just the right size to lay out my bivvy, with my tarp protecting me from frost over the top. It was the cosiest home I could have imagined, me nestled into the earth, protected by Pachamama. The Aymara and Quechua communities would frequently refer to her throughout my trip and I admired how she was acknowledged in everyday life for the people in the Andes. The cloud had lifted again, and white peaks glowed around me. From my descent, I had noticed that the valley was entirely devoid of human influence and, for once, I felt safe and alone.

FROZEN FACE

In the morning, I woke later than usual, well after dawn, curled tightly inside my down sleeping bag. It had instantly become the biggest comfort item I had with me in Bolivia, a bright blue bag that had been a considerable investment piece, but which I now decided had been worth every hard-earned penny. As the sunlight hit my stone-grey tarp, I realized how much frost was built up on it, which only did less to inspire me to get out of my cocoon. Curled up in the small sheltered space underneath my lean-to style shelter, held delicately in place by one of my trekking poles, I looked out on the pale grass leading to the shore of the small pond I was camped next to. The grass was white with frost, and even the pond had clear ice formed at the edges. I shivered violently as my body tried to awaken and muster the courage to unzip the cosy sleeping bag and step out to go pee. That was when I noticed something that woke me with a panic – I could not feel my face.

I tried to form words and speak out loud, challenging the muscles in my face to perform as usual. I was able to speak, even if it made me feel (even more) crazy to be talking gibberish all by myself in the wilderness just to test my face, but I had no sensation in my lips. Once I had made a cup of coffee – what I hoped would be the cure – I struggled to drink without a good sense of when my lips hit the titanium mug. Was it just *that cold* in the night that my face had simply frozen? Is this what I got for sleeping out in the open without a tent?

I fumbled for my prescribed medicine from the doctor, and made a second cup of hot coffee to wash it down and try to inspire some sensation in my face. My feet and hands tingled as well, which I knew to be signs of altitude sickness. As I was already diagnosed, and taking the maximum dosage to remedy it, there was no point panicking any further. As all of Bolivia on this side of the Andes is at high altitude, my only backup options would be to climb over the Andes and drop all the way down to the Amazon, or leave the country entirely to recover on a beach in Chile. The idea of the warm climate either option promised was momentarily tempting, and I imagined myself wearing flip-flops and jumping in the water to cool down – a far cry from wearing four layers of wool and down, and the only available water literally frozen on the surface. I let my mind daydream a little longer on the fantasy of descending somewhere warm to recover while I delicately packed up, trying to shake all of the ice off of my tarp before folding it away inside my bag.

Sometimes – well, truthfully, often – a lack of phone signal is a blessing. Goodness knows that googling your symptoms can be a quick dive into a terrifying rabbit hole. Standing in a desolate hidden corner of the Bolivian Andes, at high altitude and more than a day's run from civilization, is a scary place to realize you can't feel your face. It's a scary place for anything to go wrong. I tapped my phone every few steps, hoping to come into signal and somehow find answers. But what good would they be for me at that point? I had nothing aside from what was in my bag. I had no access to transportation for medical assistance. It would take me *days* to evacuate to a lower altitude if I needed to – involving a long run to the next village, a long hitchhike to the nearest town, a long bus ride to the nearest city and finally an extremely long bus ride (or two or three) out of the country. I had known the risks when I started. I had known that if anything went wrong in the Bolivian Andes, I could be stuck with my situation. And there I was, potentially crying, although I couldn't feel my own tears on my cheek, wandering through a foggy (literally and emotionally) plateau, unsure what my next set of choices should be.

Failure is always an option. I don't care what it says on a poster at the gym. It is always an option. It's just usually not an attractive one. I've always considered myself a quitter. It's one of the voices in my mind – one that I'm pretty sure is not originally mine, but possibly something hissed at me as a child when I refused to do something hard – there, constantly teasing me for my weaknesses. Cutting short a run and turning home early because my legs are tired. A pile of books I never finished because I got bored. Asking someone else to open a jar for me. Still being incapable of committing myself to learning French. The list goes on. I give up all the time, and each of those failures haunts me.

But quitting an expedition is an entirely different breed. Quitting is actually the hardest thing to do. You go into an expedition with a plan, a clear direction of what you want to achieve. When you hit that point of exhaustion – a point I usually reach only days in – you then rely on following the plan in a stupor until you reach the goal. Quitting is a logistical nightmare – quitting means coming up with a new plan in order to get home. And you're no longer in a state to make plans. You're deep in the wilderness, completely committed to the location you find yourself in. You don't know the transportation options for the towns in between because you didn't plan on using them. You don't know how to change your flights because you didn't pay for that ticket upgrade. Quitting takes a clear mind, willing to tackle the logistics of a foreign place. Putting one foot in front of the other, stumbling along the dotted line towards the end, takes no mental energy. Even when it physically harms you, it is mentally and emotionally easier than leaving the plan.

I didn't have a plan for quitting. I knew if my life was at risk that I *could* quit, but I never knew if I *would*. I rubbed my cheeks, pinched them and made elaborate movements with my jaw. *Stop that,* I begged my body. *Snap out of it.* This couldn't be happening. I refused to acknowledge it.

I walked the whole day, except for the brief downhills, which are always easier to run. I convinced myself that walking couldn't cause as much harm and, besides, I had to move under my own steam. There was no road – even if I started crawling, that would still be my only chance. Giving up was not viable. I had to move. So, I walked. I followed the dotted line. I got confused and frustrated looking for alternatives on the map, and decided following my planned route was far better than nothing. I walked all day and hardly stopped, conscious that I was moving slower than planned, and therefore remaining exposed longer. I walked until well after dark.

I thought of nothing. Thinking would bring into focus my reality. I was ill. I was scared. I was tired. Sore. Struggling. In bad shape, both body and mind. No, thinking would be a bad route. I walked. Practically marched. Thoughtlessly and alone, I moved towards Sorata, making no advance decisions. All I needed to do was reach Sorata. Then I could deal with thinking. Until then, one foot in front of the other. I ignored the fact that the numbness in my face was now also present in my feet and hands. *Just keep moving. You can't stay here.*

MAKING A DECISION

In Sorata, I collapsed into the guesthouse I had stayed in a few nights ago. Normally, the explorer in me would want to try somewhere new, but I was in no place for extra effort. I realized that I needed to start making every part of my life as simple as possible – fewer strains, decisions or taxes on my energy. And, truth be told, I just wanted to cuddle up with the small dog that lived in that guesthouse one more time. Petting a dog for an hour can make almost everything go away – although probably not HAPE. But it was worth a shot.

Once more I indulged in a routine of good rest, drinking endless cups of coca tea and big bowls of vegetable soup while I lay in bed, devouring another book. If nothing else, this expedition had been great for reading time, although I had really hoped there wouldn't be so much lying around like this. That's what holidays are for, and this was no holiday.

Sorata was my chance to call it. I knew it was one of the easiest places I could get on a bus back to La Paz, and from there make my way down to sea level in Chile or Peru. That would really be a holiday. I imagined myself drinking Chilean *vino tinto*, hanging out on a beach, maybe going surfing when I got my energy back. I imagined throwing out my wet shoes and letting the sea air heal the blisters on my feet and collarbones. Most of all, I imagined myself feeling safe and comfortable. Not scared of any dangers around me, not stressed about my health, not anxious about the impending failure.

I tapped into my calculator, not for the first time today, my remaining mileage divided by the number of days until my flight. It was well, well over the current average pace I was moving. It didn't look good. I could just call it. I could walk (well, barely, more like shuffle) up to the town plaza and get on the next micro to La Paz. It wouldn't be a catastrophe, anyone could understand that I was seriously ill and had to bail. Actually, anyone would admire my strength of decision to give up in hazardous circumstances.

If you're going to do this, then do this.

Some of the best advice I'd ever been given was to just make a decision and stick with it – rather than wasting days of your life dithering about something. Choose, and commit. Even if it's the wrong choice, at least you've made a choice and stayed in motion. Not choosing is stagnant. It's stressful. I knew I didn't want to spend every day of this journey wondering what I should do about it. I needed either to decide that I would make it work, or to decide that I would give up on this attempt and come back another time. The pros and cons to each were heavy, but it was time to commit to a choice.

STAY THE COURSE

The advice always works: once you've made a choice – even if it's potentially the wrong one – a weight is lifted. Your mind is cleared to focus on other things than constantly stressing about what you should do. I started late, as I knew there was a *real cafe* just outside of Sorata where I planned to stop for a flat white and stock up on some homemade food. As everywhere had been on my journey so far, the cafe was completely empty when I arrived, and the Swiss owner was surprised, but obviously delighted, to welcome me in. After he made my coffee, he sat down with me at the small table in his cafe garden and told me his story of discovering the Andes, and never wanting to return – *not even to the Swiss Alps,* which says a lot. I guess the Bolivian Andes really are just that good. He advised me that Dia de Todos Los Santos – the Day of All the Saints – was around the corner, and explained the tradition: people go to cemeteries or their family homes to spend the day with their deceased loved ones, which is a really beautiful thing to do. However, this family holiday will ultimately lead to copious amounts of public drinking, so I was duly warned what populated areas would be like by mid-afternoon and into the evening.

Of course, I grew up with Halloween, a spooky day where children are told all sorts of haunted stories. It's a far less beautiful, more commercialized and candy-wrapped reinterpretation of the original Latin event, and if my simmering levels of fear and anxiety needed anything to feed on, the image of all of Bolivia's deceased rising from the dead for a day was plenty.

The endless days of rain had taken their toll on the Andean roads. The wet season, as I understood it, was like this all the time – dirt roads so thick with mud that they became impassable and the towns would be somewhat disconnected from each other, until the dry season rolled around and ordinary tyres could once again travel. But that year, as the locals were regularly updating me, the dry season hadn't really come. It was too early for the roads to be turned up with mud, and many tiendas were low on supplies as a result of fewer trucks making the slow journey. I followed the dirt road from Sorata, linking a few pueblos and smaller communities, and even on foot struggled to pass the thick, peanut-butter mud. At one point I even tightened my laces, so high was the risk of losing a shoe to the suctioning ground beneath me. I used my poles for balance, and slowly dragged my way along, my feet becoming heavier with each step as more mud latched on.

The extra strain couldn't bother me today. I had made a

decision – I was going to finish this journey. I was going to make it. The Bolivian Andes had already shown me that they weren't kidding around, and this was going to be hard for me. I couldn't expect things to get better – I could only accept that they probably would not – but *I* could get better. I could get stronger. I could be tougher. I could rise to the challenge. So I hauled my mud-weighted shoes through the puddles and kept moving. There was no use complaining. And there was absolutely no use waiting for things to get better. Just pull your hood up, and get on with it.

In seven hours of marching relentlessly forwards on the muddy road – the main transport line in the region – I didn't see a single vehicle. I reflected that this was either a) an indication of how poor the conditions were or b) a reflection on the place I was going to – no man's land. During one of the heaviest downpours, I reached a small pueblo with a beautiful school set on a dark green field overlooking the deep mountain valley. The white, single-storey building was lovingly cared for with simple gardens and a mosaic made from broken glass bottles and dinnerware on the entrance. With no sign of anyone around, I stopped under the veranda to have my first break of the day and pull on some extra layers. It was only when I stopped moving that the pueblo seemed to come out of the woodwork. In minutes, the few residents came out to say hello, most of them politely passing – *No tienes miedo?* – but one older woman sat next to me and chatted away. I only understood bits of her ramble, but I enjoyed her vitality. She referred to me as *gringa señorita*, and mostly talked to me about the dangers of being a woman in Bolivia. My Spanish was steadily improving with almost no interactions in English, but sometimes I wondered if ignorance wouldn't be just a little bit of bliss at some point. My familiarity with *muy peligroso* was seeping under my skin. I repacked my bag while my new *tia* (aunty) continued to list all the possible ways I might die, as she simultaneously played with one of my trekking poles. I had 'adopted' the poles from a gear review shoot that the magazine I was working for had put on just before this adventure, and they were slightly too tall for me – hilariously oversized for her, the grips coming up to nearly eye level. Despite the clear mismatch, Tia tried her best to persuade me to give her my poles. I would have helped her in a heartbeat, but the reality was that I still needed them, as I had made my commitment now to finish this expedition, and I couldn't move at the pace required without them. Not to mention they were essential to my rustic tarp dwelling each night. I've always hated that a minimalist pack means there is no space for gifts, but I have also come to prefer that way of engaging – without the presenting of wealth or stuff, but rather simply the exchange of stories and laughter. Tia shook her head at me as I set out in the pouring rain, all alone and, in her mind, towards my certain death. She wished me good luck nonetheless, and gave me a warm hug. Sometimes, we all just need a good hug from an aunt figure.

Thunder bellowed overhead while the rain pelted me, the noise over my waterproof clothing enhancing the effect. The brief stop on the veranda had let the lactic acid flooding through my leg muscles truly start to scream, and I felt stiff all over. Running was awkward, and I had to consciously conduct the mechanics, swinging my arms furiously to promote leg turnover. I refused to stop. Thunder and lightning wouldn't stop me. Washed-out roads wouldn't stop me. Danger warnings from every local I had met so far wouldn't stop me. I would make it to the end even if I was forced to crawl.

Sunset wouldn't stop me either and, despite the searing pain in my lungs and legs, I had settled into a decent shuffle-jog when night fell. I knew if I stopped at all – even just to fill my water or tie my laces – I would never start again. I kept jogging. The thunderstorm had been replaced by a dense fog, and the beam of my head torch bounced off the thick water particles ahead of me, offering me nothing but a bright cloud to run to. Just after sunset, people working in the fields began returning to their homes, and the mud road was suddenly filled with pedestrians, mostly men in dark clothes and not using a light to help them see. Their bodies would come into view only metres away from me, and I would jump out of my skin every time. It was eerie, to say the least, to be moving through the dense cloud knowing that there were so many people nearby, also moving silently past. I took comfort from the thought that they couldn't see me either, so any sinister activity that so many had warned me would befall a solo gringa wouldn't have a very good chance of materializing. At least that's what I told myself.

Late at night, I reached the bottom of the muddy road and landed in the larger pueblo. At the outskirts of town, a group of men standing around smoking cigarettes – truly a universal staple of rural towns – flagged me down and asked me what I was up to. They seemed friendly enough, so I told them.

I asked if it would be cool if I slept in the town plaza – my new change in tactic was, rather than hiding in the mountains, to just head straight to the epicentre where *everyone* knew where I was. With the approval of the self-appointed elders of the town, I felt safe. They knew I was there, and they now had adopted responsibility for me. I walked to the gazebo in the centre of the plaza, a grand wooden structure with a roof – my favourite feature, as the rain settled back in – and surrounded by a simple garden. Locals walked around the edges, either visiting the two opposing tiendas or returning home to eat. It was a quiet place, and I felt comfortable enough to set myself up in the darkest corner of the gazebo, starting with lighting my stove to make dinner.

As I flicked at my lighter, struggling with cold and pruny fingers to roll the flint, the local police officer walked up. I gave my best casual smile, as if to say, 'Oh, hey.' He lifted his heavy combat boot and dropped it with a thud on the concrete step next to my stove, leaning a macho elbow onto his propped knee. It's a power stance refined by alpha males the world over.

'Are you sleeping here?'

'Yep.'

'You can't.'

Fair enough. I took a step back at the situation I had led myself to believe was completely normal: rolling out a sleeping bag in a local park and cooking dinner there. I realized I was glorifying homelessness.

'You can't sleep here. It'll be way too cold for you. We'll find you a place.'

And soon the town mayor was also involved, unlocking the

town hall that towered over the plaza, and even pulling out a mattress for me to sleep on the floor of the second storey, where I would be warm, safe and have access to electricity to recharge my devices.

A *salchipapas* stall opened shortly after a rugged bus arrived, depositing the high-school-aged children who had to make a long trek every day to receive their education, arriving home late at night and hungry for fried-up saturated fats. I was enthusiastically dragged to the stand and given my own cardboard plate of fries (*papas*) and sausage (*salchi*), smothered in a spicy red sauce. It was like holding a press conference, with me sitting on the high ledge I had been offered while teenagers and adults took turns asking me questions that I did my best to understand and respond to in Spanish.

'How do you stay safe?'

'How do you charge your phone?'

'What about pumas?'

I'll admit that one surprised me a little, and made me worry that the long bus ride to the nearest high school wasn't a good use of time.

After managing to duck out from the plaza and return to the town hall, I was asleep in seconds. The pueblo of Combaya had taken excellent care of me, and my heart was filled with the kindness I had received.

At 7am on the dot, my troop of Combaya chaperones was at the front door, ready to greet me. I stood for photos with the mayor, police officer and a few *tias*. After scanning my passport and taking some diligent notes on my whereabouts, the policeman insisted on giving me directions that I knew were completely wrong, and then they wished me luck, with a final reminder that I was going somewhere very dangerous and should reconsider.

My feet felt lighter as I climbed the dirt track. As I had arrived after dark, I hadn't seen where I was, and now in the bright morning sun had a view of the valley I was winding my way through. Combaya was a colourful pueblo built on an impossibly steep mountainside. The dirt track snaked around the jagged hills, clinging to the almost vertical ledge of the hillside. Below, the river valley plunged hundreds of metres away, and above, the snowy peaks of the Andes were even further out of reach. The scale of the place was staggering, and the unlikelihood of building a pueblo as well.

It was hot and sunny, the way I had imagined my journey would be, but hadn't been for longer than a few minutes up until that point. After the previous day's mammoth effort, I was particularly tired and hungry, so I pushed on to the next pueblo, imagining a tienda that became more and more welcoming the more that I dreamed of it. My first image was of all the tiendas I had come across so far – a dusty, dark shed with a few shelves that were mostly bare except for old packets of dry biscuits or bags of pasta, maybe a few tins of tomato sauce. A few stacks of plastic bottles, mostly unnatural-coloured fizzy drinks from local brands, and then maybe a few bits and bobs for the household that I didn't need to worry about. My imagination then installed a fridge, full of cold, sugary drinks, and – heck, why not? – some ice creams. I imagined the room now air-conditioned, with a comfortable seat and table for eating a cooked meal. Everything was clean and bright, unlike me, covered in dust and mud, my sweat mixing with the film of dirt on my skin to turn me a couple of shades darker than my naturally pale skin.

Finally reaching the tienda, I was snapped back to reality. The small shop, serviced through a window that a short and stout Cholita stood behind, was almost bare inside. It was clear she had received no supplies for a while, so I bought some salty crackers that had already been broken into mainly crumbs, and a bottle of Coka Quina – Bolivia's brand of Coca-Cola. I sat in the plaza, as had become my custom for visiting Andean pueblos, and leaned against the gazebo while inhaling my salt and sugar. The pueblo was quiet, as usual during the middle of the day when everyone is somewhere in the mountains, either mining, farming or herding, but a few locals passed by, all with the same question: 'Aren't you afraid?'

I wondered if I had a negative mindset, or a paranoia, that I kept imagining that the daily thunderstorms always hit me at the worst time, but I did seem to almost always be at the top of a climb when they came. The top of the pass was a beautiful green area, with small ponds the perfect mirrors to the stormy sky above. There were more llamas in one place than I had ever seen, and no humans in sight. The Bolivian Andes continued to surprise me, with every mountain pass delivering a new view, and each small region somehow different from the one on the other side of the mountain. I wanted to sit still and breathe the place in, and let the llamas relax to my presence. But as soon as I stopped, I got cold. Really cold. It's a cold I'm familiar with: an exhausted body goes into terrible thermoregulation, and I reflected that I had been overheating just hours previously and now couldn't control my shivering, even with extra warm layers on. There wasn't really anything actionable about this intel – I still had to keep pushing my daily mileage, so physical discomfort would just have to be accepted. I tightened my hood around my face and kept moving, shivering all the way down to the next pueblo, where I once again confidently strode into the plaza to set up my home. This time, I arrived so late at night that the village had already gone to bed, so I had a quiet night, save for all of the barking stray dogs.

I had adopted a habit of setting up my campsite for defence, or even a quick escape. I never left any items rolling around – either I was using it (my bedding) or it was packed. My shoes were placed next to me with the laces loose and the tongues pulled back so I could step into them quickly. The trekking pole that wasn't holding my tarp up was laid next to me, a pathetic weapon, but a weapon nonetheless. My knife stayed in my right-hand pocket. That part I was least comfortable with, but every time I awoke when I thought I heard something coming, I clenched the folded blade in my hand.

HAPPY HALLOWEEN

It was afternoon when I realized that it was Halloween. Remembering the advice I'd been given on Dia de Todos los Santos, which was the next day, 1 November, I decided to be far away from human settlements that night. By now, I was among the tallest, most beautiful mountains in the entire Andean chain, and Peak Illimani rose before me. I'll be forever grateful that the sky cleared just long enough for me that afternoon as I jogged down an overgrown, disused path straight towards her. Illimani is without a doubt one of the most beautiful mountains I have ever met.

As I reached her flanks, a stone circle caught my eye. Almost completely reclaimed by nature, I discovered the remnants of an Incan structure. The remains of the walls were about waist height, and thick branches grew around and between the uneven stones. I explored them, wondering what history they might have witnessed, and marvelling that for centuries these stones had laid at the feet of Illimani, and now were simply left here, forgotten by time and free to be explored by a lone gringa runner. While I explored, I realized there was dead and dry firewood everywhere, a clear stream coming from Illimani's glacier, and flat, soft ground. It was the perfect campsite. Although there was still nearly an hour before sunset, I decided to allow myself this one break. I couldn't pass this opportunity, even if it meant missing my goal for the day.

I found the best place to make my fire and set up my camp, and then went around collecting a pile of firewood. Darkness fell as I got my fire roaring, and I made a hot chocolate and simply chilled, leaning back to look at the stars above the white-blue glow of Illimani, keeping warm with my fire. I took a deep breath and, for the first time in weeks, relaxed completely.

As if building a fire with my hands and running to the edge of this beautiful mountain weren't enough, I even managed to repair the puncture in my sleeping pad – in the dark. I felt unstoppable, and couldn't wipe the smile from my face as I scanned my surroundings.

This is the life I've built, I thought to myself with nothing but satisfaction. I let go of the guilt of leaving anything behind, let go of my apologetic nature for the 'danger' I continued to put myself in. I didn't worry about a thing. I drank my hot chocolate and threw more sticks on the fire, proud of myself for the choices I had made that had led me to that exact, magical spot in the world.

The rain eventually returned to put out my fire and let me know it was time for bed. When the storm picked up, I watched from underneath my feeble tarp as lightning pierced the sky and flashed the bright ice on Illimani. It was beautiful and scary at the same time, and although I knew I was vulnerable in my makeshift shelter, I was also in total awe of Pachamama and the powerful forces I was watching. The scale of Illimani's glacier and the ferocity of the storm it was withstanding. I had never experienced lightning strikes at such a high frequency, as if the sky was putting on a show. Remarkably, I stayed dry under my tarp, having finally figured out the nuances of setting it up just right so that it stayed tightly in place and no wind or rain came in from the closed sides. I had never felt so at peace, despite the raging thunderstorm and the spookiness of sleeping next to the remains of an ancient civilization on Halloween. I felt like everything was just right, and I trusted my own instincts and Pachamama to see me to the end of the journey safely.

FRAGILE MOJO

In the morning, I felt like I woke up with my mojo back. There was even a small spring in my step as I strolled around my campsite, trying to get a photo of my little tarp with Illimani in the background – very difficult to do, given the scale. I was behind where I had planned to stop the previous night, but hot chocolate by a fire under a mountain was clearly all I had needed to get my mindset back, and I felt confident again. It was a relief, if nothing else.

I ran strong on the muddy track, losing elevation as I left Bolivia's tallest mountain behind me. I passed through colourful pueblos, and even found one selling ice cream, which I devoured gleefully on the cracked pavement while Cholitas passed by – 'Aren't you afraid?' Nothing could get me down. I noticed that this was the first time I had seen Cholitas dressed with short sleeves – it had hardly occurred to me that I had never seen their skin aside from their face, and I realized that I had entered into a different climate zone with the drop in altitude. Gardens sprung up around brightly painted houses, and fertile land was farmed by hand. I was losing height fast, and would have to go all the way down to 1,700m before hitting the final subrange of Qimsa Cruz. I was, of course, warned against this. One woman I spoke to advised me that if I continued into that valley, I would never come out.

'It's a very poor region, and the police don't bother going there. It's lawless, and there is a lot of crime. You're rich, and you will simply be murdered for your things. They won't think anything of killing you.' Then, 'You do have a gun, right?' I responded that I did not have a gun. She tried and failed to disguise the fear in her eyes. 'You really need a gun if you want to go there.'

I had grown so used to warnings at this point, but that one stuck with me a little. I told myself it would be no different from what I had experienced so far, but every pueblo lower in altitude gave me a slightly more wary reception. Around noon I stopped in a larger pueblo, desperate for a drink, now that I was in the much hotter lower climate and abundant groundwater had been diverted into farming irrigation. For the first time in the journey, no one in the pueblo greeted me. At best, I was deliberately ignored. At worst, the younger men stared at me with disdain. Although no words were spoken, I realized quite clearly that I was unwelcome. I took my drink bottles and biscuits and crept out of the pueblo, feeling too awkward to sit in the plaza as I had grown so used to doing. Suddenly, the warnings against this valley seemed very realistic.

My anxiety increased in tandem with the drop in altitude. I removed my watch and, along with my camera and iPhone, stuffed it deep inside my pack. A feeble gesture – I was still a white gringa on 'holiday', no one needed to see which version of the latest GPS watch I was using to know that I had more money than them. I had already ducked off the main track, instead slowly bushwalking my way alongside the route, hoping to avoid detection. Trucks carrying workmen passed now and then, and as soon as I heard the engine roar from around a bend, I made sure to be out of sight. My fear escalated at every corner and gripped my throat. I decided that if I saw a public bus – or maybe even a cop car? – I would get in and skip this section. Doing the full length of the mountain range meant a lot to me, but surviving meant slightly more. All I knew for sure was that I didn't want to be where I was. If I was going to trust my instincts, I had to listen to what they were screaming at me.

Get out.

Nature dictates everything, and I had no choice but to keep moving until I found flowing water, which would be at the very bottom of the valley. From there, I knew it would be a long way until I reached an altitude that had water again, so I had no choice but to make camp at the bottom. As every drop in height made me more nervous, the prospect of spending the night at the lowest possible altitude was hugely unattractive, but I knew I had to do it. When I reached the bottom, a beautiful clear river rushed through the red rocky valley, with a few trees clinging to the banks. Beyond this strip of blue water and green leaves, everything was dusty red and brown, completely dead under the intense sun. It truly was the only place to spend the night, so when I reached the only bridge that crossed the river, I decided to wade upstream as far as possible before dark to be well out of the way of any passers-by.

The water was clear, rushing over smooth grey rocks, forming small falls in sections, but there were enough areas that were safe to cross. I found a small island in the middle of the river that had trees with large, low-sweeping branches, and decided it was the safest home nature could provide. I would be almost impossible to spot, with my tarp matching the shade of the riverbed, and the trees sheltering me from all sides; additionally, the ford to reach the island was hip deep. My tarp setup had become such a routine above the treeline that I was confused by all the extra props. There was an abundance of help in the way of branches and roots that I could tie the corners of my tarp to, and it took me ages to pick the right combination to finally set my canopy up with the help of the trees. After making the island my temporary home,

I stripped completely for a bath in the beautiful river. It was a wonderful feeling, after all this time wrapped in all of my layers against the elements, to be totally naked in nature, letting the water soothe my aching muscles and clear the days' worth of dirt, scratches, sunscreen and sweat. My legs were covered in insect bites that I had scratched open in the night, and my ankles completely swollen from the full day of running downhill. I sat on a submerged rock, facing downstream so the water could cascade over my back, curling around my neck, massaging my strained muscles. I cupped water in my hands and washed my face, rubbing the stress from my temples. There is something so purifying in a nature bath, and I wished that I had been able to enjoy more of these so far, but the stormy nature of the Andes and the need to keep my core temperature stable had prohibited this until that moment.

As dusk closed in, my high state of anxiety pricked up again. I noticed a few lights on the hill above me, and remembered that at this hour field workers return to the pueblos, and of course the area around this river would be farmed. Wary of attention, I ducked back under my grey tarp, and with its shelter cooked my dinner. I slipped back into my running clothes and assembled everything neatly, as was now my custom, always ready for visitors. I had the sense of being watched, and poked my head out to see. There were more lights on the hill now, and my heart beat hard in my chest. *Just don't come down here.* I remembered my Atlas encounter, and I have always assumed that it was my lights that gave me away that night, so I operated without my torch and, as soon as my tin mug was boiling, switched off the flame.

Huddled under my tarp, sitting cross-legged on top of my sleeping bag, I ate nervously, gulping down my quinoa and tomato soup far too quickly – definitive emotional eating. I watched anxiously as the lights on the hill increased. Workers criss-crossing the goat trails (or llama trails) that would lead them back to the main route towards their homes. I kept my eye on their movement, overwhelmed with thoughts of what I could do if any of the lights came down to the river. I thought back to my own path up here – was it really that sneaky? Was I really that far from the bridge? Of course not. I was tired, exhausted from over ten days of HAPE and running, and it was probably a mere few steps away. Had I really concealed myself that well? I doubted it. I looked over my belongings – bright colours favoured by the outdoor industry back home. Reflective details and bright zippers.

Ridiculous, I thought as I stared at my things.

The things I was told I would be killed for.

And then it started. I noticed one of the lights winding its way down to the water's edge.

Don't come closer. Please, don't come any closer.

I thumbed my knife in my pocket and silently pulled my shoes on. The light had reached the edge of the foliage, and would soon make it through the trees that would lead to the river. Only a small ford stood between us now. If I had been seen, I was trapped on an island in a deep valley with knackered legs. I was a sitting duck.

The light was now hovering at the water's edge. My mind raced. What would I really do? Could I really use a knife? I had heard the case for not fighting back, and just letting them take what they would. How would I recover? The sickest thoughts that every woman pushes down came rushing to the front. The worst news stories I had been aware of. Movies I had to close my eyes for. Things that I knew women all around the world endured every single day. And now I had to choose – how would I handle it?

The light began moving across the water, and then it picked up pace. Suddenly, it moved incredibly fast – too fast.

Firefly.

It was a fucking firefly.

RETURN TO ALTITUDE

I woke to an aching body – which, I'm aware, has been mentioned most mornings of this global challenge, but this time it was *really aching*. A full day of running downhill from over 4,000m to under 2,000m was fun, but physically absolutely ruinous. My lower back screamed, and my quads trembled. I heaved myself out of bed, determined to get an early start. I just wanted to get out of this Valley of Fear. Literal and emotional.

After wading down the river, returning to the bridge that would take me over the large estuary to begin my climb back up into the mountains, I felt that I had woken up in an entirely different place from the one I had been living in for the past couple of weeks. Gone were the white peaks, the gloomy skies, the big open air and the short alpine grass. Instead, I was in a red-hot landscape of only dirt and mud, almost no green or grey in sight. The sky was clear and blue, and the sun stretched down to me in the deep valley, warming my skin – and then dehydrating me quickly. I was about three-quarters through my run now, and the familiar feeling of my body falling apart had never been so potent. I knew I was entering the segment of these things where getting enough water and nutrition is vitally important, and practically impossible due to the deficit already racked up from days of exertion. I could see the brown gravel road winding up the dry mountain ahead of me, and worried that I might not find enough water. It was a long way to the next village, and it was a public holiday. I filled my bottle and the bladder I carried just in case of these situations – and hadn't had need for yet – and then began my long walk up towards the final subrange of the Bolivian Andes, the Quimsa Cruz.

The sun beat down on me and sweat literally dripped from my forehead, a sensation I had almost forgotten over the course of this journey. I was so used to wasting too many minutes every day changing my layers to shield out the cold or the wet, that this concept of simply being too hot and having no more layers to change was remarkable. *Is this what the Atlas was like the whole time?* I tried to remember how I got through that for such a prolonged period of time, and passed the morning recounting all of the environments I had run in so far in my life, weighing the pros and cons of each. Naturally, your least favourite is always the one you're enduring at the time, and I was struggling to see the benefit of the intense dry heat. *At least I now have a chance of going home with a tan,* I thought – without it, no one might even believe that I had been away at all.

The climb was punishing and relentless. I had to get back

to 4,500m that evening to make the village that started the Quimsa Cruz, and also my final resupply location of the journey. I imagined a cosy Andean cafe and filling Bolivian food as my reward – but mostly I imagined cold drinks. I was now savouring the last drops of my water, and getting nervous that the red, dry rock was still the only landscape around me. At every dried-up riverbed, my anxiety heightened. How many more *hours* until I reached an altitude where water ran again?

My high state of fear from the previous day was still very much on my mind, and it was strange that in so many hours on a 'main' road (that is to say, a road that a vehicle could technically use), I never saw a single soul. I didn't know whether to be grateful that I was alone, or fearful of what might happen if someone did arrive. There was certainly no one around to hear my scream.

The answer to that question finally arrived. A lone minivan wound its way up the road behind me. I could hear it coming for a while, the climb proving difficult even for an engine, and I listened to it labouring its way along the hairpin turns that I had needed to stop and catch my breath on. There was nowhere to go, and so high was my desperation for water that I decided I would rather take my chances with whoever was driving. When it eventually reached me, the driver slowed his car and pulled up alongside me.

Inside the suburban-style minivan was a typical family: a father driving, grandfather in the passenger seat, and mother and children bouncing around in the back. Yet again, my fear evaporated in an instant and I was glad to meet someone.

'*No tienes miedo?*'

I had plenty of *miedo*. I shrugged, but declined his immediate offer of a ride.

'*Agua?*' I was so grateful that I didn't have to ask that I nearly teared up. The relief and joy on my face must have been obvious, because while his wife filled my bottle with cold water, he upped the ante.

'How about an ice cream?' he patted the cooler that was wedged between the front seats, and the grandfather produced a pink ice lolly, which, given the circumstances, was the best thing I had ever tasted. As the van continued labouring upwards, leaving me in a cloud of dust, I sat in a shaded patch of a steep corner and enjoyed my ice cream, wondering if I had at least reached the altitude where people were kind again, if not the altitude where nature could provide me enough water to survive.

By the time I made it to the first village on the climb, which I had by now begun to refer to as Bolivia's True Death Road – the real one sold through tour outlets in La Paz seeming far too mild compared to this desolate experience – I was verging on delirious. I dropped my pack with a thud at the door of the tienda, which was thankfully not only open, but one of the largest I had encountered so far. I walked in a zombie state through the aisles, collecting items that made little sense – sugar, hydration, salt, more sugar. The clerk as well as the only other patrons watched me in stunned amazement, as if a giraffe had just walked into the store and purchased these things. I ignored the obvious silence, returned to my bag outside and sat on the concrete steps eating a bag of crackers while greedily drinking my Coka Quina.

Whether it was the vibe of the village or just the *siesta* hour on a public holiday, the silence of the place was unnerving. The plaza, a sunny expanse of concrete, flanked on one side by a large white church, was empty. Until I showed up. Soon, the spectacle of a gringa beckoned attention. A middle-aged man on a motorcycle wearing sandals that appeared to be made from a car tyre stood over his bike next to me, peppering me with uncomfortable questions while I tried to regain lucidity through the diet of salt and sugar. He inspected every item within his eyesight, constantly asking, 'How much did that cost?' In South America, this is generally not a conversation a gringa wants to find herself in. I declined to answer, but he persisted.

'How much money do you have?'

'How much money do Canadians make?'

'How much did it cost to fly here?'

I was deeply uncomfortable, and deeply embarrassed at the answers, even though I wouldn't ever provide them. I knew I had a lot more than he did. And I knew that being both much younger than him *and* a female, this was an unsettling reality for both of us.

'At home', I'm proud of what I've earned. As a self-employed, independent woman, it feels good to be able to buy myself a camera or a plane ticket. The first time I came to South America, I was 18 and could barely afford to scrape by; I learned how to be the ultimate frugal backpacker, buying overnight bus tickets to save on hotel expenses and subsisting on cereal from the grocery store for days, keeping my daily budget less than $10. I was proud of myself that ten years later, I was back, and in completely different life circumstances. I had worked and built a life that allowed me to travel and enjoy the experiences. The first half of that decade had been riddled with uncertainty and insecurity, and I was finally coming out of that phase of my life and feeling like I could truly support myself and live without total financial anxiety.

But that didn't ease my anxiety for global inequality, and travelling to places that were significantly poorer – where I knew that an equal woman to myself could work way harder than me and yet never be able to enjoy the same experiences as I had already had by my late twenties – always confused me. I wanted to be proud of everything I had built, taking a lot of left turns in my life and designing an alternative path that suited me, and it was finally paying off so that I could live the life of my dreams. But my preference for travel in places where life has far fewer advantages will always keep me humble. I'm proud of what I have if I only measure it in the Western economy. On a global scale, I'm constantly embarrassed.

I said none of this to the man on the motorcycle. His hungry eyes were already fixated on my camera, watch and iPhone, and the closer he edged himself to me and my stuff, the more obvious it was that his curiosity could turn sinister. I wasn't ready to get going, the sun still baking hot and the climb still impossibly long, but I needed to move on. I downed my Coka Quina and, with a bag heavier with fresh water and juice, continued ever upwards.

It was late when I collapsed into Viloco, the active miner's town that had been on my mind for months now – the final stage of the route. I'd expected it to be wealthier than the pueblos I had encountered so far, and it certainly seemed that way from the distance of an internet search. Viloco sits nestled among the jagged peaks of the Quimsa Cruz and serves as a central station for the heavy mining activity in those rich mountains. A paved road led into town, and then the pavement ended and the gateway into the mountains began. The pueblo was fantastically colourful against the gloomy greyness of both the foreboding mountains and the stormy sky above, but I was surprised to find most of the buildings crumbling to some extent, and even some of the larger structures completely derelict and deserted. Strolling up and down the streets of Viloco's grid system, it was like visiting a place that once was. I imagined its history as a wealthy centre of resource extraction, but today found boarded-up windows, broken cement and shabby homes with stripped paint and leaking roofs. I never did find the cafe that I had dreamed of – the hotels and restaurants that once served the town were all closed. I visited the small market to buy enough to get me through the final stage of my journey – pasta from a large drum, delicately measured out into a plastic bag, and some dehydrated tomato soup to go with it. I looked forward to fresh fruits and vegetables on the other side – if Viloco had any at all, I never found them.

There was perhaps an hour of daylight left, and I knew my legs were too shot to make much use of it. Disappointed that the hotels had all closed, I strolled the streets, watching pueblo life in a daze. Piles of litter were swept into mounds on the muddy streets, and ageing Cholitas shooed stray dogs from their small verandas. Clusters of teenagers giggled around mobile phones, and young men paraded their motorbikes around the uninspiring football field. On the eastern hillside, the local cemetery was full with families still visiting for the holiday weekend, and occasionally loud and colourful buses pulled into town to drop off and collect people carrying huge bags of picnic supplies for more Dia de Todos los Santos celebrations. Satisfied with my quiet tour of the pueblo, I climbed up the steep gravel switchback above town to find a sheltered place to bivvy.

The top of the climb led me to a landscape that could have been out of a Dr. Seuss story. The peaks of the Quimsa Cruz were nothing like the Andes I had met so far – they were jagged, like a dinosaur's spine, with sheer walls towering above. The valley between, where I now stood, was covered in boulders larger than cars, and I carefully weaved my way between them, occasionally climbing over and jumping from one to the next.

I found myself a patch of softish earth between the boulders just big enough to roll out my bivvy, and with a clear spring nearby. Exhausted, I decided against the difficulty of setting up my tarp, relying on the rocks to create my home for the night. The clouds had cleared, and I lay back looking at the stars above, knowing I had little time left with them now. Gunshots and fiesta music occasionally wailed up through the valley, bouncing off the large walls of the surrounding mountains, but I no longer feared civilization.

Strangely, the sounds of revelry were comforting, and I slept deeply.

THE QUIMSA CRUZ

I woke before dawn, and lay in my warm sleeping bag gazing up at the stars. I had three – perhaps two – days left. I looked over my route for the Quimsa Cruz, still tucked inside my warm bag, and reckoned that two days wasn't unreasonable. My pace had steadily picked up over the last week, and my HAPE was hardly bothering me anymore. *Finish on Sunday night.* I let myself, for the first time in two weeks, fantasize about that finish. Beer. I would definitely have a beer. A hot shower, a clean hotel room. I could throw my shoes away. And then head back to Peru and make my flight home. *Peru. Warmth.* Now I was really letting my mind run wild.

Before the sun even began to float over the towering peaks above me, I had already packed up, determined to finish strong. There hadn't been many strong days to get me to this point, but I was certain that I could finish on a high note.

Two days. I've got this.

It turned out I wasn't the only one making the most of the day: seconds after crawling out of my bouldered-in campsite I met a herd of llamas and their young shepherd on the trail. I pulled to the side as they strutted past, their bright pink tags worn around their long necks standing out beautifully against their white and brown fur. The shepherd was stunned to see me, and looked around us in all directions as if to ask *where on earth did this gringa just come from?*

I smiled and chirped, *'Buenos dias!'* before breaking into a jog, finally free of the llama traffic jam. I never looked back to discover the look on his face.

The sun rose and a beautiful day greeted me, as if Pachamama herself had agreed that I would finish strong. I hiked determinedly up a 5,100m pass. Snow covered the trail, and near the top I had to fold my poles away in order to scramble the last ascent. It was great fun, if not fairly terrifying, me, alone, at altitude and constantly slipping on ice concealed under the snow. It was a pretty steep drop, but I never looked down. Only up.

Like something from a movie, the minute I hit the top of the pass and lifted my arms to rejoice, a thunderstorm arrived like a punch in the face. Perched on a precarious thin ledge between the scramble I had just come up and the one I would now need to find a way down, I yanked on my waterproof jacket and pants, pulling my hood tight around my face. *Two days.* I kept muttering this, and the knowledge that I wouldn't be uncomfortable much longer made the experience infinitely more fun. Instead of fearing the thunderstorm or regretting that my bag was getting soaked again, I took pleasure in the elements. Sleet pelted me, and I scrambled down the pass with an agility I hadn't yet displayed in the Andes. I felt natural. In my right place. Moving with nature, not against her. It was remarkable to me that my waterproof layers were all that I needed to be able to enjoy this wild experience – alone in a remote, inaccessible and technically challenging terrain at high altitude. What a gift it really is for anyone to find themselves that isolated on this crowded planet we share. The thought was truly astounding to me, and I began to swell with emotion and gratitude for the journey I was now two days away from completing. Snow stuck my eyelids and soon the white blanked the earth, and I lost all sense of navigation, to the point that I walked directly into an ice-cold river that had been concealed by the layer of ice and snow. The pang of cold shot up my leg and I pulled back, dancing around and shaking my foot to send blood flow immediately. *Two more days, and you can get rid of these wet shoes.* It was now the only cure for my discomfort: get to the finish line.

I worked my way across a valley that was entirely strewn with boulders. The work involved mainly scrambling and the occasional parkour move to get between them without falling in the many crevasses. The thunderstorm and snow/sleet persisted, adding a serious level of danger that I felt the route did not truly need. *Are you testing me now?* I asked the mountains out loud. I had come so far, and pushed through so much, would this be my final test to find out if I really had what it took to cross the Bolivian Andes alone?

As if to answer that question, the final 5,000m pass loomed before me, and I dug my toes into the slippery scree side with a fierce determination that didn't entirely feel like me. *I will not accept defeat, not when I've come this far.* I started picturing the white sand beach that stretches along the coast to Lima: if I really nailed this, I could have a whole spare day enjoying the sea before my flight home. While the storm enveloped me in a whiteout as I inched closer to the top of the climb, I let my mind drift to that warm, sunny beach, and a day of relaxing and not having to lift a leg for anything.

I hardly stopped that whole day. Storms came and went, but by mid-afternoon the clouds seemed to relent, and I came out of the fog to find the view I had been expecting ever since I began planning this trip: a deep blue-green lake, sheltered on all sides by white, jagged mountains, lush green slopes, and llamas absolutely everywhere. If you were going to make a postcard for the Bolivian Andes, this is exactly the picture you would take. A smile spread wide across my face, and I made easy Spanglish conversation with a llama as I meandered my way down to the shoreline, still delicately scrambling over slippery ledges. In the distance, I could see a gravel road used by one of the mines, and I knew the last miles of the day would be fast ones once I hit that strip of laid gravel.

The sun was lowering when I finally made the road, and as I looked back on to the lake, I saw one more sight that I had been dreaming of and not experienced yet: a sunset. In 16 nights of the Bolivian Andes, I had never once had a sunset, only the gradual darkening of stormy weather. But that last night, the clouds lit up fiery red and pink, reflected in that beautiful lake below. Tears welled up in my eyes as I stood in silence, just taking it all in, committing that moment to memory.

I kept moving until well after dark, making the most of the easy navigation of following a gravel road, grateful that it was still a public holiday, so the mines were all deserted. I was truly alone in the entire landscape, the workers all either congregated in Viloco or home with their families in the cities. It was a special feeling, and a perfect way for me to say goodbye to the Andes. Just us.

When I found something that appeared to be either a stable or a lazy shed, I confidently decided to make my home in it, grateful for a roof already built to keep me dry on all sides, and I laid out my tarp underneath me instead to create a clean ground to make camp on. My home for the night was a three-walled wooden structure, built on the side of the gravel road on one of the many switchbacks near a cluster of a small mines. I suspected it was a break area for the men, but really I had no idea. I felt safe and cosy inside my little roadside structure, although at 4,600m my last night was one of the coldest I had gone through on the whole journey, and I spent most of it awake and shivering, reminding myself over and over that I would be warm in Peru very soon.

FINAL PAYMENT

On the last morning, there was no fear, only excitement. I practically sprung from my bivvy, despite the biting cold and my frozen-solid shoes that I had to force my tender feet into. I stuffed everything into my bag haphazardly, and began running as fast as I could. In reality, that was not very fast at all, but it's the spirit that counts.

Over the first 10km of the day, I weaved through small mining settlements, all eerily deserted for the holiday. I had been so afraid of these places in my planning phase, knowing that they would be almost exclusively male, so finding them empty, aside from the stray dogs who had been left behind, was a relief. I wandered the streets alone, as if attempting to understand the local life through the visual tour of their buildings and objects. I sat on a bench in one of the camps and made myself a coffee, reasoning that there was no need to save anything still in my pack – if I wanted to use up my fuel and last supplies, I could. I was going to finish this thing by nightfall.

The final test was as brutal as I should have expected it to be. A severe hailstorm erupted at the worst possible location, just as I was wading through yet another field of boulders and ice-cold streams. The hailstones hit my hood with force, many of them the size of medium-to-large marbles. In the middle of the valley traverse, there was no hope of shelter, and I could only hope that the stones never got big enough to cause injury. I moved as fast as I could although, without any visibility or trail to follow, navigation was infuriatingly slow. I shook with cold as I delicately pulled myself up and over boulders, risking the leaps between them and imagining the worst if I should fall and break something here. I had to engage all of my efforts to stay calm, and not lose my temper at this last hurdle. I was anything but home free, even with less than 20km to go, and Pachamama was letting me know it.

Finally, I passed the test. The sun came out and a clear blue sky illuminated the wonderful landscape around me. The final climb of my journey was decorated in waterfalls, as if from a painting, and the sun gave warmth to my bones as I sprang my way up the last mountain pass.

At the top of that pass, a cloud enveloped me once more. I sat down on a rock to try and celebrate the end, knowing that only a 12km pure downhill lay between me and the Yungas rainforest, the end of my traverse, but sitting on a snow-covered rock in a cold fog wasn't the celebration I felt I needed – although it was entirely apt for the journey I'd had. I yanked my backpack on tightly, ready for the descent, and made my way down, out of the Andes and into the jungle below.

The end is always anticlimactic, as I've come to learn. For one, there is no place I love more than the solitude of the mountains. And secondly, I never find my way back to civilization fast enough to enjoy that first night 'back'. I found a hotel just after dark, and carried a *cerveza* and *fritas* to my small room. The shower wasn't exactly hot, but I took my time slewing off the adventure from my skin, soothing the aches, pains and open wounds left all over my body. I slept soundly in a large clean bed, completely warm and safe. But I never felt overjoyed. I only felt relief – I had overcome the series of tests that the Bolivian Andes had put to me, and now I would go home. But my heart stayed with that green lake with the llamas, the hot springs in the north, the vibrant Cholitas and the overwhelming grandeur of the glaciers that topped the highest peaks in all of the Andes mountain chain.

*

Fear is a companion we all travel through life with. The ilk of adventurers I watched growing up – an industry I could not see myself in – constantly proclaimed 'fearlessness' as an entire value system, banning weakness and hesitation.

I don't believe in fearlessness. Fear is an important function of your human brain that can help alert you to danger. When fear is triggered, I listen to it.

But fear can be limiting. If you let that fear take up too much space, let its voice grow too loud, it takes the helm, controlling your journey through life. It's a companion that, like any other long-term relationship, requires work. My time in Bolivia forced me to really listen to my own voice of fear, and find new ways of working with it. It was uncomfortable, but I'm grateful for the experience. Ever since that journey, my relationship with fear is healthier than ever.

I cut it so fine to make my flight home that I travelled straight from that small town to La Paz to gather my things, then onwards to Lima to fly back to Scotland. I landed first in Heathrow, which was alit with Christmas decorations and blaring capitalism and wealth. The contrast hit me harder than it ever had before. The world I actually live in, and the world I feel most alive in, are two very different places.

I had been mostly on the road for six months at that point, living my very best outdoors life, getting to travel for work around Europe, competing in endurance races in Ireland and Kyrgyzstan, and spending as much time as possible in nature. I was thriving in my life of adventure and had no intention of slowing down. A busy speaking season lay ahead, and then I would dive into the next mountain range in just a few short months.

CHAPTER FOUR

Doing It My Way:
The Southern Alps

There were countless occasions in the Bolivian Andes when I reassured myself that if I could make it through that difficulty, I would get to go to New Zealand next. I pictured the Southern Alps as a land with permanent sunshine and rainbows, no threats to my safety, easy and established hiking trails, abundant healthy food, Hills Alive with the Sound of Music, etc. It was going to be nice.

Throughout the winter leading up to my departure, I kept this image alive. I would escape the worst of the dark and dreary days in Scotland, and head to the other side of the planet, where it was summertime.

As I neared my departure date, I began to worry that things were *too nice*. Was I letting the challenge down? Going into Kyrgyzstan, Morocco and Bolivia, I had been facing huge amounts of uncertainty and fear, tackling mountain ranges that had no recorded crossings on foot. No guidebooks, easy maps or guarantee that the route would 'go'. This time around, there was nothing to fear. I had multiple gpx files added to my phone, I had friends picking me up from the airport in Christchurch, and trail notes from loads of people in my network who had already been running on the South Island. The intimidation factor was zero. I worried that this was a poor follow-up to how hard I had worked for the last three. Was I getting soft?

HERE I GO AGAIN

Whitesnake's 'Here I Go Again' came on the radio as the bus neared the trailhead to drop me off at my chosen start line. A smile cracked my face at the perfect timing of the lyrics – *here I go again, on my own*. My legs were twitching with excitement – the bus ride couldn't have been more different from the ones I had taken in Morocco or Bolivia. It was a comfortable, air-conditioned minivan, filled with hikers going to various trailheads in the region. I had the smallest backpack by more than half, and the bus driver had asked where the rest of my stuff was when I appeared, assuming thereafter that I was only heading out for one night.

'When are you coming back? I don't have your reservation to collect you . . .?'

'I'm not coming back, I'm heading north.'

'How far? You mean like Wanaka?'

'Umm, yeah, and then some more.'

I was still hesitant about revealing my full plans, the past three experiences having taught me to keep quiet in order to avoid the ridicule and doubt. Looking at my small backpack again, the driver eyed me with concern.

'You know they don't have any amenities at the huts, right? It's a long walk to Wanaka.'

There it was.

'Yep, all good. Don't worry.'

I didn't want my good mood crushed by returning to the familiar defence of my lightweight equipment and ability to cover more distance than the other hikers who were loading upwards of 70-litre packs into the trunk for their weekend adventures. I was confident in my 30-litre setup, currently stuffed to nearly overflowing with enough food to get me to Wanaka, my first resupply.

The driver had me note down his schedule and locations for collecting hikers the next day, just in case.

The Southern Alps welcomed me in by letting me know their tolerance level for happy hikers: within minutes of leaving the trailhead and the concerned bus driver, I hit knee-deep mud with no way around. My brand-new shoes, donned that morning for the first time, would have to lose their bright pink cheer – a colour I had chosen intentionally to constantly brighten my mood. I figured that I spend most hours staring down at my feet and wanted to give myself something nice to look at for this journey. But straight out of the gate, the Southern Alps took that away. After 20 minutes of smooth and easy jogging, my shoes would already never be dry again.

By midday, the reality of coming from winter in Scotland to summer in New Zealand hit hard. The heat was intense, and my head was already swimming. I had been warned incessantly about the hole in the ozone layer and to never remove my hat, but the blazing sun felt like it was reaching right *through* my hat, into my skull and melting my brain. When the waves of nausea that heat exhaustion always brings me showed up, I slowed down and took a breather under the shade of a large tree. I mixed up some electrolytes in my small soft flask, and decided to finish that ration before moving on.

Sitting still invited sandflies, who began biting my foreign northern skin, so I cancelled that vow immediately, attempting instead to jog and drink at the same time.

The first trail was everything I had been looking forward to: a stunning clear blue sky, views of white peaks, and a fun single-track hiking trail snaking through the forest and up into the high alpine. As the sun lowered, I reached my first DOC (Department of Conservation) hut, this one quite popular and attended to by a ranger. The main room was already filled with hikers, mostly Australians who had come over for a long weekend of trekking. I found an empty bunk bed and then joined the main hall to boil some water for my dehydrated dinner, which I enjoyed at a large table of weary hikers having the same. My small backpack was greeted by surprise again, but I couldn't stop smiling at the difference – here I was, surrounded by people with the same enthusiasm for long trails as me. Sure, their methods and mileage were different, but we were all on the same page.

I needed to find the ranger to show him my DOC pass, and was surprised when he took a keen interest in my trip. Andre was a young guy, perhaps only a few years ahead of me, and spent his summers manning the huts. We were stationed at the high point of a popular three-day through-hike, so he was mostly busy with the 'weekend warrior' crowd, and seemed stoked to meet someone taking a different route. I showed him my plans on the map, and he took his time to thoroughly inspect my route. To my huge relief, he confirmed that it was well planned, but couldn't resist constantly teasing me for how hard it would be. I had no sense of what a Kiwi scale for 'hard' was yet, but I was about to learn.

DAY 2

My first test was the Cascade Saddle, which had earned a few *ooohs* from the rest of the hikers I shared the hut with; even Andre the ranger had suggested it was a treacherous route. I made quick work of reaching the top, where I was greeted with my first proper Southern Alps vista. Wildflowers decorated the rolling grassy hilltops, and glaciers dominated the peaks around me. I stayed at the top for ages, too happy to waste the moment. Finally, when I went to make my descent, I did so past a sign warning of the falling hazard, and I remembered Andre's final comments last night:

'Most of the rescues here are for dislocated shoulders of people trying to catch themselves from falling. The rest of the rescues – are dead bodies.'

I folded up my trekking poles to leave my hands free to down-scramble my way to the next valley floor, and was relieved to make it without incident. I was getting my sense of scale for Southern Alps passes and, so far, I was okay.

Aside from the ample route notes and gpx files for simple navigation, the other logistical bonus of the Southern Alps was the abundance of DOC huts. In popular hiking regions, there are some luxurious, large huts with full kitchens, bunk beds (with mattresses!), ample firewood and other adventurers to mingle with. In the more off-route areas, the huts are more basic – some of the ones I found consisted of only a single room that hadn't been slept in for days or even weeks. Although I always preferred sleeping under the stars, the availability of these shelters was a great comfort. At the bottom of Cascade Saddle I took some time in the large DOC hut, empty in the middle of the day, to mend my Day 2 blisters and top up my hydration. The heat was going to take me a while to get used to, and I knew I had to be careful in these early days not to run into trouble with it.

I was like a kid in Disneyland throughout my first few days on the trails of the Southern Alps, constantly bumping into other outdoors folk who greeted me with nothing but positivity and encouragement, and I felt like I fitted New Zealand like a glove. It was my first time there, but I was at total ease in the culture and landscape.

Despite the enthusiasm of the people I was meeting, I was craving the solitude of the inner mountains, and eager to find myself in the true back country. The days had been physically demanding, with the high miles I was trying to put in and the steep mountain passes required, but the physical endurance was the only challenge I had faced so far. I longed for the adversity that I had become so accustomed to in the isolated depths of mountain ranges, where the environment and my own emotions would test me and make me work for my progress. I felt guilty for wanting to get away from the wonderful people I was meeting, but it was time for me to head into the true wilderness.

A rough single track carried me along for a while, but then I would leave the incredible NZ network of 'tracks', via a Kiwi footbridge: a precarious construct of simply three cables, two at waist height for each hand to grasp onto, white-knuckled, and below *just one* cable for your feet. The cables swung violently in the slightest of wind, and trail shoes slipped easily on the thin metal. One had the choice of whether it might be safer and more comfortable to forget the 'bridge' altogether and swim across. At the end of the precarious crossing, I was dropped onto a new Kiwi concept: routes. On the map, there were 'tracks' and 'routes'. 'Tracks' were proper trails, with clear footing. 'Routes', I would learn, were simply a game of wild connect-the-dots, where the dots were small orange triangles held up on stakes or bolted to trees at relatively long intervals, with no discernible path in between. Every time I found an orange triangle, I breathed relief and then began hunting for the next one while trying to find decent footing.

At least my first route was up a riverbed, so navigation was impossible to mess up, but moving over a rocky riverbed was slow and tedious as my feet slipped on every movement, while a fierce headwind tried to dissuade me as I trudged up Ruth Flats. The loose ground was hell on my exhausted legs, and I put my head down against the wind and tried my best to simply get the segment over with. The day had been gently raining until now, and a few angelic rays of sun were reaching down to the river between the grey clouds, as the wind continued to rip through the valley.

With every bend in the riverbed, taller peaks were revealed in front of me as I trudged upriver back towards the central divide of the Southern Alps. On one such bend, I discovered a campsite, whose resident was a wild-haired older man in just his shorts and sandals. He had a campfire going, two tents set up and a tarp between them. From a distance I could see him cooking over his open flame, and when he spotted me, he enthusiastically waved me over.

The man could only be described as a caricature of a crazy wilderness guy. His hair was remarkably similar to Einstein's, and his skin (mostly exposed, save the small shorts) was leathery from years of sun exposure. He was rushing around his campsite, keeping his fire going and pinning his tents down against the howling wind. I took in his setup: real pots and pans – not camping ones, but those from a kitchen, in addition to the ample shelter. I wondered how he'd carried it all in.

'You'll stay for a coffee?'

I didn't feel I could say no. To my surprise and, admittedly, delight, he produced another stove, a coffee grinder and an AeroPress.

'Wow, I'm impressed.' I motioned at his clutter.

'You've got to be comfortable!' The crazy chap spread his arms appreciatively at his outdoor kitchen.

I sat perched on a rock while he expertly made us each an espresso, and felt bad I had nothing to offer in return – my luggage was considerably lighter than his. But to that, he had some wisdom.

'Weight is all *just in your mind*,' he declared, pointing at his temples.

While I've always believed in mind over matter, and a human's ability to persevere through mental toughness, I also respect that a heavier backpack has genuine consequences for the body underneath trying to carry it. As delicious as the espresso was, I am still not considering a backpack the size of his (I checked it out – you could have fitted a husky in there).

We chatted about our adventures – he was a professor from Czechia (contributing further to the 'mad scientist' look I already couldn't stop seeing) on his summer holiday, living outside and going at his own pace in life. I couldn't help but laugh at the idea of him walking back into his economics lecture in a few weeks' time, fully clothed and prepared to talk sense to an auditorium. I've heard it said that many of us possess at least a couple of spirits inside of us, and I was glad that I met his wild one, although I got an inkling that his work one was a surprisingly accomplished and professional dude. I've always enjoyed meeting people abroad, knowing that I'm getting a privileged glimpse into that spirit that they seldom get to let out of the cage in their daily lives back home.

It was getting late already, but I wanted to get some considerable distance up the valley. Crazy Czech guy had suggested I stay at his campsite, but I wasn't totally into that idea. I spent another hour dragging my feet through the rocky valley, before it began to narrow and the shoreline next to the river disappeared. I would have to wade through the river itself, waist deep in most places. As the river ebbed, I would need to constantly cross in order to walk on the bank on the opposite side. The water was beautifully clear but alarmingly cold, as I was nearing its mountain source. At the deeper places, I could feel buoyancy start to take over and the bottom half of my backpack submerge. I had unclipped my straps, should I tumble over and need to free myself, and used my arms to 'swim' as my tiptoes tried to push along the sandy floor. I regretted getting completely wet so near the end of the day, and knew I would be cold in my campsite.

My aim was to make it as close to Rabbit Pass as possible before nightfall, which I almost did. In fact, it was completely dark when I began searching for a patch of ground large enough to roll out my bivvy in the midst of the substantial boulder field tumbling down from the mountains above me, and the fierce wind made setting my tarp up incredibly challenging. I found brick-sized rocks to peg it down, and huddled underneath as another rain shower passed through.

Despite the weather, I felt utterly at home, curled up underneath the presence of some of the biggest peaks in the region, in my cosy sleeping bag, with everything I needed to keep myself safe, warm and happy.

By midnight, the storm had passed, and I woke to a beautiful starry night sky. I smiled as I fell back asleep, feeling that contentment that comes from knowing you are in the right place at the right time.

RABBIT PASS

I started early, rising with the sun to a cloudless sky. The wind from yesterday had died down completely, and a stunning day was clearly on the rise. I packed up quickly, my eyes cast skyward at my first challenge of the day: Rabbit Pass. The mountains loomed over me, and I was still in their shadow from the morning sun. I had camped at the base of the climb, and it appeared completely vertical from that spot. I had heard a lot about this pass – it seemed to hold legendary status among the mountain community, and I was *going the wrong way*. The concept of trails being one way was mind-boggling to me at first – surely if you can walk it north to south, you can equally walk it south to north? Not in New Zealand, apparently: here, many trails are designated either north–south or south–north because of the differing challenges involved. I had decided to run the entire length of the Southern Alps, so found myself heading north on a segment that was intended for southbound travel. And there was nothing I could do about it.

The ascent of Rabbit Pass was a test of mettle. Within minutes of leaving my campsite, I had my hands on the rocks, scrambling my way up, until I realized I was in the full-commitment zone: any mistake would be very, very serious. I vowed to continue looking only forwards as my whole body shook with fear. The rocks were loose and unreliable: I scanned the face for good holds as I wedged the toe of my running shoe into the best cracks I could find, and my hands reached for stable rocks. Many times, I sent a cascade of rocks down the steep slope, the intensity of the slides a very audible reminder of the potential consequences of getting it wrong.

Just breathe. Stay focused. You've got this. I muttered to myself out loud, promoting only positive thoughts. I had learned enough about these moments and settling my nerves by now, and I was oddly excited to be put to the test.

About 2m to my right, directly across the vertical rock face, I noticed the bolts used by climbing groups. *I must be on the wrong route,* I thought, assuming the bolts were in the most obvious line. I considered side-climbing over to the bolted route – if nothing else, the bolts offered stable holds, even if I didn't have any rope to secure myself with – but I was so close to the top now that I decided to just make a big push for the final stretch.

Go, go, go, you've got this! I coached myself, the quiver obvious in my voice as the final moves steepened beyond my comfortable climbing limit. Pulling myself up onto the ledge, to finally sit down on safe, horizontal ground, was the last awkward and challenging manoeuvre, but as soon as I sat there, legs dangling over the route I had just 'free-soloed', the adrenaline of what I'd done came crashing through. I heard the involuntary *whoop* I had let out echo through the mountains.

I could hardly walk on my shaking legs, so sat there for a few minutes longer, breathing deeply to reground myself.

In the frosty morning, with the shadows of the surrounding peaks still long, I was wearing all of my available layers – long tights, thermal base layer and windproof. Now, I had climbed higher than the shadows and was under the direct blazing southern sun; while letting my heart rate come back down to earth, I rearranged into shorts, t-shirt and plenty of sunscreen. I had already sent out my resupply boxes on the trail ahead, each of them containing top-ups of factor-50 sunscreen. I wondered if I would even make it that far before running out again.

The journey over Rabbit Pass was one of the most pleasant running experiences I think I've ever had. The glorious sun welcomed me to the high altitude, and views of glacier-topped peaks around me were endlessly drool-worthy. The rain from the previous evening had delivered a fresh dusting of snow to the peaks, and they were shining like jagged pearls. I was torn between wanting to run, fast and free, with a big grin on my face, and wanting to stop, sit down, soak it in and perhaps never leave. This is the paradox of a perfect mountain moment.

The magic came to an abrupt halt at the precipice of the descent – here is where I learned why Rabbit Pass was only meant to be travelled in the opposite direction. A sheer drop, much steeper than the climb I had come up earlier, plummeted to the valley floor. I couldn't see a feasible route, but began noticing those teasing orange triangles sticking out in unlikely locations, indicating the best route. The 'best route' was just a bit above my comfort level.

I folded up my trekking poles once again, had a quick snack – assuming my hands might not be free for a little while – and turned around backwards to begin my down climb. I shuffled my toes along granite slabs, finding tufts of grass sticking out where I could get a stable hold, while my hands grasped for cracks in the rock that I could hang myself on if my feet slipped, which they sometimes did. The familiar wobble of my knees returned in an instant, and I still had a long way to go down.

Slowly – painfully slowly – I picked my way down the vertical slope. To my left, a beautiful cascading waterfall broke the silence of the still valley, but I couldn't let my eyes drift that way for long. Each point of contact with the earth was crucial, and I sidestepped along the 'route', often facing the wall, clutching with my hands. When I had shuffled to the left for long enough and it was time to make a switchback to the right, a sheer slab blocked my path. I could see it was the only way forward, but the vertical slope of it and lack of grassy knolls to grasp sent me over the edge with fear – my entire body betrayed me, and I stood there shaking, incapable of taking a step forward. I turned around to climb down once more, but couldn't convince any of my limbs to move beyond that. I don't know how long I stood there, clutching the grass in front of my face, my toes teetering on the precipice of the slab I needed to climb down. Below it, no barriers blocked the vertical fall to the valley floor. I was still over 100m from the bottom. I could just about make out some climbers walking up the valley now, their figures small as ants in the vast mountain wilderness. I had a long way to go before I could walk safely on that valley floor. I considered waiting for the climbers to come up, but knew they were hours away, and I was now shaking so violently that I could just as easily have collapsed off the wall before even attempting to move. I had to find a way to keep going.

I spotted a bit of trail that didn't seem so far away, where there was a clear, flat footpath. I unclipped my backpack and attempted to delicately lower it so it wouldn't drop the entire way. As soon as I released the top loop of my bag, it gained momentum rapidly and tumbled down. The sound of my water bottle hitting rocks at high speed assured me that any fall would be deadly. I was considerably lighter and more agile without the pack, but the fear I had confirmed by dropping it only made me shake more.

Stop being an idiot, I mumbled to myself. I had no idea how long I had been 'stuck' in this same location.

These are the moments when being alone sucks. A partner or friend could easily help you through these fear moments, being your eyes and coach, guiding you along the rock face. I desperately wished someone would come and tell me where to put my feet and what to grab with my hands, assuring me that it would hold. I peered down to the blurry valley floor again. The climbers weren't even at the base of the wall yet. I would not have that external validation – I would have to get myself through this.

Move your right foot down, I said out loud. My voice was shaky and high-pitched. *Breathe,* I reminded myself as soon as my right foot found a bit of a hold on the rough granite. There weren't any cracks or protrusions to make decent footholds, so

I had to trust that the tread on the bottom of my shoes would stick to the rock as I delicately lowered my left foot next. With my arms stretched above my head, clutching the edge of the slab, I took another deep breath before letting go with my right hand and searching for a lower hold. My feet both slipped, and I heard myself try to scream – but only a breathless whimper escaped. Somehow, I stopped myself slipping further, but now I was spread across the rock wall, with my backpack far below me, and well over the edge of fear. My belly lay flat against the cold rock; I leaned my forehead on it and closed my eyes. I felt the tears coming, and begged them to stay back. I was holding on with everything I had, and starting to cry would only make my body weaker. I needed to pull it together and be as strong as I could possibly be. *Move, please keep moving,* I pathetically begged myself to try. I hated my weakness in that moment. I knew that while some trekkers used ropes and climbing equipment to tackle this route, plenty of people also managed it without gear, and I was more than capable of being one of them. I despised myself for falling apart like that, for losing my cool in the crux of the moment.

OKAY! I forced a breath out.

Enough.

I was tougher than this.

I could do this.

Let's go, you've got this.

This time, my voice sounded more like my own, and I even nearly believed myself. I took those emotions of fear, desperation and self-loathing, and jammed them into a bottle, put the lid on tight and pretended to be confident enough to make it down the route successfully, toting that bottle to be opened later.

Somehow, through self-coaching, fake-it-till-you-make-it talk and breathing, I crawled and slid my way down to my backpack, and didn't stop until I got to the bottom. I let out some sort of animalistic cry of relief when my feet hit solid, horizontal ground. The climbers I had watched setting up from the valley had now made it to the base, and were casually enjoying the sun while preparing their equipment for the climb. I smiled at them, but moved swiftly past. I needed to open that bottle. I found a clear stream where I could rehydrate and reset. I kicked my shoes off, dipped my toes in the cool water and lay down with my backpack – now sporting some battle scars where it hit the rocks – as a pillow.

I slowly pecked at a melted energy bar while watching my chest rise and fall – deep, relieved breaths. I looked up at the wall I had just come down and winced at the sight – I did not like it up there. All of the muscles in my body were still shaking, so I focused on deep inhales and long exhales – *in, two, three, four . . . out, two, three, four* – focusing only on my breath and ignoring flashbacks that tried to stay in the forefront of my mind. It was time to brush it off and keep going.

The rest of the afternoon was a treasure of mostly downhill trail running. Kiwi hiking groups I passed were astonished that I had gone 'the wrong way' over Rabbit Pass, and it was unclear whether I was impressive or stupid. Either way, that was the only way I could have done my Southern Alps traverse, so there was no use dwelling on it. This wasn't a hiking holiday, after all.

I set a target to make it to a DOC hut that night, and my legs were wobbling like Bambi by the time I collapsed on the front porch. The hut was full, with a few walking groups cooking dinner, hanging laundry and playing cards. There were only a few bunk beds, but I was pointed to the last remaining mattress. It was a single-room hut with a separate outhouse, overlooking the wide Wilkin River where one of the groups had come to fish. I made polite chitchat while I changed my clothes and got my dinner going. My body was knackered, and I didn't have much strength for banter. Despite being the latest arrival at the hut, I was the first to bed. Unfortunately, so many men in one small cabin meant a symphony of snoring, and I hardly slept. While sleeping in the huts seemed to be an advantage to moving fast – no campsite to set up, warm shelter and, theoretically, more comfortable beds – I wondered if sleeping outside, alone, would be a wiser strategy. I was truly enjoying the social nature of this journey, but that enthusiasm quickly died with the snoring.

First to bed, first to rise. I waited, awake in bed, not wanting to be 'that guy' who gets up too early – another reason that staying in crowded huts might not help me. Finally, I crept out of bed, taking my stove out onto the porch to make my coffee and breakfast. I had an easy day ahead of me to my first resupply point, but I wanted to get there early to make the most of the recovery. I had a strategy in mind to arrive in resupply locations as early as possible, and then leave as late as possible the next day, giving myself as close to 24 hours of recovery as I could. This way, I intended to not take any 'rest days' on my journey, but stay in motion.

I followed the Wilkin, crisscrossing as the orange triangles dictated. Sometimes the crossings were waist deep and I was glad that it was a scorching hot day as the cold water flowed over me. The river was beautifully clear, so I could even see my pink shoes on the bottom. It was strangely pleasurable to do so many river crossings, even if it was slow and slightly risky in the deeper sections. My entire body was feeling rough from the last day of climbing, and sometimes I even lingered in the river a little longer than necessary to let my muscles relax in nature's ice bath.

I reached the highway and found a cafe only 5km from my destination. I was so exhausted that I didn't even question stopping for a break, and enjoyed fries for second breakfast without any guilt. I sat with an elbow on the table, resting my head on my palm, leaning over my food. I could have fallen asleep right then and there.

My resupply had been sent to a hotel/campsite, where I booked into a small, basic cabin for the night. After washing my clothes and myself and plugging in all of my devices, I flopped onto the bed for an afternoon siesta. I may be an outdoorsy girl, but nothing makes me feel better than washing my hair after a few days in the wilderness.

The morning brought violent rain and wind, so I waited it out in the cafe until mid-afternoon, chatting to backpackers, drinking flat whites and reading and writing. I felt guilty for sitting it out, but my legs were begging for more recovery time. The first segment had taken a far deeper toll than I felt it should have, and I wondered if my February body was really up to the task. Having just come through Scottish winter, I wasn't in the same type of shape as I had been on previous journeys, all of which had taken place at the end of summer, when I had a lot of outside days already under my belt.

ONE WEEK IN

I passed the one-week milestone, but didn't feel as if I had settled in yet. My routines were seamless – my campsite rituals were nailed, my kit choices were true perfection and I had avoided losing time or distance to navigation, for a nice change. But my body was not keeping up. The route was harder than I had anticipated, sure, but I wasn't willing to let myself off with that excuse. My daily mileage was consistently well below what I had imagined I would be doing. Every night, when I conceded defeat for another day after the sunset, I would stop my watch and despair over the number I saw looking up at me from my wrist.

Next to my watch was a bracelet I had engraved with one of my favourite mantras, especially for this journey: 'Don't be shit.'

I had set an intention. I wanted to achieve something out here. The last three journeys had been difficult in epic magnitudes due to the logistics, terrain, culture, navigation and the sheer challenge of entering the unknown. New Zealand lacked these factors, so I had decided to 'balance it out' by making this journey *physically* hard. I figured if I put in a really hard run, and really challenged myself in that way, I could make this journey worthy of the project. But that relied entirely on my own mental strength to keep pushing myself and not take my foot off the gas – to not be shit. 'Being shit', as

I defined it, was letting myself down, taking easy options, holding back instead of giving more. Choosing comfort instead of hurtling myself towards the edge of my comfort zone and finding out what was beyond it. Every time I looked at my wrist, I saw that mantra, next to a watch face displaying data that I constantly regarded as 'shit'. I was frustrated.

Perhaps the gods were listening. When I looked down at my watch on Day 8, I noticed the numbers hadn't changed in a while. I tried to sync it to my phone to reset, but it didn't work. I fiddled with technology for as long as I had the patience for, to no avail. I didn't want to stand on the trail messing with my smartwatch and smartphone, looking profoundly anything but smart. The watch was not coming back, it needed to be plugged into a computer for a software update, and I was a very long way from one. I sighed. I could use my phone to track my run, but it would drain the battery. I had my inReach, but it was incredibly inaccurate on the battery-saver mode, as I had learned in Kyrgyzstan when I returned home to find I only had a strange connect-the-dots map to remember my route by. It didn't provide insightful data like my average pace or my cumulative paused time – numbers I was relishing punishing myself with when I reviewed them every night.

I was going to have to keep going without recording any data. I was going rogue, off-grid, moving forwards and not getting any quantified feedback on how shit or not shit I was. I put my devices away, and jogged forwards, totally analogue.

It was wonderful.

Never again did I torment myself about stopping to walk, pausing to look at something or checking my pace. I ran by feel, not by expectation. I looked at the map and estimated distances, rather than recording totals to the nearest 100m. I let go.

That's not to say I wasn't still focused on not being shit. I continued to push myself, day after day. At my next resupply, lying on a cheap hotel bed while my clothes hung to dry in the room around me, I admired my swollen ankles and tried to massage my failing muscles. I had just tiptoed around a grocery store, desperate for food but unable to bear the pain of standing on the hard tiled floor. I felt weak, exhausted and uncomfortable. I wondered if I was getting sick, as spells of dizziness had begun to plague me and I couldn't take in enough water to offset them. My skin went through waves of overheating and then suddenly shivering.

This is what pushing yourself feels like, I told myself. This was a good thing, this was what I wanted. I wanted to know what it took to be a hardcore ultra runner. I wanted to find that level where the goal is more important than anything, where you can dig deeper than your body is willing to let you. I had admired elite ultra athletes from afar for so long, seen how far into the 'pain cave' they can take themselves, and now I wanted to know if I had what it took. I knew I didn't have the physicality to reach their level in an objective sense, but did I at least have the mental toughness? There was a satisfaction in the slow physical destruction of my body. It was proof, in my mind, that I wasn't mentally weak. At that juncture in my life, it seemed I needed to prove that to myself.

THE HEAT

My days through the middle of the range blended. I was usually packed up by sunrise, and tried to move until sunset. Sometimes I was so tired by evening that I would be tripping over anything on the trail as my eyes tried to shut themselves and send me to sleep as I stood. I mostly bivvied on river or lake beaches, and most nights I was too tired to bother setting up my tarp, hoping instead that it wouldn't rain while I simply rolled out a sleeping bag and an ultra-ultra-light inflatable mat.

I had my first full-body swim (as in, not a river-crossing accident) in Lake Tekapo, which glittered like a pool of diamonds under the hot summer sun. I realized that there hadn't been a cloud in the sky for more than three days, and I was starting to suffer seriously from the effects of the heat. I was drinking as much water as possible, and had picked up more electrolytes in the last town I went through, but for nearly 12 hours a day I was slogging under the sun with no protection or relief aside from my hat. Swimming felt amazing, and I started jumping into water whenever I saw it, but I couldn't reverse the sun exposure I'd already been through. I began hoping for rain – practically sacrilege for someone who lives in Scotland.

I was having this train of thought while climbing a ski hill, the abandoned chair lifts waiting for next season, and it was impossible to imagine deep snow and crowds of skiers in thick jackets while I went dizzy with the intense dry heat.

As I clawed my way up Stag Pass, memories of the Atlas Mountains came to mind, and in the overpowering heat I felt confused – was I back in Morocco? Or was I somewhere else? How long had I been out here alone? I began obsessing over finding water, a problem the Southern Alps hadn't given me yet, but I was at a lower altitude now, my route zigzagging around glaciers and impassable terrain. The landscape down here made for much faster moving, but I yearned for the big pointy peaks of the interior, and all of its challenges – especially the high-flowing, clear-blue rivers.

That night, I made it to the wonderfully named Royal Hut, a lone tin structure in a grassy field. Although it was a medium-sized DOC hut, I had it to myself that night – unless you count the resident mice who I had to secure all of my food and toiletries from with the use of pots and lids that had been left on the dusty shelves. I stopped before sunset, preferring to stay in the hut rather than keep going until dark, so I wandered down to the river to collect water, bathe and wash all of my clothes. It was a nice luxury to have so much nature in isolation, to shed my natural self-consciousness and be naked in the wilderness. Without anyone around, most especially my own gaze in a mirror, I felt relaxed in my own skin, if only for a brief amount of time as I carried my wet clothes back to the hut to hang to dry. I did some yoga outside in the sunset (definitely wearing clothes for that) and then went in for a very restful sleep, feeling safe and warm inside the hut while the wind loudly shook the tin roof. There is something so charming about the white-noise effect of any weather on a rustic tin roof, and it sent me right off to sleep.

In the morning, I felt weighed down onto the bed. The hut had only a small, dirty window, so I woke up late without the bright sun reaching me. My body was heavy and everything ached. I knew I needed to get up and stay on task, but rubbing my sleepy eyes I found it impossibly hard to move. Eventually I did, and through a series of very slow stretches, each accompanied by an audible *'ooft'*, I staggered my way across the concrete floor to my stove and got the coffee going. I had soaked my porridge overnight to avoid having to cook it, so in no time I had breakfast. Sitting at the little wooden table in the centre of the hut, I studied my plans for the day, occasionally breaking from looking at my phone to rub my eyes some more. They didn't want to stay open. Although I was trying to be fast in the mornings, I needed a second cup of coffee to have any hope of ever leaving that hut.

More dry heat pushed me over the Two Thumb range. I had hoped to be further into the interior of the mountains, but glaciers blocked my path – running solo without mountaineering equipment does have its limits, so having to drop down to this lower, much hotter altitude was what I had decided to do upon inspecting the conditions a few days earlier. I had to preserve my water for yet another day, convincing myself that I could be a bit like a camel and just drink a lot when it was available, and then be fine for these long days without any drinking.

While a wide double track aided me up the day's climb, I was left with a vertiginous, off-track descent on the other side. I don't know whether the route truly was that technical, or if my body had just given up on holding itself together, but I crashed down through the majority of that forest descent. I fell so many times that I began to consider not getting back up and simply sliding my entire way down the mountainside. On one particularly thrilling fall, where I slid a good distance on a muddy ramp and had absolutely no control, I finally heard a snap. When my sliding came to a stop – thanks to a tree that I hit – I frantically turned around on myself to verify the location of the noise. It was my trekking pole, sadly amputated in the middle segment. The wound was fatal. I stared at the pole in my hand, the bottom of it now dangling from the sad cord inside, and told myself that it could have been one of my bones. These falls were completely out of hand – I needed to find a way to get my legs back under me and, if I couldn't do that, I shouldn't be on technical routes.

I picked my way down the rest of the hill daintily, growing increasingly frustrated at every error. There was no obvious line to take, and I clutched onto branches of trees while easing myself down steep slides that I couldn't have any hope of walking down without slipping. It took hours to move only a few kilometres, and not for the first time on this journey. Again and again I found myself moving across terrain that was impossibly slow. My progress on the map was pathetic. I was beyond disappointed at myself. When I finally reached the bottom, I was in a total huff. A small flowing river trickled over the rocky valley floor and I sat in the shade, throwing my pack down with a *humph* beside me, and splashed water over my dusty face and bleeding legs. I then sat there, rehydrating and fuming. I had lost my patience with this route.

When I was done being stubborn and grumpy, I uncrossed my arms and began walking. My broken pole made me feel off-balance, so I folded them both up and strapped them to the outside of my backpack. For a minute, I had no idea where to put my hands – I had become so accustomed to my setup. I didn't have enough positive energy to generate a run – and my head was truly swimming from the sun exposure at this point – so I continued walking, sometimes letting my arms go back to the folded stance as I stomped my feet into the rocky ground, letting myself have a bit of a toddler fit about the frustrations I was feeling. I tramped like this through a pasture, and eventually the hilarity of frightened sheep loosened me up a bit.

'Stop running away, I'm no threat . . . you woolly sillies,' I sighed at them as they freaked out and scattered at my approach. Cycling offroad in the UK, I've had more than enough close calls with dumb sheep jumping out in front of my wheel, but on foot there was no danger to either of us. Only the sheep didn't see it that way.

Finally, a gravel road came into view, and the mighty Rangitata River. It had been a big question mark – a question mark of many, many additional kilometres, whether I would be able to ford the river, or need to add nearly 50km to my route to get down to the nearest bridge. At the sight of me meandering through his sheep, a farmer driving past in his pick-up truck noticed me, and stopped to wait. I began to stress. Farmers don't typically take kindly to anyone disturbing their livestock or trampling through their property. When I finally reached the gate, I put on as big a smile as I could muster in my low mood, and came forward with the best Canadian-esque greeting I had.

'Ah, you're not her.'

'I'm not?'

'My mate is into running around in these hills, I thought you were her. Never mind. You're crazy being out when it's hot like this, eh?' He leaned forwards to open the metal gate for me, holding it open while I passed through, his collie dog inspecting my shoes.

I shrugged, then asked him about the Rangitata. 'Is it high or low right now?' Although I would inspect it myself, it was impossible to judge without local knowledge, so I jumped on the chance to have a local's attention.

He measured his response, looking out in the direction of the river. 'It's a big river, eh. And when it's hot like this and all the snow in the mountains is melting so fast . . . Well, let's just say that if you muck it up, it's *not flash.*'

I assumed I only wanted things to be *flash.* I had also learned that the Kiwis are the only nation I've discovered so far that understates mortal danger, so I took the negative expression on his face to be a severe warning.

I thanked the farmer, who continued up the gravel road while I jogged down it. My pole was broken, the Rangitata wasn't a go, I had heat exhaustion and I was grumpy. I had no idea what would happen next. All I knew was that I needed some form of a pause.

Another pick-up truck trundled down the road in my direction, a group of farm dogs chasing their master. The driver waved and continued on, as did all the dogs save for one, who left the group and decided to run with me instead. I was much slower, and very much up for playing with sticks. After a few moments of fetch and pats, I looked up to realize the dog had completely lost his group and was probably now my dog. I kind of worried about the burly-looking guy in the pick-up truck who the dog previously belonged to. My new pet and I walked/jogged for some time, him faithfully coming to heel alongside me, as if we had always been companions like this. The time with this new friend lifted my spirits immensely, so when we finally found his master stopped at the side of the road waiting for us, I was in the mood for strangers once again.

'I'm so sorry – I seem to have stolen your dog,' I smiled, quickly adding, 'Not on purpose!'

'He's a pup, kind of dumb still.' The young, burly farmer had the hardest accent I'd come across yet. He looked like he was washing about as often as I was, and empty cans were rolling around the back of his rusty pick-up. I asked him about the Rangitata as well, hoping a second opinion would be more positive, but I didn't get the result I was looking for.

'Straight-up suicide right now,' he shrugged matter-of-factly. He told me there was a nice campsite at the end of the road with a cafe attached, and that sounded like everything I needed. I said goodbye to my dog as he was put in the back of the truck, and reluctantly declined a lift along with him.

When I reached the cafe, nearing sunset, I was devastated to discover it was the one day of the week that it closed early. The cafe managed the campground, so without one I could not have the other. I was stuck. But, as fate would have it, the owner of the cafe pulled up at that moment in her small car to drop off a delivery of produce for the next day's orders. She began to explain that they were closed, and so was the campsite, but didn't even finish her speech before taking in the entire sight of me: bleeding knee caps, dusty clothes, sunburn, fatigue and a broken piece of pole swinging off my pack. She stopped mid-sentence and told me to hop in the front seat.

'I just need you to promise to come to the cafe and pay when my till is open in the morning,' she said, in the sternest voice she seemed capable of. I assured her that, as I had already peered through the window and seen the breakfast menu, there was no risk I wouldn't be in her cafe in the morning. She asked about the cuts down my legs, and I told her about my pole-snapping fall. In an instant, she offered me a ride with her husband in the morning to nearby Geraldine where I could replace the pole. I was so stunned by her continuing kindness. She unlocked a small cabin for me on the outskirts of the campground, and seemed genuinely concerned with instructing me to get lots of good rest. I said that it was my intention and, after a cold shower and rudimentary laundry, I flopped onto the thin mattress, a small fan making a very weak attempt to cool my skin.

The cafe owner's husband, Matt, was at my doorstep in the morning with a latte in hand. On our drive into Geraldine, we became fast friends, and covered a lot of deep topics like our families, politics, nationalism and hopes for the next chapters of our lives. He had business in town while I went to an outdoor shop which had just one pole available for purchase. It didn't match my nice remaining carbon one, but I kind of liked the mismatched, raggedy pairing. I then sat in a nice cafe, catching up on internet access and stuffing my face with healthy food while I waited for Matt to take me back to my route. By the time I got going again, I was completely reinvigorated through the amount of kindness I had been receiving on this journey. It was truly humbling how every person I met was willing to help make my adventure happen.

STRONG AND TOUGH

Again, I suffered the consequences of having to route out of the Alps, as heading back into them meant battling a strong headwind. This time, it was one of the strongest winds I had encountered, to the point that after nearly half an hour of trying to set up my tarp without losing all of my belongings in the wind, I eventually gave up and slept on top of it, huddled between some boulders to offer some protection. It was a short sleep that night, when close to 5am I was awoken by truly howling wind, and I collected my campsite as quickly as possible – frantically trying to hold onto all of my belongings as they were lifted by the wind – and dashed to a nearby private cabin. I took shelter on the porch steps – luckily, it was empty inside – while a storm touched down. In the small veranda, I made my breakfast and repacked my things properly, while keeping an eye on the gathering storm outside.

All morning, I battled against winds so fierce that I could barely walk. A few times I was blown sideways, and miniature tornadoes of sand and small rocks blew by, forcing me to pull my hood tight around my face and shield my eyes. I had hoped to get back to high mileage, but the next move was over Browning Pass, one of the highest of the journey and an exposed and technical scramble. I knew I couldn't go to altitude in these conditions, so in the early afternoon I pulled myself into a small, picturesque red hut situated at the base of snowy peaks.

A lone hiker was already inside, a middle-aged man hoping for a good weekend trek, but also now sheltering from the storm. He informed me that it was going to get much worse, and I had made the right call not to try the climb. He was already in his sleeping bag with a book and a cup of tea when I entered, so I decided to respect his vibe and pretty much do the same, taking the upper sleeping platform all to myself while he had the extent of the lower. We chatted now and then, and both got up to make our dinners (noodles for everyone) around the same time, and it was a truly lovely experience for quiet people coexisting in a tiny space. We had to lock the door as the wind pummelled the small structure, and hoped that we would be able to tell if any more people showed up so we could let them in. The impressive storm literally shook the hut, and it was so cold we had to stay in our sleeping bags even before sunset – I was beyond grateful to be inside.

When it was finally safe to leave the next morning, I had been locked inside for 18 hours straight. I had been drinking bottomless cups of peppermint tea and reading my book, and I felt amazing. Just when we each went to sign the DOC logbook, I noticed my companion's name.

'Strong? That's your last name?' I pointed at the page with utter delight.

'Yes, real name,' Mr Strong replied with a sigh, as if he had heard this many times before. I knew the feeling well. I pointed at my name, and his face lit up and he let out a huge laugh.

'No way!'

The river that had been perfectly clear to the bottom the previous day was dark and filled with silt. The sky above was still moody, and high winds continued to push me around. I knew I had made the right call to sit out the worst of the storm, but it wasn't completely exhausted yet. The climb started from just about the front door of the hut, and lived up to its reputation almost immediately. Without any tall trees to hold the slope together, the steep trail wound in tight, rocky switchbacks. Loose rocks made for careful footing, and a long drop to the valley floor without any barriers to catch me ensured that I kept my focus. It was hard work, but with 18 hours of blissful rest under my belt, I saw no need to slow down. As I climbed higher and higher, my legs began to shake – I wasn't sure if it was the effort or the physical reaction to heights. I was now so far above the valley floor that I couldn't spot the red hut, and the steep drop truly terrified me. Any mistake would be fatal.

In the final stretches before the top of Browning Pass, there was a small scramble before I eventually pulled myself up onto it. The wind pushed me down the minute I crested the saddle, so I sat down sheltered by a bit of rock to recover from the breathless climb. I couldn't take more than one thing out of my bag at a time, as I had to hold onto all of my belongings to prevent them from blowing away. Staying low to the ground, frequently grabbing any available holds with a spare hand, I walked quickly along the saddle. Ponds created by the storm reflected the gloomy dark sky, and ripples from the fierce wind turned to small waves in the larger pools. Even with the dramatic weather – or perhaps because of it – the views from Browning Pass were breathtaking, and I was brimming with gratitude to be in such a place. Although 18 hours doesn't sound like a long rest, the absence from this wilderness made me appreciate it even more when I went back outside. I was getting severely hooked on the Southern Alps. It was true love.

Unfortunately, the howling winds wouldn't permit me any time to soak in the love at the top of Browning Pass. My hair felt like it was being ripped from my skull and my eyes were crying to combat the dryness of the gusting wind at my face. I had to get a move on. I descended, this time onto the west side of the divide, excited to see the 'other' half of the Southern Alps that I hadn't ventured very far into yet.

The west side was as I pictured it: lush, dense forest. Once I dropped below the treeline, I was back into the familiar frustration of obstacle-course negotiation; the hook grass on the path was so thick that I had to pull on my long pants and sweater to protect my skin, and eventually even pull my hood up after my braid got snagged. Within an hour, my pants were completely ruined, hilariously coated in hooked seeds that would take me for ever to get out, ripping bits of thread with each one. Although this time around I had the financial burden of such things taken care of by my sponsors, I was still gutted to ruin a new piece of clothing, and played out in my head the conversation I would have with the designer in England who I give feedback to on the products. 'Yes, great trousers, wore them a lot, but they just don't stand up to thousands of relentless tiny hooks.'

The treachery of the course continued, and I fell multiple times. In one spectacular incident, I slammed my shin into a rock so hard that I nearly puked, and on the way down my trekking pole stood rigid in the mud and the handle went into my eyebrow with force. Or, rather, my eyebrow dove into the handle of my trekking pole with force. Either way, it was a bad fall, and I wasn't sure whether to laugh that I had just given myself a black eye, or cry because I was seriously bad at walking.

I beat my estimated timing to reach the hut I had set as a target, and decided to stop anyway at 20.15. I was sweating from pushing so hard through the humid forest with all of my clothes on for protection, so I washed off in the river before heading in. The hut was one of the smaller ones, with only one metal bunk bed, a little wooden table and an old wood-burning stove in the corner. Since I was there early enough to still have the energy to light a fire, I decided to wash all of my clothes in the river and hung them out to dry in front of the stove. I read my book by the light of the fire, casually stretching my limbs as I did. The windstorm was still howling, shaking the tin roof and making ominous noises in the forest. I got the fright of my life from a scratch at the door, which only turned out to be a wee possum.

'How dare you scare me like that!' I shouted at him above the wind as he scampered away. Maybe he just wanted to share the warmth of my fire. Too bad.

GOALS

I was slow to get going in the morning. I made a coffee on the small table, then dragged it back to my bunk bed to drink inside my sleeping bag. I could hardly hold my eyes fully open, and couldn't fathom putting weight on my legs again. It was Day 16. I reviewed my route to the finish, just to confirm that my secret goal of finishing in 20 days was truly out by now. The route to my next resupply didn't seem that bad: a very short mountain pass was ahead of me, and then it seemed like a decent fast run to the road end, where I had mailed ahead a box of supplies that definitely included some chocolate. If I got going, I'd be having that chocolate later tonight.

The way up Newton Saddle was another 'route', not a 'track'. It was a pure bouldering course, following a river gorge with no chance of footing outside of the riverbed. Steep grassy banks led into the narrow gorge, where trekkers were simply left to clamber up the rocks that fresh mountain water poured over. The bruise on my leg from the previous day was throbbing, so in my infinite ability to discover the bright side, I was grateful that the river route included frequent ice-bathing for that injury. It took me three hours to reach the top of the pass, which, judging from what I had seen on the map that morning, seemed astonishingly slow. I didn't stop to admire the view – I vowed to bomb down the other side and get to that chocolate.

The other side turned out to be more river gorge, just much further and now climbing *down* rather than *up*. There were a few literal leaps of faith where I either hoped I wouldn't miss the wet boulder beneath me and hurt myself, or at least if I hurt myself badly enough I could get to the chocolate by other means (rescue plane). The storm had fully disappeared and another cloudless, scorching hot day beat down on me. When the route demanded jumping in pools of water, sometimes neck deep, I appreciated the cooling effect. But there was no denying that the movement was far too slow. Frustrated,

I never stopped to rest. Never drank any of the abundant mountain water, or ate the remnants of my snacks that would be replenished that night if I could make it. My full body ached from the bouldering – my feeble runner's arms strained with the work, and I vowed to take the gym more seriously at the end of this journey.

Finally, I stood on flat ground at the bottom of the pass. The small back-country hut had been my goal for the previous day, and I knew then that it had been a wise choice not to attempt it. In all, it took me seven hours to move the 4km over that pass. I stared at my watch face, tapping it with my fingers, assuming it was broken again – it simply couldn't be late afternoon already. I still had over 20km to go, and nowhere near enough daylight left to achieve it. I knocked back a small drink of water, and then took off at a run.

Smack. Almost instantly, I fell, quite literally, flat on my face. Stunned, I peeled myself off the ground and tried again. The route hadn't found a track yet, and so I entered the river that stood between me and it. I jumped in at, on reflection later, the deepest and dumbest place I could have chosen, soon swimming, kicking pathetically while my backpack dragged me downstream. About halfway across, clinging to a boulder to catch my breath, I noticed the orange triangles indicating a very easy place to walk across without getting wet. Right next to me. No matter, I pressed on. Minutes later, and, to this day I still don't know how, I found myself entirely lost and enclosed in deep forest. I could not find my way back out to the trail, and it took me a long time, causing more shreds to my skin as I pushed through deep vegetation to get out of where the forest seemed to have simply swallowed me alive.

I looked at my watch again as I steadied myself against a tree trunk. There were two hours of daylight remaining, and I wasn't going to get far. I also have a 'three strikes rule', and in the last hour I had made three really stupid mistakes. I had got away with each – I didn't hurt myself (badly) falling, didn't drown, and made it out of the forest prison . . . But I have always believed the fourth chance would get me. I looked up at the sky and let out a big sigh. With my head hung low, I returned to the hut I had so briefly stopped at. There was no use pushing on in my condition. I needed to eat something and get some rest. I knew the rules.

Like the previous night's, this hut was also small, rustic and empty. A glance at the logbook indicated that no one had been there for weeks, and almost everyone who had been there had left a dramatic story about how difficult Newton Pass had been, which was some small comfort. I curled up on the small mattress in the corner, hugging my knees to my chest. *Four kilometres.* I had a target of 50 per day. I couldn't believe how terrible I was. If I hadn't been so severely dehydrated, I'm sure I would have shed a tear at my disappointment.

Sometimes you just need a good feed, some proper rest and a lot of perspective. I spent some time reading all of the logbook entries in the Newton Hut, and the sheer joy and stoke coming from past trekkers made its way into me eventually. They all commented how physically taxing it was, but also added the *fun* involved in the brutal effort. And they were right – if I hadn't been worried about my arbitrary targets, that would have easily been one of the most enjoyable days on a trail I had ever experienced anywhere. I had spent an entire day bouldering in the most beautiful mountains on a clear sunny day – it was literally my dream to get to spend my time this way.

This was the turning point. I finally accepted that my goals – arbitrary, made-up targets that not a single other person on the planet cared about – were robbing me of enjoyment. I thrived on the challenge of trying to achieve something, but I had set my targets too high for this place, and it was causing me stress in what should have been the most enjoyable journey a woman could hope for. I felt silly. I tried, but couldn't think of any acceptable reasons that my 'goals' really mattered. As long as I did it – and did it with integrity – then who cares what my average mileage was? A real athlete – pretty much anyone who trains – could come to the Southern Alps and destroy my achievements. They were never set to stand up on a global scale, they were just what *I thought I could do*. They were, therefore, meaningless, except for the meaning that they held for me and me alone. And in that moment, they had lost their meaning to me.

I made a vow to enjoy what remained of my journey across the Southern Alps. I threw my ego in the imaginary garbage and let go of my aspirations. I had plenty of time, but a trip all the way down to New Zealand was a rare and special thing, and I needed to savour it. So, from that night onwards, I did.

ON MY OWN TERMS
Have you ever woken up with a smile already on your face? It's a pretty spectacular thing to be that happy. I'm sure we all

chase that feeling, and perhaps many haven't experienced it long-term. On the morning of Day 17, I woke up that way. My body was feeling as wrecked as usual, but rays of sun were leaking into the small wilderness hut and the dawn chorus of birdsong was rising in the forest around. I had a small bag with only the few items I needed to live in the mountains for 17 days and more. I had an amazing playground, and still much more time to enjoy it – why had I ever hoped to be done in just three more days? I wanted many more days out here.

Following my new regime to enjoy everything, I sat outside with my coffee, zooming in my focus on the minutiae of the wilderness. The incredible plant life, prints left by small crawling animals, bees pollinating bright flowers. I did some slow yoga to attempt to open up the battered muscles throughout my body, and massaged my stiff neck and shoulders. After breakfast and packing up, I signed the logbook with a smiley face next to my name, and set off on the rest of the journey, however long that needed to take.

The trials of Newton Pass weren't done with me, and I negotiated two hours of difficult bouldering, still downhill. A blue and white tit flitted around me, singing for me the whole way. I spoke back to her, chatting away as she responded in song. I held out my poles and she perched on them, so I could get a closer look at her beautiful feathers. I felt like a Disney princess, bonding with the forest creatures. It was a truly special wilderness encounter, and in total contrast to the chaos and carnage of trying to force my stiff and aching body to clamber down the steep boulder course, requiring many jumps, drops and climbs, and even taking my pack off on many occasions to make the moves a little easier and less risky. It was physically brutal, but the bird and I sang to each other (her songs much, much better than mine) and enjoyed the sweaty work. Well, I don't think it was much work for her.

In case you're wondering – I do have a photo of the tit perched on my trekking pole, so I know this wasn't a hallucination. I realize it sounds like one, though.

It was mid-afternoon when I finally made my resupply, where bad news awaited: my resupply box had never made it. The campground had a small store, but as they mainly catered to RV campers, options were limited and extortionate in price. The new me, however, couldn't be easily fazed, so I cleared the shelves and made do. The next segment would be powered by ramen noodles and soda crackers.

After going 2km in the wrong direction the following morning, I realized how real the struggle was – those four extra kilometres were both painful and distressing. I fretted over the cost to my body. Back at home, I would never 'count' a run that was less than a 5k, and yet that morning a 4k was a monumental effort. When I returned to where I went wrong, by the side of the highway, I stuck my thumb out and took a lift to Arthur's Pass, where I knew there was a touristy cafe and shop targeted towards campers. I decided to have a proper meal and a good resupply, rather than continuing to push myself when I was so exhausted that I a) couldn't navigate and b) got distressed over errors of only 4km because I was too tired to handle that extra mileage. I didn't have to wait long before a Spanish hiker in a rental car picked me up, and she and I delighted in briefly sharing our solo adventures before she left me at the cafe. I ordered two flat whites, a panini and some cake, and nearly choked on the price. After eating enough to probably be able to safely make better choices, I went to the small shop and found some dehydrated meals to make up for the ones I had posted to the campsite that never arrived.

With my bag bursting at the seams, laden with as many calories as I could force into every spare bit of space, I went back to the highway to hitchhike back to the start of the next segment, only making it by noon. Although I had decided this new methodology was more fun, there was still a part of me struggling to let go of the early starts.

I arrived at a hut just before nightfall. It was placed high on a river bank, so I decided to take care of my water needs – bathing, washing my socks and then filling my bottles – before making the short climb. I was truly so tired that I couldn't fathom doing it twice. I hauled myself up to the hut, feeling a bit fresher after a river bath and ready to meet people.

The hut was enormous, with two separate sleeping areas and a large common room with long dining tables and wooden benches. It had the air of an old hunting lodge, unlike many of the DOC huts I had stayed in so far. It was dark and musty and everything was made of wood, from the hut itself to all of the furniture. There were already two hikers there, both solo trekkers on the same popular trail that I was crossing. The three of us sat together at one of the large tables, where we compared notes on which of the dehydrated meals available in NZ were the most palatable, and exchanged stories of our solo missions in the wilderness. It was a pleasure and a surprise for each of us to get to share the evening with other people – and people who understood us. People who were in the same frame of mind. It was validating for all of us, and we stayed up later than we knew we should have, chatting away by candlelight, three solo adventurers sharing a comfortable camaraderie.

The two men took one sleeping room and let me have the other one to myself. The hut was clearly built for popular seasons, and the beds were stacked three high, comfortably fitting dozens of bodies into the stead. It was eerie and also luxurious to have such a big room for myself. Obviously, I chose a bottom bunk – I probably couldn't have climbed a ladder for any amount of money in the state I was in. My feet throbbed and my aching legs kept me up late. A heavy rain started soon after we turned in and pelted the roof all night. I felt grateful and cosy inside our harmonious wooden hut.

When my alarm went off in the morning, the rain responded with new vigour. I took it as a sign to snooze for a while longer. One of the men, Ronin, stayed true to his plan to get up early and I admired his resolve as I pulled my sleeping bag over my head to bank another hour. When the rain stopped, I pulled myself out and hit the trail.

The clouds were low, and I couldn't see more than a few metres in front of me. When I reached the saddle of the climb I was apparently on, I only knew it from the green and yellow sign marking the pass. I figured the Southern Alps had more than spoiled me with views so far, so I couldn't be sad to be stuck in a cloud this once. The rain fell gently, but beneath the canopy of the forest the humidity was stifling.

As I jogged downhill, I dug my heels into the rocky trail to stop as quickly as I could – two kiwi birds waddled along the bushes. They were the first I had ever seen. I held my breath and watched silently, trying to hold my camera down at their height to capture evidence. Their distinctive long, slim beaks and armless bodies were a true spectacle to see up close, and so I stayed and watched them until they disappeared into the forest. I later realized that it was on Kiwi Pass that I saw the kiwis, and was especially delighted by this.

I never stopped again that day. I had set a goal to get over 40km – although I had vowed to slow things down and enjoy myself, I still relished a physical challenge, and I felt I was up for it. With the cooler weather, it also seemed like a good opportunity to gain some ground. In the final hours of daylight, I was bonking – running out of energy completely, and struggling to push myself onward. I had resorted to putting my headphones in with a charged playlist and, as I stumbled on weak legs, found more enjoyment in the challenge than I had previously on the journey.

When I made my target DOC hut, I lifted an arm in the air for victory. Then I flopped down on a bench and lay motionless for some time.

The hut I had made it to was one of the biggest I had seen, but again it was deserted. It was slightly creepy to have so much space in a wilderness hut while the weather picked up outside, so I lit some candles to brighten things up, and closed the doors to all of the dormitory bedrooms so there was only the dining room left. I boiled water to rehydrate my dinner, then promptly fell asleep on a bench next to the grand window looking out over the wilderness. During the night, I was awoken by the roar of stags in the forest nearby. For a moment, I thought I was back in Scotland, and smiled at the sound of my favourite Scottish animal. It took me a while to remember where I was, but I kept smiling at the Scottish heritage that can find you on the other side of the world.

I slept to the sound of the stag roars and the howling wind and rain, occasionally waking to check the door that creaked ominously. The hut seemed like a good set for a horror movie, and I wished that Ronin had made it – this hut had also been his target for the day, but we both knew it was a massive goal to reach before sunset, which had moved up considerably since the start of my journey.

NATIONAL TRAGEDY

I woke up in the Mega Hut and realized it was Day 20 – my target for finishing. I knew that my best-case scenario was to finish in another three days – not even close. I stretched my limbs and pulled myself upright, staying in my sleeping bag to slink across the dining-room floor and turn on my stove to make coffee. The mornings were now distinctly cooler, the autumn arriving rapidly on the South Island. The changing weather may have been the only pressure I felt to get to the finish line. Actually, my destroyed feet also wanted me to finish. But everything else was great. I was living my best life, enjoying the way I was spending my time. It's such a pleasure to do the thing you love every day, and to get to do it while feeling safe, happy, free and capable – well, that's just beyond great luck in this world. I didn't want it to end.

I celebrated the start of Day 20 by watching the dawn light with two coffees and an extra-large bowl of muesli. Perhaps the diet was another good reason to get to the finish line. Very few fruits or vegetables had been on my plate in nearly three weeks, and that was slightly concerning. I made a quick video recording of my thoughts that morning – not something I do often, but I have found myself looking back on that video now and then. In it, I see myself at my best. Granted, I look visibly worn, but it's clear in my voice how much inner peace I held in those final days of the journey. I like looking back on it to remind myself how easily I can access that level of happiness and overall life satisfaction. All I need is a backpack and a trail. It would be wise of me to never forget it really is that simple.

I entered the final days of my traverse feeling as settled and content as I can ever remember feeling in my life. I was nearly moved to tears by the beauty at the top of Waiau Pass, where I sat for a while simply taking it all in. Months later, I found the 'shoe selfie' I took of my feet dangling over a boulder, and was surprised to see my legs covered in swollen insect bites, trickles of blood from my knees, pudgy swollen ankles, and bruises and scrapes everywhere. Those discomforts never stayed in my memory. In fact, I don't remember those final days being difficult at all, and only my body can tell the story of whether the trail had its challenges. My memories are only of the awe-inspiring views, the magical waterfalls and clear rushing rivers, the abundant birdlife, and overflowing gratitude to be moving through that landscape.

Knowing I was nearing the end, I started really dragging my feet. When I arrived at an already packed hut (the only way I could tell it was a weekend), I decided to stop early and stay with the friendly Kiwis who had already welcomed me in. Hikers ate various dehydrated meals shoulder to shoulder on the packed dining benches, while strings crisscrossing the ceiling hosted everyone's merino wool layers from the day of trekking in the rain. The atmosphere was convivial as groups and solos joined up and made one large hut family. There were perhaps 20 or more of us that night, and as the chatter died down when we all turned to our sleeping platforms, those of us with satellite devices had the messages come through – there had been a mass shooting at a mosque in Christchurch. We collectively roused from our bunks, almost everyone at a loss for what to say. All we knew was that the hut had been filled with New Zealand love and compassion, and hearing news from the city of one individual trying to destroy that love was a pain we all felt personally. Heads hung low as we grappled with the limited news that short satellite communications could deliver. We would have to wait until we got back to phone signal to find out more, which for most of us would be a few days.

When I finally tried to sleep, I drifted off feeling the love and warmth of the hut, knowing even more how lucky I was to be safe and surrounded by kindness.

It took only two days after that for me to reach the end of the Southern Alps. I could have done it one go fairly easily, but at the last minute I decided to alter my route to take in a ridge, rather than the easier valley trail to the end. I wanted one more view from above the clouds, and boy did it deliver. My legs wanted to run, but my heart wanted to stay and linger as long as possible. I sat down on nearly every comfortable-looking boulder or lookout along the Angelus Ridge, filling up on gratitude and memorable mountain views as much as possible. An easy run would have taken me downhill to the finish, but I wanted to wake up with this view, so stopped early, doing some mountain yoga and taking photos to enjoy my last day.

The final morning greeted me with my favourite spectacle of nature: a cloud inversion. I jogged along the Angelus Ridge in the bright sunshine while all around me were white, fluffy clouds. It's exactly what I have always imagined heaven would look like – just some mountain peaks above the clouds. It was an emotional morning, and when the trail finally descended me into that cloud, down towards civilization, I felt part of my heart stay behind.

The trail switchbacked steeply down to St Arnaud, and I passed many groups of day hikers on their way up. I told every one of them how beautiful it was at the top, while they just watched in bewildered awe as I sprinted as fast as my long legs would spin down the hill. It was nearly lunchtime when I finally made it, so I quietly ducked into a cafe for a real flat white and a sandwich, soon joined by a German hiker I had met several days ago taking a different route. I sheepishly told her what I had just accomplished, and she bought me a slice of cake and gave me a big hug before she set off on the rest of her journey. I wandered down to the main intersection of the highway, and stuck my thumb out to begin the long ride back to Christchurch. I wanted to be around the people there – a community that had shown me so much kindness and hospitality, and was now feeling so much incredible pain. I still don't know what words I can say about the event, but one thing

I *do* know, after all the travel and experiences I've had in so many cultures around the world, is that the world is full of far more good than evil, and in New Zealand that goodness is in spectacular abundance.

*

It would end up being nearly a year and a half before I was able to take on the next leg of the project, and in the time that passed it seemed as if everything changed. My schedule was filled with work projects and travel, and I barely touched foot at home. 'Home' itself changed, as my long-term relationship came to an end and I moved on to live independently. And in the weeks before I was due to head to the Caucasus to take on the biggest journey yet, lockdowns swept the world and paused us all.

When flights to Canada opened again, I decided to return to my birth country. I had always hoped the Canadian Rockies would be the final leg of the project – some romantic finale of returning home after discovering mountains all around the world – but I would have to work within the confines of the situation. I did not want to pause the project any further.

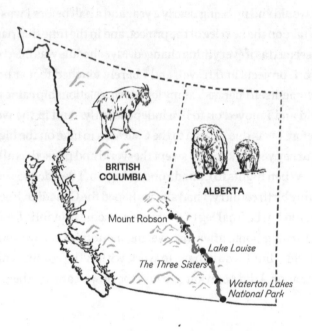

BRITISH COLUMBIA

ALBERTA

Mount Robson

Lake Louise

The Three Sisters

Waterton Lakes National Park

CHAPTER FIVE

Where Are You From? The Canadian Rockies

I sat cross-legged on the motel-room floor, surrounded by small plastic bags and piles of technical outerwear. For the first time in a few months, things were feeling incredibly familiar. The room had that faded, uninspired decor scheme favoured by chain motels worldwide. With the blinds closed, I could have been anywhere in the world. But I was home. If home is defined as the place that you were born, that is – Scotland is still the home I've built, and mountains remain the home of my heart. I was back in Alberta, and tomorrow morning, I planned to begin my run across the Canadian Rockies.

I'd always intended to end with the Rockies. What better way to close this project that had literally taken me around the globe, taught me about mountains and mountain cultures, than to finish where I started? But of course, this was no longer the last run – as the pandemic grew in force and the reality of the changing world became clear, I had reluctantly cancelled my plans to fly out to Georgia that summer to run the Caucasus: my European adventure would have to wait. At fairly short notice, I found myself back in Canada and, after a cramped two-week quarantine, had the full green light to run the length of the Canadian Rockies. The National Parks had opened up just weeks previously, and the vast wilderness seemed like the best place for me to be. In a lot of ways, I felt unprepared. I had scrambled to put this plan together, given the little notice I had had. As I sat on that motel-room floor, surrounded by piles of things that I couldn't decide whether to take or not, I looked down on my post-pandemic body – that lockdown weight gain was clearly visible, and I wondered if those pale legs had what it was going to take. I dropped my face into my hands, and let myself sit there in that pitiable state for longer than necessary. It was well after midnight, and I still didn't know what I was taking.

On the desk sat the latest issue of *Canadian Running*, where a six-page spread on me described 'the incredible runs of Jenny Tough'. I didn't feel anywhere near incredible. I didn't feel that anything I would ever do was incredible. The photoshoot from New Zealand showed a smiling woman with tanned legs, next to an interview that did nothing but highlight my 'achievements'. I felt embarrassed that magazine racks around the country were selling an image that I couldn't currently stand next to.

I was in a darker place than I could ever remember descending to. I had fought against the warp-like pull of the dark hole in my mind for all of my life. I had fallen in a few times, and clawed my way out through brute force, but this time I felt the edges crumbling in around me, and I had lost the will to climb back out. The contrast between my reputation and my reality was not lost on me. To anyone who knew me, I seemed to be this tough, resilient, powerful woman. To me, I was weak, depressed and hopeless. I remember catching my reflection in the window of another closed-down shop in downtown Victoria that week, and it struck me how hunched my shoulders were, my head hanging visibly lower. It was as if I'd lost several inches in height. I hated looking at myself in the mirror during that time, and had started to lose touch with how I appeared. I had given up on making my hair look nice or wearing clothes that made me feel attractive. I actively avoided interaction and shrank as a person. The guise of social distancing made all of this easy, and my shrinkage went completely unnoticed by the people I know. Into the deep dark hole I sank.

START LINE

The sun was baking when my dad dropped me off at the start. We had driven in total silence – he had obviously reached his limit with my melancholy by now. I had hoped he could drive me up the 12km paved road to the true start, but the road was blocked for construction. Neither of us bothered to read the sign, he simply let me out and snapped a few photos while I reluctantly shrugged on my backpack and began dragging my feet up the hot pavement towards my favourite mountains in the world. I couldn't even muster the positivity to run, even just for him to see and know that I would be okay. I kept my dark sunglasses on, avoiding letting him see how depressed I was, and wished he would put the camera away – I never want to see how low I was that day.

Eventually, I unfolded my trekking poles to try and inspire some speed walking. The click-clack of the poles' metal tips broke the deafening silence. I put in my earphones – unusual for me to already turn to blocking things out only minutes into an adventure – hoping that I could distract myself and inspire some enthusiasm . . . It seemed like I spent more time upset than not, and yet I still couldn't verbalize my pain. *You're hopeless,* I muttered to myself as I turned the music up. Speed walking eventually led to jogging, and in a respectable amount of time I was nearly finished the 12km road, nearly ready to turn off the pavement and head up the trail. Finally.

With less than 100m to go before that happened, a Parks Canada truck pulled up alongside me. I nodded a polite hello, then the ranger pulled over and stepped out.

'I'm actually here to see you,' he said.

Flashbacks of Morocco, but this time in the same accent that I speak in.

'Problem?'

'Yeah, didn't you read the sign? They're working on this trail, it's been closed all year. I can't let you continue.'

What a start.

Mike, a third-generation ranger of Waterton, couldn't have been more charming as he bundled me into the back of his truck, the only seat where plexiglass protected us from each other, and drove me around to a trailhead I could use. I looked forlornly out the window as the 12km of paved running wafted past. I quipped to him that this was my first experience being in the back of a cop car, to which he replied that I 'haven't lived'. I then filled him in on my adventures with the Gendarmerie, observing that my only interactions with law enforcement so far in my life had been due to running alone in the wilderness. He was quick to assure me that his objections were completely different from his Moroccan counterparts, and took interest in the book that I was about to launch – *Tough Women* – promising to buy a copy when it came out in Canada. It was a powerful distraction and pulled me out of my depression to return, momentarily, to my outward-facing persona: the professional writer/adventurer on a grand mission to change the world. He seemed fooled.

We reviewed the map on the hood of his truck before he let

me go once more, and I nodded politely as he showed me trails I was already incredibly familiar with. If I have learned anything by now, it is that they'll feel much better if they think they taught you something and you were receptive. So I thanked him sweetly, and ducked out of having to take his heavy paper map away with me, assuring him that I did indeed know the way.

Start again.

Let's have a good one this time.

The do-over seemed to do the trick. Mike had dropped me off at a fairly popular trail on a hot Sunday afternoon, so for the first couple of hours I had plenty of passing runners, hikers and mountain bikers to chat to. The brief interactions, and the nice conversation I'd had with the handsome ranger, seemed to lift my spirits and I was already feeling better. This is how the first day is meant to feel.

It was my first time back 'home' in over a decade. Familiar vistas on the skyline of mountains that I had grown up looking at, and locals who shared a (literal) common ground with me were something that my life of adventure had completely lacked. It was a strange shift, with this project having so far taken me to corners of the globe that I had previously known nothing about. This time, the land was familiar. It was only me that was strange.

At a junction about an hour in, the well-trodden trail became suddenly more rugged, and the passing traffic of Albertans disappeared instantly. From that point, I didn't see another soul for three days.

The freshly laid gravel behind me, the thin trail ahead was

soft, with large puddles in places and jutting roots to trip over if I lost focus. Rivers were no longer graced with bridges or stepping stones, and my feet got wet for the first time. I smiled, knowing they would stay this way for about three weeks, if past experience was anything to go by. I wasn't wrong.

My stomach was writhing in a tense knot, so I frequently stopped running when the cramp became too intense. I wondered if the knot was entirely in my head – a result of my sad moods, my late night spent worrying and my lack of sleep over the past weeks. The muddy trail abruptly turned skyward – the first pass of the journey began. I started climbing, my stomach tensing painfully, but my disposition gradually improving. I was surprised and relieved to discover I made quick work of the pass, and stopped at the small, green Parks Canada sign marking the spot.

Looking at the sign, I remembered something vital: *I am resilient.* Sitting on that motel-room floor the previous night, feeling sorry for myself, I had forgotten this important trait. *I can do hard things.* I lightly high-fived the sign and took a picture. I'd got this now.

A forest fire in 2018 destroyed much of the landscape in Waterton Lakes National Park, and it was haunting to move through the dead forest. The ground was still dark and ashen, and the spiny branches of dead trees twisted and reached out to the still air, with no pines left to sustain them. It was hauntingly still. No wind, no animals, only me and the ash. It looked like something out of a Tim Burton film. Instinctively, I turned my music off and tried to move silently, not disturbing the scene. The sun was dipping low, and I was certain I didn't want to spend the night here. I couldn't even find moving water – it felt like everything truly was dead. Quietly, I propelled myself across the pass, eventually descending at a point where green forest appeared in the distance.

It was nearly 10pm when I finally made camp. The ground was completely saturated with snowmelt, but the remnants of a horse camp – a true Rocky Mountain back-country scene – suggested that it was the best ground I'd find that night, so I rolled out my bivvy next to a flowing stream and some cut logs that had been made around a fire pit. There was no hope of finding dry wood for a fire, and I was too tired anyway. I threw my thin ropes pathetically up at a branch in an attempt to make a bear hang, and the result was genuinely laughable. I still didn't seem to care enough about anything, so I eventually left my backpack filled with all of my food hanging just slightly higher than my own height – welcome treats for any wildlife that might be milling around, but at least it was far enough from my bivvy that they might choose the pack over me.

I'd forgotten how incredibly cold the Rockies get at night – it defies logic to change from such blissful, scorching summer heat during the day into sudden below-freezing chill at night. In planning this journey, I had honestly told myself that my memories were based on a younger, weaker version of myself, and it *couldn't possibly be that bad*. But lying there, in the best outdoor equipment available on the market, I made my judgement: the Rockies are way too fucking cold at night. At 2,044m altitude, and above the snowline, I shouldn't have been so surprised, but after the scorching July weather we'd been experiencing, it was a shock to the system. With my mind running wild, the way it normally would on the first day of a long adventure, and the cold leaving me shivering until dawn, I hardly slept at all.

At 4.30, dawn began to break. I hadn't had enough time lying down, but I was grateful the sun was back to warm the earth. I begged it to rise a little faster, just this once, and thaw the land around me. Although it had only been dark for a few hours, the grass next to my bivvy had frozen solid, and I couldn't bear to pull on my iced shoes and make the journey to my bear hang. I knew that coffee was the only way I'd have a hope of warming up, but the sacrifice needed to get there was a brutal price to pay.

I switched on the stove, which I had intelligently prepared last night with water ready to start, and gingerly made the trek across the partly frozen ground. Seeing it in the light, I truly was embarrassed by my pathetic bear hang. In a project spanning six continents, it was sobering to realize that this was the only mountain range where wildlife were a concern, and I knew I'd need to hone my skills – quite quickly – to avoid interaction with it.

I wrapped my sleeping bag around me and hung my dew-soaked bivvy sac on a nearby tree. Finding my perch on a log next to my warming stove, I already knew this was a two-coffee morning. Despite my early start, it was nearly seven by the time I had packed up and started moving. Another thing that would need to be honed.

The morning of Day 2 always feels like The Proper Start. The chaos of getting there has finally settled, and now the real work lies ahead. It is on the second day that the routine of a new life starts. My connection with civilization, comfort and connectivity are now memories. There is only me, my small bag and the mountain range unfurling before me. Time to get to work.

The work that morning started with a new mountain pass. Soon, I was above the snowline but still inside the forest, making navigation almost impossible. With no visual signals to point me in the right direction, I was hooked to my compass, held under my nose, if I was to have any hope of finding the right direction. Countless times, I lost my route. I spun in circles, and every direction looked the exact same. Endless forest growing out of a snowy ground. It took me hours to move a painfully short distance.

Finally, I found my ridge. La Coulotte is no less than six peaks along a glorious, trepidatious Rocky Mountain ridge. There is no Plan B. Once the ridge starts, you are committed.

No water.

No shade.

No escape.

No mercy.

The trail over the ridge was faint at best – I was easily one of the first set of human prints to cross it since the snow melted this summer. Above the treeline, dry scree ribboned over the jagged ridge before me. It was easy to see why the ridge was selected as a route across this region – the steep slopes on either side plunged to impenetrable forest, and a network of mountains jutting into one another at various angles rolled over the landscape ahead. Staying high was the easiest way to make progress – but the steep scree slopes on either side of my feet made my knees knock together.

I walked swiftly across the scree flanks, desperate to get this over with. Memories of that terrifying day in Kyrgyzstan, four years ago, shrieked through my mind. In truth, I thought I had moved past that. I thought that day didn't scare me anymore. My abilities and confidence had grown so much in those four years through consistent experience. The fear couldn't really be that logical. And it infuriated me that it was back so suddenly – and so potently. I bent over almost double to keep one hand on the ground while I picked my way across the side of the slope. The ridge had become impassable in some segments, where rock cliff faces blocked the route, so the thin trail led me down along the steep side, where loose gravel tried its best to sweep me down the mountainside with it.

Just breathe. Keep breathing. I counted my breaths, attempting to deliver enough oxygen to my brain to calm it down.

I was furious at myself. The vista around me was absolutely jaw-dropping. The Rockies, the home of my heart, rolled out in their highest glory all around me. With a clear blue sky and a perch at high altitude, I could see the chain of my favourite mountains stretching towards the horizon. The adventure that lay before me, snow-capped jagged peaks and a big Albertan sky. But I couldn't enjoy any of this. My legs shook and my heart raced. I was suspended in a state of total panic. I wanted off the ridge. I wanted solid ground. I used to believe running a ridge was the highest pleasure on this earth, and here, on one of the finest ridges I've ever met, I was ruining it.

You suck!

Where a single tree protruded from the rocky slope, I stood at its base and took a break to try and calm myself down. A sign of hope appeared – a track. I hadn't seen footprints since leaving the main trail yesterday morning, and, finally, here were signs of life. I followed the footsteps with confidence, thanking this unknown person for guiding me across the precipitous scree. As the trail snaked around the mountain, the scree dissipated for a brief segment and gave way to more solid dirt. It was only here that I could discern that the footprints I had been following were not laid by an early hiker, but by a grizzly bear. My panic was shattered by humour – what a genius bear to leave a trap for hikers! I would have dumbly followed him right to his lair. If I ever get to be a bear in a future life, this is definitely how I will hunt.

When I finally reached it, I ran with glee and gratitude down the solid, wide, double-track muddy trail that led away from the end of the ridge and down to the valley floor. The fear had left, and I could move freely. More importantly, I could finally replenish my water – the exposed ridge, so close to the sun, had taken a toll and I had let myself get dehydrated and sunburned, a mistake I knew I would pay for over the next two days, at least.

RE-ENERGIZING

Despite the heavy fatigue dragging my legs down to the ground, I surprised myself by putting in a good run. A gentle rain had descended on the Rockies, and the drop in temperature and abundant availability of water were slowly resuscitating me from yesterday's heat troubles. I put a lot of importance on my ability to run that day – if I could just show myself that things were okay, maybe they would be okay. I settled into a steady run, and kept my feet shuffling for hours. The low trail through the deep green forest felt like a shelter, where I was hidden from the world. Only one startled moose interrupted my steady progress, otherwise I kept trundling along, not giving in to the temptation to walk.

Late in the afternoon, my body screamed back at the near marathon I had run on untrained legs. I knew that if I kept my pace, I could make Coleman that night, a day ahead of schedule. And at Coleman a B&B that specifically catered to hikers attempting the Great Divide Trail – which I would use much of – waited with my first drop box and a home-cooked meal. Lactic acid flooded my thighs and I began to truly stagger down the trail. The rain had stopped and mosquitoes replaced it. So frustrating was their cloud that I had to layer on all of my Gore-Tex and cover my face in a head net, which would turn out to be one of my most valuable items. I slammed my trekking poles at the earth, trying to spur forward motion. In a few steps, I would falter again and dig deep to propel myself forwards once more. Soon, the noise of the highway reached me through the forest, and my phone came into signal. I called the B&B to let them know I would make it, and was told that I'd 'be a little late for dinner'. Eager to be a good guest, I pushed hard, desperate not to show up too late.

Barbara, a hiker celebrating her 65th birthday by walking

the Great Divide Trail, was the only other guest and had just finished her dessert and second beer when I fell across the threshold. Food showed up in front of me, along with a beer, while the hosts and Barbara brought me back to life with cheery conversation. I wanted only to get in the shower and drink as much water as could come out of it, but I was delighted to meet Barbara – she exuded the aura of a woman with a million stories of adventure to tell. I instantly fell in love with her and sat with her much later than my tired and smelly body should have done. Finally, I limped to my bedroom, where the finest bed I had slept on in a very long time beckoned. I decided there was no chance I would start early the next morning.

True to form, I indulged in a late and gigantic breakfast with Barbara, listening in awe to her life of adventure, entrepreneurship and championing young people and women into the outdoors. She was a great connection, and I felt no need to prioritize running over this conversation.

Finally, when I had stayed so late that our host had even made us lunch, I got my gear together, stuffing in my resupply of dehydrated meals (Barbara and I exchanged recipes for dehydrating at home, filling me with new ideas to execute if I ever wanted to make my own dehy meals again). We wandered into Coleman for coffee, and to fill my already bursting bag with extra cinnamon buns – Alberta-sized, each the approximate width of my face and soaked in sugar. The sheer weight of the small brown takeaway bag promised substantial calories to power me until at least the next afternoon. Leaving the cafe, I finally insisted I would indeed leave Coleman and continue my journey north, and we wished each other luck and promised to stay in touch.

The extra rest provided ample energy to produce a steady run along the muddy double track north from Crowsnest Pass. It lifted my confidence immensely that I wasn't taking walking breaks, although my feet scuttled so close to the ground that I frequently stumbled on rocks – notifying me that I was barely committing to a jog. Still, I was moving, and that was truly something. The familiar knots in my stomach persisted, and I hoped it was just indigestion, not related to any emotional state. The drenched road left ample puddles for mosquitoes to breed, and as dusk rolled around the little terrors came out in significant force. I decided to keep running late, completely intimidated at the thought of trying to set up camp with them around. Of course, they were not the only wildlife present and I had to consider the bears, too, who had been reported at great frequency in the past few days. Finding the strongest breeze I could – a minor clearing with a gentle whisper of wind, at best – I stopped to boil some water for my dinner. The mosquitoes descended. As soon as the water was warm enough, I poured it into my small mylar bag of homemade dehydrated mac and cheese, then put my bag back together and started walking, holding my dinner in front of me and attempting to stuff sporkfuls under my mosquito net. There are easier ways to consume your dinner, I'll say that much. But at least I was doing the bear-safe thing and eating far away from my campsite, while doing the mosquito-safe thing of never standing still.

With a belly full of warm, cheesy calories, the world

became a more beautiful place. It's funny how mac and cheese can do that. Wildflowers burst through every available patch of sunlit grass. Enormous pine trees swayed in the faint breeze. The forest, stretching for unimaginable extensions on all sides of me, buzzed with life. The chain of blue, layered mountains that make up the Crowsnest Pass area glowed in the late sunlight. My feet pattered rhythmically along the muddy ground, the occasional ting of my carbon-fibre trekking poles hitting a rock the only abrupt noise – until the rev of a truck sliced through every sense. A red flatbed truck rolled slowly around the corner. Its windows already down, it stopped to check in.

'Are you okay? Do you need a ride or something?' the middle-aged man with tufts of blonde hair sticking out from his trucker cap leaned one wrist casually on his wheel, the other arm dangling out the window.

'All good, just jogging,' I shrugged.

'Okey dokey, lots of bears out there, just so y'know.'

I shrugged again.

'We've been hunting rabbits,' the man indicated his son in the passenger seat, who couldn't have been more than eight years old. 'Have a look-see,' and at this, he nodded into the bed of his truck. I knew I didn't want to look, but I also wanted to be polite. These would likely be the last men I saw before making camp that night, and that's always a group of people to make a positive impression on. In the back of the truck lay three brown bunnies, their dead eyes glaring back at me as thin streaks of blood trickled down the bed of the truck. I took a deep breath, hoping to steady my face.

'They look . . . uhh . . . well done!' I nodded at the two beaming Albertans.

'Okey dokey, well, if you're sure you don't want a ride, just be real careful!'

I thanked the men for stopping, genuinely grateful for the human compassion in these parts. But I frowned as the dead bunnies rolled away, wishing he could bond with his son over any other outdoor activity. Looking at his Albertan plate, I reminded myself that my first car had also had one of those white and red plates with the wild rose symbol on it.

Not long after meeting the bunny-hunters, I conceded that my legs would go no further. My watch showed after 10pm, although the sun was only beginning to fade. A small bridge over a stream provided a welcome place to lie, and I could no longer resist. I set up my bivvy on the soft green grass, sheltered by trees and close to the clear stream. The bridge offered the easiest bear hang I'd made to date, letting my backpack suspend from the concrete with little effort on my part.

After a few short hours of rest, a beam as bright as a torch shone into my bivvy: by the time I realized it was a nearly full moon in a clear night sky, I was already awake and halfway to collecting coffee and breakfast from my less-than-impressive bear hang.

About an hour of uphill plodding on sore legs later, I came across the closest animal encounter so far – a herd of cows refusing to clear the path. I asked nicely, then held out my trekking poles, mildly shooing them along. Cows kill more people than sharks each year, and as they huffed steaming clouds of breath in the cold morning air while stamping their heavy hooves and lowering their horns – longer than the width of my torso, ample hornage to pierce any essential organ – I sheepishly moved past them, embarrassed as the apex predator in the situation.

Slightly beyond the posse of bovines, I realized why I was moving so well, and why my bag had closed so easily – I had left my bivvy behind. While enjoying a second coffee by the river, I had hung my dew-heavy bag to dry in the breaking morning sun. And, despite its being a bright red parasol, sticking out like a sore thumb in the natural landscape, I had somehow missed it when clearing up my campsite.

Absolute. Idiot.

It was an easy downhill back to the campsite, although a second encounter with the cows was less than ideal. I apologized in advance that we would be meeting thrice this morning. Half an hour later, with my bag at its full, expected weight, I turned back up the track I had now stamped twice, reluctant to meet the cows again and kicking myself for the wasted mileage.

That evening, an open, rocky bank with access to the river promised some relief from mosquitoes, and two camps of fly-fishing enthusiasts were already set up – promising better targets for bears. My legs wobbled and I decided it was time to give up. The neighbours watched in utter surprise as my small blue backpack produced my ascetic red home for the night, which I rolled out under some trees to provide shelter from the onsetting rain. Next to the multiple trucks that had accessed the fishing spot via the rugged dirt road towing campers and setting up large awnings, comfortable camping chairs and folding tables, my meagre campsite with less than no luxuries was a true spectacle to the locals. I had to remind myself that *I am a local*. Despite the life I live now, I was brought up here. That was once what I knew of camping, too. Those trucks never used to seem too large to me. Bringing a fully enclosed breakfast tent in order to be in nature without ever touching it seemed reasonable. This was my first time running *not* as a foreigner, but every time I mixed with the local population, I felt as strange and foreign as I did back in the Tien Shan or the Andes.

'Where are you from?' one of the colossal RV-owners, kitted out in an impressive number of khaki-coloured pockets favoured by fishing enthusiasts, came by to ask.

It's always been a tricky question, but never more so than when I'm genuinely only hours from the place where I was born. My parents both come from different countries – Scotland and Newfoundland – and they had my sister and me in different parts of Canada – Ontario and Alberta. I had spent most of my adult life in Scotland. With a life of travel and identifying as a local in many places, but equally in no places, I have never known my answer. In the Tien Shan, it's easy to reply, simply, 'Canada.' Rarely will anyone ask for further details. But now, I was in Canada. I would have to give an exact postcode. Was I even *from* Calgary? I hadn't been there since I was a student, ten years ago. My accent had evolved. And at this exact moment, the red bivvy rolled out next to me was my only real address – I was currently without a fixed abode.

'The Island.' I told a half-truth. Vancouver Island was my banking address and where my parents lived, after all. I knew it better than Calgary.

For a lot of people, 'Where are you from?' is a basic question. It has an obvious answer. But, for a growing number of people in the modern world, it's not as straightforward as that. And, furthermore, it can be a divisive question. It can be a way of determining what side of a line you fall on – in Canada, it may be as innocuous as wanting to know what hockey team you cheer for. In other places (or times) it can be a way of deciding how you feel politically or what cultural norms you adhere to. It can be an enquiry into whether you're 'us' or 'them'.

As a Scottish–Canadian, I have almost never experienced a downside to this question. Giving either of these nations as an answer typically produces a red-carpet welcome. We are adored nations of the wealthy, liberal classes with cute and fascinating cultures. I have been literally high-fived, bought drinks, even given places to sleep solely by announcing these nations as my homes. For a solo female traveller, it's a pretty good safety blanket to get to wear. But that's a privilege I inherited. It is not lost on me that I have in no way earned that welcome.

I've tried for years to come up with another basic question for strangers. 'Where do you live?' is an obvious, easy replacement. It lets people tell their stories, rather than be confined to their histories. Or, sometimes even better, forego the entire subject and instead focus on their present moment – 'What brings you here?'

THE 'I GET EVERYTHING WRONG TODAY' DAY

I've come to know that there is an infuriating yet valuable day that appears generally within the first week of any big adventure. I call it the 'I Get Everything Wrong Today' Day. The day that will be riddled with mistakes, many driven by the onset of fatigue at that stage of the challenge, but many due to my own avoidable errors. In this journey, it came on Day 6.

I started insanely late, after deciding to linger and enjoy coffee with the family that had set up such a remarkable camping spot in order to fish for a week – Covid had cancelled their vacation plans, but they were certainly making the most of the situation. Finally, I set out on my way, which after less than an hour took me to the end of the gravel double track I had been on for nearly two days now. Before turning into the forest, I noticed the largest grizzly print I can ever remember seeing. I stopped to photograph my own foot next to it, clearly displaying how great this creature was next to my feeble human body. It had rained last night, so the likelihood of this print being fresh seemed pretty high. I started trying to remember to ramble or sing out loud, to make a bit of noise as I bimbled along.

I thought I spotted an enjoyable shortcut. I was desperate to leave the boring double track behind and head onto a thrilling trail in the forest, and I took my chance. Within little time, the forest had closed in around me. Impenetrable green flooded out the bright sun, and I was utterly and hopelessly lost. Jagged branches reached their dark arms towards me, folding me into the forest and holding me back from ever getting out again. It was eerily quiet, and I had lost all sense of direction. I was furious with myself. All of the negative emotions that had been bubbling for weeks surged forwards. With every misstep or branch scratching my sunburned skin, I cursed myself. I was stupid. I messed everything up. I was never going to make it. I was hopeless. I was the worst.

I repeated these messages to myself endlessly, unable and unwilling to change the record.

By the time I emerged, I was bleeding everywhere, twigs stuck in my dishevelled braid, and beyond grumpy. Piercing blue sky welcomed me back after leaving the forest behind, and the warmth instantly soothed me. I dropped my pack and sat on a bare log, more out of an unwillingness to continue than any need for a rest. I knew I needed to keep up a good pace now – the amount of food and battery charge left would barely cut it for me to get to the next resupply and, with Covid restricting the hours on that resupply, I knew there was a good chance I would be waiting an extra day for it.

Stubborn and irritated, I continued north. I lost my trail multiple times. I didn't put on sunscreen. I dropped things, literally and figuratively. I didn't fill up when I crossed a clean river. I spent hours of the day on wrong trails, and by 8pm I was destroyed. My sunburned legs ached and dragged across the ground as I fumbled around a river valley attempting to find my route up the next pass, which would take me into British Columbia for the first time on the journey. When I noticed the time, I decided to sit down and regroup. I took my shoes and socks off to reveal the saturated, mushy flesh of my feet that hadn't properly dried out in nearly a week, and would stay that way for probably a couple more weeks ahead. I set up my stove on a pebbly beach, protecting the small flame from the wind with a larger rock acting as a barrier on the west side of it. Tonight's meal was a mushroom risotto I had made a few weeks ago – how I yearned for a glass of malbec to go with it. That would settle me down, if nothing else.

I sat in total stillness aside from cooking and eating. I didn't think of anything or make any plans. I knew I had spent the entire day making mistakes. Some trivial, some irritating, some costly. I was falling behind my targets to make my next resupply point, but much worse than that, I was not enjoying myself. I needed to get my act together.

Wordlessly (I use that term in the sense that there was no dialogue in my own head, of course), I packed up and set off uphill. Leaving the pebbled river area, I soon entered knee-deep grass that was completely flooded. A snowmobile trail led through the woods, a clear cut in a perfectly straight line through the trees. Wildflowers sprouted along the trail, the absence of trees giving them space to be reached by sunlight. Colours of red, yellow, lilac and pale blue decorated the forest carpet, and I delicately tried not to step on any as my shoes traipsed through the wet ground. I tiptoed on the sides, closest to the trees, so I wouldn't fully submerge my feet into the muddy centre of the track. Water rushed downhill, the last few days of heat moving most of the previously snowy peaks down to the grateful river valleys.

The sun lowered and the Rockies in front of me lit up with alpenglow. I reached a high enough point on the trail to find drier grass and where the wind reached me, so I could sleep comfortably and without the nuisance of biting insects. Losing the last of the daylight, I set up my bivvy and another abysmal bear hang by the light of my torch.

There was something ominous about my campsite. The woods behind my bivvy had a haunted quality, much like the one I had been lost in earlier that morning. I recalled the large bear print. The wind swayed the tall trees, which creaked and rocked loudly, while my red bivvy flapped and threatened to turn over. I left the door open, glad that the absence of mosquitoes granted me fresh air for a change, and with one arm out read my book on my phone for a few minutes until I must have passed out.

The 'I Get Everything Wrong Today' Day is always a positive turning point. The mistakes are lessons, and some of them strong reminders that I have to heed in order to be successful. It comes around the same point on every journey – when I'm far enough in to start being tired and making mistakes, but not yet far enough to have my routines and systems dialled in. But after the 'I Get Everything Wrong Today' Day, those systems dial up really fast.

With my bivvy door open all night, I woke at one point, glaring up at an intense, glittering display of stars. I had never seen them so beautiful. With no cloud cover and the wind still ripping through the forest, it was fairly cold, but the fresh alpine air reached into my lungs and revitalized my tired body. I felt the Rockies taking me back into their embrace. Back to my home. Back to the air that I breathed as a child. The night skies I shivered under for so many of my first camping experiences.

Soon the stars faded away, and a rose sunrise faded in. I lay on my stomach, my head out of the cocoon, watching the dawn with my head propped up on my hands. I inhaled deeply, and centred myself anew.

This is going to be a good adventure.

I climbed higher until the trees became smaller, and the forest thinner. Wildflowers erupted over rolling dark grass, like a postcard fairytale with the Beehive Range as the backdrop. I knelt on the grass, trying to photograph the beautiful and individual flowers. So many different species mingled next to each other. I didn't know the names for many of them, always having been so animal-crazy as a child that I completely ignored the botany of the Rockies. But you don't need a name to love something – Shakespeare wrote something about that, I'm sure of it. At one point I found myself standing tall, face to the sun, with my arms outstretched, as if to embrace the Rockies fully. I'm almost certain there was a smile on my face. With no self-consciousness about what I'd just caught myself doing, I allowed the smile to grow, and began running. Not jogging, not dragging my feet. Running. And it felt amazing. There was no trail to follow underfoot, but small orange markers the size of my palm hinted at the way through the trees, each marker far enough apart to lead to doubt, but not so far that I got totally lost again. It felt novel to hit such a steady pace without any compass work.

By midday, I reached the top of the pass, with views of the looming mass that is Baril Peak. The pass was a wide open area, just above the treeline but dotted with wildflowers, patches of snow and large slabs of rock basking in the sun.

I relaxed on one, lizarding myself on the rough rock. An alpine wind ripped across the open area, fooling me into a chill while the intense sun scorched my bare legs. I sat still, simply marvelling at Baril. I picked out the lines that I thought would make interesting routes to the summit, and even checked my map to see how far the ridge went on the other side. I fantasized about mountaineering, pursuing summits instead of traverses. I loved traversing mountain ranges – at number five, I was confident in saying that – but a little part of my heart always wanted to skip off-route and take in some summits. I never allowed myself the spare time for frivolous pursuits like that, and as I craned my neck to look up at the 2,998m summit of Baril, I let that piece of my heart run up to the top while the rest of me began assembling my pack again to keep going. A big descent lay ahead.

When I crossed the border into BC, the little orange markers disappeared, and my day of strong progress took the hit. I got lost multiple times, and when I finally reached the bottom I was thigh deep in the river, wading my way out of the wilderness and towards the dirt road that would take me to civilization again. The long wade reminded me of the Southern Alps, although the glacial melt was considerably colder, and it was not far from my mind that the water's edge is a favourite hang-out of bears. Letting my memory scroll through my most recent journey in NZ was a happy escape, and a smile crept across my face as I went through the highlight reel of that adventure.

It is a bittersweet moment when a challenging trail intersects with a clear path. I emerged from the river and stood on solid gravel road. The earth was compact, even and stretched in a straight line for miles in either direction. There were no obstacles in my way. I would make a lot of miles tonight before the sun set, but they would be painfully dull. I rotated through a walk/run setting, giving my shaking legs some rest, then trying to speed things up when I simply couldn't face the boredom of the road stretching so far into the distance ahead of me. I knew I would spend all of tomorrow on it as well.

Ahead of me, an obstacle. Finally. And the finest of obstacles: a herd of horses strutted down the road, dust kicking up from their hooves, illuminated golden by the lowering sun. At the sight of me, they gained pace, all heading towards me at once. I was overwhelmed with delight as they jostled for position to receive a muzzle pat from me. The alpha – the one wearing the bear bell, hanging from his neck and piercing the still evening air with its rattles – hogged the attention, and I was glad to give it.

The horse procession slowly continued on its way, but not without each animal ensuring it received a cuddle from me. I wished they had been walking my way. I almost considered abandoning everything, turning around and heading off south with them.

SPIRITUAL HOME

One of my deepest memories of the Rockies in July is thunderstorms. When I was a child, my dog would hide under the coffee table as pounding storms clapped through the big prairie skies. Now, hot days built into intense evening storms, and I knew they would be a problem for my limited outdoor sleeping hours. That night, I collapsed into a terrible bivvy location, long after sunset, and paid the price in the middle of the night when a torrential storm hit. I scrambled, half-asleep, to gather my things under the thin footprint of my bivvy in an attempt to keep everything dry. I placed my shoes under the canvas, unwilling to take them inside, and pulled everything else in and stuffed down to my feet. A bivvy sac is not nearly big enough for a full-sized human and all of her ultra-light possessions, and I cowered, cramped, attempting to stay in the middle where no wet fabric would touch my face.

I have had a quirk since birth – perhaps from being born in summertime in this region – that I sleep better than ever during a storm. Once I was certain that my belongings wouldn't be soaked in the morning, I blacked out again almost instantly, and slept in later than I had yet on the journey. It was only the whirr of rising mosquitoes – the greatest drawback of a good storm – that alerted me to the need to get moving.

Less than an hour later, I crossed the border once more into Alberta, where the trail infrastructure was restored – the maintenance of segments of parks is covered by jurisdictional budgets, and these sudden changes marked only by imaginary lines in the maps were a typical feature of travel in this vast back-country region. Just beyond the wooden stump signalling the border crossing was a lovely wooden picnic table that would have made an excellent shelter in the storm. If only I had pushed a little longer! I sat on it for a few minutes, enjoying breakfast, to ensure I got my money's worth anyway.

As I neared Canmore, the population of trail users picked up considerably. Up until this point, I could have counted every single person I met in over a week. Suddenly, I was coming into the epicentre of Canadian endurance athletes and weekend warriors. I met several people who warned me that many of the nearby parks were closed due to recent grizzly bear activity, to which I had no backup. Going without phone signal for days at a time, I simply could not know when a bear, wolf or mountain lion had been reported and a trail closed until I had already run through it and come out at the parking lot (or not).

Canmore was not how I had left it. Social-distancing orders, plexiglass counters and pedestrianized streets all marked the global situation and sobered me up again. In eight days, I had mostly been able to forget about the pandemic. But here, I witnessed a place I had known my whole life, completely unrecognizable. Before arriving in town, I fished out the facemask that my mom had sewn – it had sailboats on it, and was slightly too big for my face – and became conscious of just how filthy I looked. And, undoubtedly, smelled. The only products that had touched my skin for a week were mosquito repellent and sunscreen, when really I could have done with more soap and deodorant. When I came into phone signal, I booked a hotel and stopped at a supermarket on my way through town, gathering enough food to at least get me to a place where I could coherently decide how much more food I would need. I planned to spend my entire stay in Canmore just eating and washing.

Within an hour of checking in, the hotel room was covered by my draped bivvy and sleeping bag, drying clothes I had washed in the tub, plugged-in devices recharging, snacks and mugs of tea I couldn't keep my hands off, and me, wrapped in a clean white towel, letting my hair dry while the scent of hotel shampoo wafting off my tresses overwhelmed my senses. On the starched white sheets of the hotel bed, I assessed my legs just over one week in: already bruised and scraped, tanned and noticeably swollen. I drank electrolytes and continued force-feeding fruits and vegetables into me, hoping to recover entirely in 16 hours through hydration and nutrition. I was so comfortable on my bed, and so delighted to be in Canmore, a town I have always loved, that I heavily weighed the pros and cons of a day off. But I knew that giving in to temptation would ruin me – and I was also going way slower already than I had hoped. I sighed, and grabbed my wifi-connected phone, then fell asleep in the process of attempting to share a post on social media.

The trail between Canmore and Banff is a well-trafficked, easy route called the Goat Creek Trail. All day, runners, hikers and mountain bikers sailed past, often in groups, but always greeting the haggard runner with the oversized backpack. It was nice company to be surrounded by my fellow tribe – not only the outdoor crowd, but folks with the same accent as me, no less. When the rain settled in and the population of the trail thinned out, further away from towns, the loneliness set in. The brief time in civilization had brought it all – whatever it was – rushing back. The pang in my stomach. I reduced to walking, holding a hand over the pain in my gut, willing myself to keep it together. I felt *sad*. Inexplicably so.

I walked into Banff before sunset, and booked a hotel again. I had been dreaming of this moment for years. Banff has always been my spiritual home, the epicentre of my mountain heart. As soon as I got a driving licence, I zipped out here as often as I could, carting my lovely golden retriever, my best companion, Tessa, with me in the summer, or my cherished snowboard in the winter. When I dream of a place called 'home', although I mostly maintain that I don't truly have one, I always picture Banff. If anything could ease the knot in my stomach, it would be coming home, after all these years.

I jogged past the Banff Springs Hotel, seeing the insane opulence with a more experienced world view. I didn't need to enter the lobby to know that nothing would have changed inside – it's a place that celebrates heritage. It's funny how nothing about that crown jewel in Banff's richness called to me anymore. I no longer saw it as a symbol of success, but rather the opposite. What extravagance.

I joined the river path, where families and dog-walkers had left work for the day, and I continued my embarrassingly slow jog as I bobbed between being caught in family photographs with Mount Rundle in the background. I slowed down finally when I hit downtown – eager to see what had changed, and what remained the same. As in Canmore, the social-distancing measures had altered the outer appearance, but the air, the light, the smell remained intact. The lack of huge commercial buses transporting crowds of tourists was welcome to me, at least, although likely not to the local businesses who were trying hard to keep their heads above water without the town's crucial income.

I stared down at my swollen ankles. The new socks I had bought in Canmore – truly a glorious feeling after spending nine days in an old pair of gym socks after discovering I had forgotten my good wool ones – had left indented marks in my skin. My calves mushroomed hideously over the memory of the new socks, and I needed no more encouragement to stay a day in Banff and let my body recover.

Later in the day, when I could face putting my shoes on my red, fat feet, I took a stroll around Banff. On almost every block, I bumped into the ghosts of my younger self. Memories of summer hikes, stopping for ice cream, meeting friends. The last time I walked these streets, I had Tessa faithfully at my heels. We would be stopped multiple times by tourists wishing to have a photo taken of the beautiful Canadian dog. She was always a willing model, and I was ever the proud Dog Mom. My heart panged for my old best friend. I felt lonely, walking through the memories.

If it hadn't been for the pandemic, I probably would have told old friends that I was so nearby, but I couldn't ever figure out if I was hiding my excuses behind social distancing. I knew I was in a funk. There was no pretending otherwise.

I left Banff late the next afternoon, the new trail-booking system stalling me, as the only available campsite was a mere 10km, and I couldn't book any of the sites further on. I decided to leave Banff just before sunset, allowing me more time to rest and ample time to get to my designated campsite. It was odd to be bound by red tape. This project had so far seen me experience the truest form of freedom, and here in my own home I was restricted heavily. Of course, I believe thoroughly in the need to protect our wild parks, so I dutifully followed the Parks Canada rules, especially when I went to collect my envelope of permits, only to find it hand-doodled with a drawing of mountains and a good-luck wish from the female staff at the Parks office. It was the touch of kindness my heart needed, leaving Banff behind.

I climbed up to the Mount Norquay ski resort, sharing the switchbacked road with a few nonchalant mountain goats. I've always loved how the wildlife in Banff confidently occupies human spaces – elk frequently stall golf games while moose hold up traffic. A raven cawed enthusiastically overhead as the goat hooves clip-clopped on the pavement. I reached the ski resort, which is always a slightly haunted sight in the middle of summer. Empty chair lifts were stacked at the end of a gravel parking lot, and a large blue map of ski terrain promoted winter fun. Behind the relics was a green slope, without a patch of snow in sight, the runs between the trees like scars on the slope. I love skiing, but it is not without consequences for the mountains.

It started to rain, so I sat under one of the chair-lift stations while pulling on my layers. It was already nearly dusk and the air cooling. Leaving Norquay behind, I was back on the trails. Entering the forest after a short stint in civilization is like lying down on a soft bed at the end of a stressful day. You don't realize how tense you were until you really finally relax. I removed the headphones I'd been wearing, instead enjoying the sounds of the forest – wind ripping through leaves, creaking branches as they sway, the distant calls of the ravens. The rain had stopped, and the orchestra of the forest followed as all the creatures made their last moves in the daylight.

I made it to the campsite I had a permit for, and found it completely empty. I was disappointed not to have gone further, but I figured it was good karma to play by the park rules; I also didn't really feel like pushing on to the next site and risking arriving after dark. I spent far too long going between each of the marked tent pads, trying to select the one that was just right. It's always easier to make a decision when there are fewer options – it's like going to a restaurant with a three-page menu. Some campsites didn't have enough protection, while some didn't have a clear view of the stars. I wasn't hungry after such a short effort, so skipped my dinner and went to bed early, largely to escape the growing cloud of mosquitoes. Moments after I had zipped up my bivvy, the rain started, so I lay in my cramped red cocoon reading my book on my phone. I slept with earbuds in that night to block out the whirring noise of mosquitoes.

LAKE LOUISE

I moved quickly in the morning to escape the mosquito-infested forest. Within hours, I was above the treeline, and the wind brushed them all away. Snow still remained, in some places in quite significant quantities, but wildflowers carpeted the high alpine slopes. Marmots darted around, running underground when I approached their small dens. I always said hi to them, even as they ran away. I found a perfect lookout spot where I sat with my legs dangled over a vertical gorge, watching around me the landscape where I grew up. In all directions were trails and places where I had been as a girl. My first camping trips, backpacking experiences, summer camps, family hikes, all of them were in this small radius where I was sitting. I thought about that young version of myself, hiking up these monumental trails. What did she dream was possible? Who did she want to be?

What would I say to her if I could, through time travel, greet her on the trail? Would she be happy with how things turned out? There was no doubt that my values and direction had changed a few times between that young age and now, but one constant in my life was how I felt in the Rocky Mountains. I always felt at home out here. In some ways, it was as if the peaks and the landscape around me had been part of raising me – always keeping that watchful gaze over my development.

I would bump into the ghost of my child and teenage self a few times in the trails around this area, sometimes completely by surprise, experiencing vistas that I had forgotten, or didn't know the name for, but could suddenly recollect having been there before. I began to appreciate the scale of the place where I grew up – the incredible awe of the playground that I had in my youth. I've always been grateful to be Canadian, but as I made my way from Banff to Lake Louise, that gratitude grew several notches.

The crowding at Lake Louise was a shock to the system. At any time, when you've exited the pristine wilderness – where I never saw another human – and returned to tarmac, commerce and crowds of people, it's pretty jolting. But, months into the pandemic, I had no sensitivity for crowded places at all. New signs directed tourists to explore the lake shore in a one-way direction, but huddles of groups and families smiling up at selfie sticks clustered around the wide pavement and

Canadian-red canoes dotted across the turquoise lake. I hadn't been there during the summer in a very, very long time, so I couldn't tell if it was normal for it to be so busy. I stopped momentarily to snap a photo – my trail shoes were almost the exact same shade of green as the lake, so I couldn't resist – but then quickly escaped via a hiking trail to the north of the Lake Louise Château, one of Canada's grandest hotels. I ducked around the service side, admiring the obstinate luxury while I tried to move my legs as fast as possible away from it.

A muddy single track snaked through the forest, and in minutes I had left the glitter of Lake Louise behind. With so many touristed routes from the area to take hikers to viewpoints, the northbound trail away from one of Canada's gems was oddly unused. It took no time to be completely returned to isolation in the wilderness. An amazing thing happened on that trail: I ran the whole way. I ran so well it was like I didn't have a backpack or over 500km of fatigue in my legs. I ran as I am supposed to run. I enjoyed myself. I felt good.

Finally! I exhaled. Finally, my body has come good. Finally, my feet don't hurt anymore. Finally, the initial fatigue has dissipated. It felt like it had taken a lot longer on this journey than the previous ones, but finally I had settled in. A smile cracked my face as I knew that I had just turned an important corner – I was now in the glory phase of this adventure.

Only 8km from Lake Louise is the much smaller, though similarly turquoise, Lake Ross. I didn't hesitate for a second before dropping my backpack and wading out into the clear, freezing water. I kept my shoes on – they were so permanently wet at this point, there didn't seem any point in wasting time taking them on and off. I let my feet sink into the muddy bottom of the lake while I splashed cold water on my face and arms. My newly functional legs responded with gratitude for the mid-run ice bath, and when I waded back to shore to begin running again, it was as if I had a new pair entirely. I ran gleefully through the forest trail, skipping over streams, bounding down descents and hopping up inclines.

My solid hours of running now had to face the greatest motivational challenge my route provided: highway. It was nearly 10km along the busy main road to reach the town of Field, my next resupply. There was no option aside from running on the shoulder while trucks and recreational vehicles blew past. I had decided from the outset that I had nothing to prove with covering these highway miles – I'd rather skip them, missing out those few footsteps in favour of not ending up as roadkill. In another time, I would have stuck my thumb out and got myself to Field that way. But this was a pandemic. Hitchhiking is illegal in Canada at all times, and ride-sharing with strangers was obviously no good in the current crisis. I watched mournfully as family vehicles pulled in and out of the layby I was resting in, knowing that I could so easily ask any of them for a ride. The highway was truly miserable. The rushing wind of every passing long-haul truck. The deafening noise of relentless traffic. The solid, flat tarmac igniting pain through my body at every footstrike.

There was only one thing for it: a cheesy pop playlist. I switched on some Beyoncé and got on my way.

It was evening by the time I made it to Field. I was over the moon when I finally exited the highway and jogged on shattered limbs to the visitor centre, where a public restroom was open. I asked the Parks Canada staff member what time the post office was open until, and she suppressed a laugh – it was only open for a few hours every day, and I'd missed it by a long shot. I now had to decide if I could wait until it opened again later in the morning and collect my resupply. With all of the accommodation in the small town booked up by holidaying Western Canadians, and the rain already setting in for the night, it wasn't a very attractive prospect to sit around on the streets of Field until nine the following morning. My only backup idea – buy more stuff and head on out, abandoning my resupply – was quickly rejected as well: the only shop in town had also closed early, and wouldn't be open until around the same time as the post office tomorrow. I had no choice but to wait.

I went to the only takeaway diner to mull things over with a salmon burger and sweet-potato fries, hiding from the pelting rain under a slightly insufficient patio umbrella.

I wandered around the streets of Field – there are about four of them, in the right-angled grid pattern of most Canadian towns. The Canadian Pacific Railway came through here, and so the small settlement had a wealth of history dating back to the development of Western Canada and the influx of immigration and industry. I read a few faded yellow signs in front of houses, shops and the lookout point over the railway line itself. I didn't really have anything better to do. Long cargo trains passed by noisily, either labouring their way up Kicking Horse Pass or flying with squealing brakes down into the BC interior. On my discovery stroll, I found the public washroom at the community centre was: unlocked, clean, spacious and had running water and a power outlet. Those were pretty much all of the things I needed in a hotel room, which I couldn't get – the bed wasn't such a dealbreaker, considering I had my own. I waited until dusk, sitting on the porch step reading my book, and when no one came by to lock up, I moved in for the night. While the rain showered Field, I was safe and warm on the linoleum floor of the washroom. They had even left the cleaning supplies in a corner, so I sanitized the place before rolling out my bedding. I slept soundly, happy not to have shelled out big bucks for a July hotel booking. It didn't even occur to me to be troubled that I found this experience so brilliant.

In the morning, I waited for the real hotel to open its breakfast restaurant, and was the first guest seated for a typically Canadian calorie-laden meal with a couple of large coffees. I had been chatting to my close friend Emily, back in the UK, who agreed that my washroom bedroom was a genius win. One of the most experienced and intrepid long-haul adventurers I know, she made me feel far more confident and grounded after speaking to her. She reminded me that the hard bits are only normal, and suggested that my newfound leg strength, and the mental ability to find a toilet a good place to sleep, were perhaps signs that I had indeed turned a corner and entered the 'highlight phase' of the journey, where everything falls into place. The awkwardness of early days in messing with equipment is over, the physical strain feels acceptable and the emotional stress has flattened out. She instructed me to eat more, and I couldn't deny her.

The sun was high when I finally collected my box from the post office. The man working there – clearly an avid outdoor enthusiast, dressed in cargo shorts and fleece vest, said he remembered my dad coming through a while ago.

'You're way ahead of schedule,' he chirped.

'Am I?'

'Yep – see?' he tapped the marker on the box where he had written a date, which he told me had been agreed between him and my father, who had dropped it off, as my realistic arrival time. It wasn't the one I had forecast when I packed the box. I smiled weakly at the classic underestimation of older men, and braced myself for the next, almost standardized observation:

'I guess you go faster with that tiny backpack.'

And then:

'Be careful you don't tire yourself out! Better to slow down and be more sustainable. People always underestimate the trails out here.'

SASKATCHEWAN RIVER CROSSING

The brief contacts with the human world were getting stranger and stranger as the journey grew. By the time I reached Saskatchewan River Crossing, I felt completely out of place around the neat resort and its paved roads. Exiting one of the gnarliest trail sections and suddenly finding myself in a parking lot where the only plants were neatly displayed in flowerpots and all of the ground underneath me was smoothly paved with arrow-straight painted lines felt completely alien. I wanted to quickly grab my resupply and leave again – back to the wilderness.

A long slog on pavement took me north. When the trailhead arrived, I was grateful to leave the pavement behind, but nervous at what lay ahead: one of, if not the, most challenging segments, with a series of high-altitude passes without any trail or infrastructure. I would be navigating and most likely alone out there. There were grizzly warnings all over the region, and once I left the highway behind, there were no exit points – I was fully committed to the five-day trek to Jasper. I wondered if I was really up for it.

Through the course of the day, I got lost several times, the final one quite severely. I had journeyed up the wrong fork in the river that I had been using as my navigational handrail, and in a weak moment decided to 'B-line' my way back on to the route – basically, B-lining is trying to move straight across terrain, rather than go around obvious obstacles. I painfully picked my way through dense forest, bouldered over ledges and slid down mudslides. It took over an hour to get back on route, and I arrived shattered, bleeding and in an even worse mood than I had already been in. I then had to pick up the route and continue climbing upstream without a trail. I spent most of the time in the water, mostly above my thighs and freezing cold, within sight of its glacier source.

It was late when I reached the top. The snow was wet, which made traction easier as my feet slid easily into footholds, unlike at the start of the day when the outer crust was entirely ice. The view that opened before me was of white peaks all around, melting rapidly into braiding rivers and flooded valleys below. The next valley and mountain pass seemed just achievable in the remaining daylight, although I couldn't see any easy line to cross them. I eventually resigned myself to the fact that my only option would be to cross the river, knowing that it was at its deepest at this point in the day after an entire day of sun on the glaciers.

I sloshed onwards, soaked completely, and then pushed my legs as hard as possible to get over the second pass as the sun lowered. A park boundary marked the summit of my climb, but I had no time to linger – it would be dark soon, and I needed to descend from the snow and on to somewhere dry to sleep.

My bivvy for the night was arguably my best yet. I stayed at altitude, hoping that the lower temperature and higher wind above the treeline would keep the mosquitoes off. It didn't work perfectly, but I assumed it would only be much worse lower down. There was no way to make a bear hang with no trees, so I buried my food under a pile of rocks by a snowbank, laughing at how pathetic it really was, and then slept a good distance away from it, hoping that would make up for my casual attempt. I sat up in my bivvy, watching the sunset over the Rockies. It was a beautiful view. It had been the hardest day, and I felt as though my home mountains were giving me the nourishing hug I needed to cheer me up, just a little.

Throughout the night, I heard avalanches crash down the mountains around me. In the still of night, they seemed incredibly close, and I had to consciously remind myself that they weren't close enough to harm me. Somewhere around 4am I finally woke to the longest thunder roll I'm sure I've ever heard. In seconds, the rain came down like a wave. I reached out of my bivvy to pull my backpack inside, then zipped up the outer waterproof layer. It's hard to breathe and extremely claustrophobic when I do this – I prefer to keep just the mesh window zipped up, allowing wind to flow into my tiny cocoon. I curled up, as if to make myself as small as possible, while the epic thunderstorm raged. It came in a series of three storms, each time with a brief interval of beautiful alpine sunrise. Clear skies would illuminate the grand peaks in front of me, before another dark cloud crested the ridge and headed fast towards me. I would zip up the protective layer once more, and hang on again. I actually managed to get some quick power naps while these storms came – as I said, I've always slept well in a thunderstorm, even in a small nylon sac at an exposed-altitude back-country spot. Between storms, I managed to collect my buried food and make coffee and breakfast, finishing just in time before zipping down once more for a last turn of head-banging thunder.

It was 8.30 by the time the last thunderstorm let up, and I could shake out my wet bivvy and get started. The morning began with a climb up snowy Pinto Pass. It was near the top when I realized my period had just started, and I laughed at the ridiculousness of that happening when I was alone in bear country – recent sightings still buzzing in my ears, attempting to manipulate a silicone cup that would hopefully be the most bear-safe solution. When I was younger, I recalled the official pamphlets handed out in Banff on wildlife safety, warning female tourists that their periods would attract bears. I always rolled my eyes at yet another perpetuated stigma against women in the outdoors – but it did seem to make me particularly vulnerable in that moment.

I descended from the snow to Pinto Lake, a beautiful, postcard-perfect vista of the Rocky Mountains in their ultimate glory. If it were at all accessible, it would be one of the country's top tourist sites but, luckily for me on that day, no one else was there. The green water reflected the grey-and-white-streaked mountains perfectly, and the clear blue sky above completely forgot the morning's storms. I waded out into the lake wearing all of my clothes, hoping that a bath could double as laundry (still being concerned about my period attracting a bear attack, I figured I should up the hygiene effort). Worried at my slow progress and the difficult terrain still ahead, I didn't stay long, although I would have loved to camp there for at least two days, just relaxing on the small lake beach and gazing at that insane vista. It remains one of the best Rocky Mountain views I've ever witnessed.

For the rest of the afternoon, I learned in a very tangible way why stunning Pinto Lake was deserted – the trail leading north was even harder than the two days of trail I had worked through from the southern approach. Perhaps because it was early in the season (and the Parks were only just reopening from the pandemic), but more likely simply because it's a remote area, the trail had not been cleared in a long, long time, and deadfall – trees that fall naturally – blocked the route, sometimes in walls of several trees on top of each other. I had to climb over or crawl under, constantly scratching my skin or snagging my backpack on sharp branches. My skin was raw with the burns of grazes, while blood trickled from my knees and elbows. To make matters worse, underfoot the trail was completely awash with sticky, gooey mud, a consistency like peanut butter that my shoes would grip onto and need to be forced back out with every footstep. There is surely no slower way to travel. *Slosh, slosh, slurp, climb over a tree, slosh, slosh, crawl under one, then over one, slurp, smack, slide, venture 20m into the thick forest to get around a wall of deadfall*, etc. When I finally reached a clearing to pause for a rest, I counted my rations: eight bars left, and I was only about halfway through this segment. I was going to have to start going hungry.

The mosquitoes, meanwhile, did not have to go hungry. Any moment stood still invited a swarm, so I got back up and kept moving. Finally, I reached the treeline again, and in a single footstep I came out of the forest and onto a beautiful alpine meadow, reaching up the mountainside towards the grey and white peaks. A gentle breeze hit me, and I could move easily out of the trees. I climbed until I was near the top of the pass, utilizing the same strategy as the previous night to stay out of the damp forest, hoping the cooler air at altitude would dissuade the hungry mozzies. It didn't totally work, and after my usual routine of feeding myself a good distance from where I would be sleeping, I crawled into my bivvy, exhausted, frustrated and deeply concerned about how on earth I might get through this part.

My morning was a repeat of the previous one – getting parts of my routine accomplished between diving into the bivvy and zipping it up tight while another thunderstorm lashed my small red home. This time, four successive thunderstorms rolled by, always with interludes of clear blue sky before the next dark gigantic cloud built its way over the surrounding peaks, dropping all of its rage on the beautiful alpine meadow before giving up and rolling off to somewhere else. It was after 9am when this performance finally ended, and I left the campsite grumbling that I was already three hours behind – with so much terrain to cover, I couldn't afford to waste any daylight. Not that you can control the weather. But still.

At the bottom of the pass, I merrily joined a popular hiking loop (unbeknown to me, given I did all of my research on the drive out over two weeks ago). I saw my first hikers in what felt like an incredibly long time, and enjoyed a bit of trail banter, disguising perfectly how stressed and chaotic I was truly feeling. I blushed when they marvelled at my pack size and how fast I moved on the trail – yet again, I felt like a fraud. In my mind, I was moving too slowly. I was no good at this. I didn't deserve any admiration.

Then I remembered – my menstrual cup. It had been in for over 24 hours, and I had completely forgotten.

At a river, I ducked behind a tree and pulled my shorts down to fish it out – but *I couldn't find it.* I had never used one before, and just assumed it would be intuitive when I discarded the packaging minutes after buying it, which I did on an excited whim after a friend told me they were a *must-have* item for back-country periods. Having no waste to carry makes a lot of sense, and I was thrilled to be having an 'eco period'. They're all the rage, apparently.

But now I was deep into the Canadian back country, trying to reach up inside myself to find the darn thing. It had gone too far 'up', and I couldn't pull it back down. I started to panic.

I stopped at every river crossing throughout the day, hoping my running might wiggle it loose. This obviously did not work at all. I got more and more scared and frustrated, keenly aware that it had been in there for way too long to be healthy, and started to imagine what awkward conversations I might get to have with a nurse when I finally reached Jasper. I had no idea how serious the consequences might be – the only part of the package I had read, before discarding it, said to under no circumstances leave it in for eight hours. I was now past 30, and about that much more time before I could get to that imaginary nurse. My deep stress was only appeased by the hilarious thought of how it would look if a hiker stumbled upon me trying to get it out – and then also a faint hope that such a hiker might actually turn out to be a nurse.

(Just so you know – they're sort of easy-ish to get out, if you know how, and if I had had any phone signal I could have watched the instructional video and been fine.)

I decided to forget about the cup. I was almost certain I was making it worse, and the only thing I could do now was to get to Jasper as quickly as possible. I was no longer on the popular trekking route, and the state of the trail had deteriorated again. At lower elevations, the trails were now completely flooded after several hot days had finally melted the snow caps on the mountains, and the river crossings I needed to tackle had started to get scary. On a few occasions, the footbridge was submerged or even broken away by the torrent. But, on more occasions, there was no bridge at all, and I had to hop in freshly melted snow up to my waist, trying with all my strength to stay upright against the fast-moving water.

Darkness closed in, and I was still tramping through ankle-deep, freezing water, down the trail through the thick forest. My head torch was insufficient in the impenetrable darkness beneath the forest canopy, and my nerves got the better of me with every passing shadow. I normally don't fear bears, but I normally don't walk around at night in the back country. I was determined to make it to the next marked campsite, and it was nearly midnight when I finally collapsed onto an old, rotted picnic table. Too tired to move, I found the bear hang, then flopped into my bed, underneath the table for extra rain coverage, and fell asleep in seconds.

THE TEST

There's always that one day. That day when it all happens. When you are tested from every side. In hindsight, you'll look at it lovingly, as if it was some sort of turning point for both the journey itself and you as a person. For me in the Rockies, that day came 18 days in. I woke early, having slept lower down and under the trees, so starting in the rain didn't feel as problematic – at least I could shelter under a great fir tree while I rolled up my bedding. My body felt terrible – my legs were heavy, feet sore to the touch, sinuses blocked, a swimming headache and period cramps. I knew I had no choice but to push it even further in order to get to Jasper. I had two energy bars and an 'emergency' pack of noodles. After breakfast, that was everything I was going to have to live on the whole day. Forget period cravings – this would be a serious caloric deficit, as if I needed any more reason to be cranky, physiologically or otherwise.

I pulled on my soaking wet shoes and began sloshing up the washed-out path. I made quick work of Maligne Pass – I had been warned it was 'double-black expert difficult' and, additionally, the current trail conditions were 'extreme'. At the top, the views were appropriately stunning, but I was concerned that, even at the highest point, the trail was still washed out. The Rockies were melting fast, a consideration I faced once again at each river crossing. More deadfall blocked my route, and I was lucky to manage 4km an hour. My breathing was heavy and I was sweating hard. Bear scat frequented the trail, and my mind went back to the fear that my cup was still up there. I had to ignore any fears – stoicism is a tool, and this was a good day to employ it. I shut down all emotions and any thoughts of the future or past. The only places my attention needed to go were keeping my legs moving and trying to stay upright with all of the deep mud, prohibitive deadfall and seriously high river crossings that I needed to contend with. This wasn't a day for mistakes, and it also wasn't a day for taking my time. I did not find a single bridge still in place on my way down the pass, and it took the entire morning until I emerged from the forest. I was now approaching Maligne Lake, where at the northern tip my mother was waiting, willing to take me to that nurse if I needed her to.

From the forest I stepped out onto a boggy marsh. The path had long since disappeared, and I wondered if anyone had attempted this route yet all year. I spotted the familiar brown and yellow sign of Parks Canada infrastructure, and gleefully speed-walked towards it, my shoes making a sucking sound at every muddy footstep while long grass tickled me up to my chin. The sign indicated the way to the bridge, which led to the trail that I knew would speed me out to a paved parking lot, the modern world and my mother. I saw the wooden support beams on the southern side of the river and rushed towards the bridge, excited to stand on solid ground. *I was going to make it out in another hour.*

The bridge, made of two thick wooden planks, extended to an island in the middle of the river, and then nothing. It had washed away on the far side. White caps of fast-flowing water licked what remained of the bridge, hinting that the breakage could have happened recently, and the rest was potentially about to be taken out, too. I shrugged – hadn't I been half-swimming all day? – stepped off the plank at the small island, and assessed the rest of the crossing. The water was moving rapidly, and it was clearly deep. Much deeper than I was tall. It would involve a swim. I dipped one toe in, and it was quickly slapped by the powerful river. I accepted the reality that the water was moving way too fast – I would have no hope whatsoever of swimming against it, and there were perhaps 6 or 7m to go. That may not sound like much, but at the speed the water was flowing at, I would be very far downstream before I made any progress towards shore. Turning my gaze to the east, downstream, I assessed the consequences. Rapids. Huge rapids, and not far enough away. Once I got sucked into those rapids, there would be very little hope for me. My body would either be pulled under enough times until I drowned, or I would be slammed into a rock and pinned down by the crushing force of the current. I knew better than to try, but I had no reason to lose hope yet – there's always another spot.

I crossed back over the bridge and started picking my way through the deep bog along the shoreline, looking for another place to cross. My eyes flicked between watching my step, as I couldn't see lower than my knees in the bog and kept sinking in and tripping, and scanning the water, looking for the widest point in the river, where it would be slow and shallow. My heart was racing as I couldn't help focusing in on the rapids, growing higher and higher in my anxious mind. At a bend, I found a widening of the river and decided to go for it. I slid down the muddy bank, where I needed to drop from the shore directly into the water – no gentle wade out. With my pole, I reached in to check the depth. The entire pole went in, and half my arm. It was deep. Still, the water was slowest in this place, so I decided to swim it. I double-checked that everything that needed to be waterproofed was secure, then sat my bum on the 'launch', feet ready to jump. I dipped one foot in the water, and once again it was swept to the side with a slap. The water might be slower, but not *that* slow. It was no safe bet. I took a deep breath, attempting to slow my heart rate and calm my mind. I counted to three, then I jumped.

Except, I didn't. I clung to the shore. Only one leg went in, up to my thigh this time, and the water pulled so hard on it that I realized in an instant I couldn't do it. I yelled out loud at myself. Another deep breath, and another. Then I counted down from five, and this time I really did jump.

Except, I didn't. This time both legs made it in, but in some instinctive, acrobatic, life-saving reaction, I clung to the shore with both arms and somehow managed to pull myself back to land. There was no way I could swim against that current. I hauled myself back to the shore, and sat facing the river once more, with my knees tucked under my chin, arms pulling my legs in, rocking and crying. I was scared. I was *really* scared.

With a cry of desperation, I headed back into the bog to look for another crossing point. I checked the map constantly, hoping for something I could have missed. Perhaps a place where the river was wider? Perhaps a bridge by the lake, where the river eventually ended? I found nothing. I assessed the distance to Maligne Lake, wondering if, as a final backup, I could swim that, where a current wouldn't be an issue. It was hours away, and I knew it was a terrible plan. I fantasized about the tourist boats on the lake, although they a) might not be running due to the pandemic, and b) almost certainly did not travel this far from the dock, and c) almost even more certainly did not pick up maniacal wild women waving from shore.

I considered the only other option: go back. It would take me three days, but I could go back to the next trailhead. Three days. I was already out of food. So that was also a terrible plan.

I lost my ability to stay stoic as I continued searching the shoreline. Perhaps if it hadn't been so frustrating underfoot, trying to pick through eye-level shrubs and impossible marsh, I could have remained calmer, or taken notice of the blue sky above me or something else to chill me out. But the situation was frustrating and scary. I tried to jump in at a few more spots that seemed sort of hopeful, where the water was darker rather than torrid white, but I wimped out each time. I hardly noticed when the sky clouded over – in hindsight, I may have genuinely believed the darkness was only inside my mind. It was certainly reflective of my grim mood. There didn't seem to be a good chance of getting out of here either way. I knew I couldn't call for evacuation – the three-day trek without any food was still technically a possibility. I felt so desperate as I paced the boggy shoreline, losing my handle on my mood entirely.

I selected a bend in the river where a few boulders were jutting out, at fairly even intervals to the other side. I figured that all I had to do was manage the short distance between each rock, where I could then stop and catch my breath before making the next sprint. The fact that they were jutting out indicated that it might be shallower near them, and the river was at its widest point. I knew it was the best I could hope for, and I had now been tramping through bog for nearly two hours looking for a place to cross. I had to get going.

I didn't count down this time. I just jumped. In one step, the freezing water was up to my chest. I fluttered my feet along the bottom, desperately trying to maintain contact with the rocky riverbed. I jammed my carbon trekking poles in, and the rushing water made them shudder violently. When I had four points of contact, I dug in both poles and one foot while I shuffled the other foot forwards. I pushed hard on all of my muscles to make myself as strong and sturdy as physically possible, bracing my core right down to my legs. I took conscious, deliberate breaths as I edged further out into the water, the depth increasing until the waves lapped at my face. I hardly noticed the cold – one slip, and I would be quickly moved downstream. Soon, the water became shallower as I reached the first boulder. I steadied myself on it, and allowed myself a few seconds of releasing the panic that was high in my chest. I hated this. This was far too uncomfortable. This was way past my acceptable line of risk.

This was not cool.

I couldn't stay there long. I was vaguely aware of the piercing cold of the river, most of which had been a glacier only hours previously. I used the same tactic to shuffle across the riverbed, not daring to lift my feet or poles off the solid ground. I approached the centre of the river, and buoyancy took over. Waves hit my face and I let go of my poles, swimming furiously with my arms while trying to dig my shoes into the rocks. With one crashing wave, I was pushed over. In a horrifying moment, I opened my eyes underwater and understood what that meant – I had lost control. The river had won. I kicked hard towards the ground until I hit shallower depths, milliseconds that stretched on for minutes. I clambered up to the second boulder, gasping for air, stunned to have made it without being swept downstream. I permitted myself to look in that direction – I had less than 10m of 'free flow' before hitting the next set of rapids. If I hadn't recovered from that stumble, you probably wouldn't be reading this.

The final stretch to the opposite bank was thankfully milder than the first two stages, but far from easy. Somehow, the submersion gave me a new confidence, and I let myself believe, for the first time since meeting the river, that I was more capable than it. When I finally hauled myself out , via a tall bank that I had to do a very awkward and exhausted pull-up manoeuvre onto, the gushing adrenaline surged forwards as I realized that I had survived.

I have no idea how long it had been raining for at this point, but it was actually lashing down from the sky, perhaps adding to the drama of the river. I had planned to remove all of my wet clothes and change into whatever dry layers I had to avoid hypothermia, but it seemed pointless given that I was standing outside in a storm. Once I found the trail – a saga that took another hour of wading through infuriating bog – I only had 10km to move, so I kept going, dripping wet and freezing cold. Later that night, I looked at the video I had recorded and had definitely never seen that shade of blue on my lips before.

The final stretch to the end of the trail was, fittingly, harder than it really needed to be. The deep mud persisted, and it wasn't until the very end that the path cleared wide enough to permit running. By this point, I was shaking from both violent cold and seriously low blood sugar. Coming out of this world of mud, weather, bears and a general feeling of being very lost and alone in a hostile wilderness into a paved parking lot, now in a bright blue sun, was wildly confusing. Suddenly, trail runners, cyclists and large groups of tourists were passing to and fro in front of me, few taking notice of my dishevelled and desperate appearance.

In my hotel room, I put on the kettle and the heating, and ran a hot bath. I stayed in that tub for as long as it took for my skin to return to its natural colour, the shaking to stop and my body to relax enough to get that stupid cup out (the instructional online videos stated relaxation was very important – no wonder it had been stuck in there for the last three days).

I washed all of my things and felt just barely strong enough to head outside to buy some dinner, which I took back to my room and ate while in bed under the covers, where I stayed for a full 12 hours.

JASPER

The day that follows the worst day frequently tends to be the best day. The lower the low, the higher the high. It's proof of resilience – you always come back stronger. Despite going to sleep on deeply exhausted muscles and head-to-toe soreness, I woke late the next morning to a surprisingly able body and chirpy mood. I returned to the lake shore where I had emerged hypothermic and frightened the previous day, and I set off onto the Skyline Trail – a highlight experience near Jasper that I had somehow never done before. Starting so late in the day, I had already decided to take it easy, letting my body recover from the last few days of hardship. I hardly recognized myself in this bright and sunny mood and, despite the initial climb, I found myself running – albeit slowly – taking photos and chatting with the marmots once again. It was a night-and-day shift from the overgrown back country I had just come through, to be on one of the most popular trails in this segment of the Rockies. The trail was easy to spot, smooth underfoot, and the small river crossings had lovely, stable bridges. I was a new woman, and this was a new Rockies.

At sunset I found my way, slowly, to one of the designated park campsites, which was already full of two- and four-man tents, luxurious canopies that I could only imagine. I didn't need a tent pad anyway, and at the edge of the tent cluster I found a tree with a dry patch underneath to pitch my bivvy, knowing that I was already the last one to go to bed and would likely be the first to get up the next day. It was an incredibly cold night, and I hardly slept as I shivered in my bag, looking up at a cloudless sky and twinkling bright stars. My body was still going through the repercussions of yesterday, my internal thermostat clearly still struggling to regain its full power.

In the morning, the ground was covered in frost, and my stove stuck to the picnic table after my water boiled. I silently enjoyed my coffee and breakfast while packing stealthily, not wanting to wake the other campers, and then made my way up to the Skyline ridge, delighted to be the first person up for the day.

No matter how many times I climb a mountain pass, even the ones in the Rockies that I have known my whole life, the revealing moment when I crest the ridge and see, for the first time, the full 180 view that I have just worked for always gets me. I let out an audible '*Wow!*' and stood in the ankle-deep snow, awestruck.

I ran the entire Skyline Trail, a true surprise both at the point in the journey (Day 19), and given my recent struggles. I had almost given up on my legs ever feeling good again, but the magnificent views of white peaks as far as the eye could see in all directions, the flowing trail and my sheer relief at entering the final stretch after fearing I would die the previous afternoon all came together to create a wonderful day of running. I let it rip on the descent, bounding down towards Jasper, where I didn't even mind the hot, sweaty, noisy run I had to make alongside the highway back into the town centre.

I reached the village early-afternoon, too early to even check in to my hotel, so I went out for lunch and waited in the sun. I enjoyed being back in one of my favourite towns in the world. I felt unshakable – and I had only one final segment on the journey.

Once again, I took advantage of the hotel room and slept in late. It was past noon by the time I got going on the final leg of the journey, although I wasn't really sure where the Rockies actually *ended*. They just kind of peter out from Jasper onwards, and I had always intended Jasper to be the end of the route. But I felt like I needed a bit more time, given my recent Disaster Day, so a semi-circle around Mount Robson, arguably the most beautiful mountain in the whole range, if not the continent, was my plan for the finale. Alberta was under a warning of heatwave weather as I turned off the final stretch of pavement and into the back country one last time.

It was baking hot, and sweat was literally dripping off me. I was grateful to enter the forest, but found the trees created some sort of sauna, and the lack of wind was stifling. The mosquitoes certainly loved it, and the only thing about finishing that excited me was returning to the coast and leaving them behind. I applied a paranoid amount of repellent, spraying my entire body, backpack, shoes and clothing several times inside each hour.

The trail was officially decommissioned, so deadfall and overgrowth persisted as a frustrating issue. I was clumsy in the heat, constantly tripping over things, slipping off muddy rocks and getting stuck in bog. I misjudged one fallen tree, stepping on it to climb over when my body weight broke the entire thing, sending me crashing to the ground, bum first. I would have laughed at how dismally embarrassing the scene was – I'm already conscious of my body weight as it is – if it hadn't hurt so much. I inspected the damage, a large cut just below the scar the Atlas left me with. At least I was consistent and keeping my battle scars to a contained area (at the time of writing, both marks are still visible, right next to each other, like a collection of bumper stickers for the places I've visited).

Progress through the forest was impossibly slow, and I wondered what on earth I was doing. I followed in the tracks of a small bear for over an hour, half expecting to meet him at any moment, given how fresh (I assumed) the tracks were. When I finally ascended out of the forest, I imagined things would improve – they almost always had, so far. But the ground was entirely flooded, and I waded through a meadow for hours, my feet submerged at all times, making infuriatingly slow progress as I attempted to find the route that had long since been withdrawn. A few white ribbons had been tied to branches, giving hope for wayfinding, but no trail existed. Running was impossible. As the sun lowered, I aimed to reach the top of the pass for nightfall, certain that there would be drier ground to camp on. The mosquitoes swarmed me in a way that I can only remember on very few occasions in my life so far. Despite the stifling heat, I had to walk in my full Gore-Tex layers and my sexy head net. The buzzing was deafening, as the whole meadow was alive with dark clouds of bloodsuckers. In short, it was pure hell.

I reached the top of the pass, still standing calf deep in water in the grassy meadow, and still peering through a cloud of mosquitoes. This wouldn't work. I had no idea what to do – where on earth would I sleep? The sun had already gone down, and I had nowhere to go.

To my left was the stunning Rainbow Range, home of Mount Robson. The towering peaks practically glowed in the moonlight. They were breathtaking. To my right were some smaller peaks, and I wondered how accessible they might be. Without taking much longer to consider my choices, I turned on my heels and began powering up the side of an unknown mountain. I was sweating heavily in my waterproof layers, imagining myself in a life race against the stream of mosquitoes that pursued me up the side of the hill. I glanced ahead now and then to pick my line, clambering up rock slabs and searching for the easiest gradient to the summit.

The moment I crested the ridge of the mountain, I was hit with the icy breeze that wasn't making it down into that valley of hell. The north side of the ridge was still covered in deep snow, the cold air coming off the snowbank instantly brought my temperature down and, best of all, it sent the horrid cloud of mosquitoes running back down the mountain to the bog mess below. I took off most of my clothes, letting the cold air cool my sweaty skin, and took in the views around me. Under the night sky, the white peaks of the northern end of the Rockies were illuminated by the bright moon, only just rising from behind the dark ridges adjacent to me. I checked the map, but the small mountain I stood on didn't appear to have a name. I was literally nowhere, and it was possibly the best place I ever pitched a camp.

I set my stove to boil – feeling absolutely ruined after finishing my mountain-pass climb of a day with a casual *sprint* up a mountain – and after the summit breeze dried off my skin I pulled on my warm sleeping layers and found a soft patch of ground to lay out my bivvy. The true ridge was rocky, and so close to the snow was actually quite cold, so I dipped down slightly to find a patch of grass and some very slight shelter from the wind. I sat on the top of the mountain eating my double-serving noodle dinner, shoes off, as the stars came in to the sky. I switched my head torch off to fully appreciate the vista. The earth glowed in a cold blue, and although the wind was chilling, it had a gentleness to it that I couldn't understand. I felt at total peace, like I was in the exact place that I belonged, sitting on top of an unnamed mountain in the Rocky wilderness.

I slept for only a couple of hours. Without the hum of mosquitoes, I had left the door to my bivvy open so I could fully appreciate the fresh mountain air (my sleeping bag did not smell particularly great anymore). I stirred in the night and was awoken by potentially the most magnificent display of the galaxy I have ever witnessed in Canada, and I have to say I have a very high bar for that statement already. I was awake like a shot, sprinting for my camera, and so excited by the wonder above me that I soon found I had no idea what I even *wanted to do* with my camera. I just knew I needed to remember this for ever. The Milky Way snaked overhead, and the stars danced over Mount Robson. I sat bolt upright, not feeling remotely tired all of a sudden. There was no chance I could go to sleep and miss out on this night.

I may have slept a little bit as the stars faded away, but they were soon replaced by a powerful pink sunrise, and once again I was bolt out of my sleeping bag, messing with my camera, never getting a photo anywhere near as magnificent as the moment deserved. I fetched my stove and made a coffee, sitting up and soaking in the sunrise, even if it was still far too early to be awake.

I must have sat there for nearly two hours, drinking back-to-back coffees, simply admiring the views around me. As the pink sky gave way to the daylight blue, a calm washed over me in a way that I have seldom felt before. A smile had permeated my face. It was one of the best nights of my life, and I knew it had only been such because I had finally got everything that I came here for. Leaving from Waterton Lakes in such a low place, going even lower through spells throughout the journey, facing fears and anxieties and deep isolation, I now sat on an unknown mountain with a permanent grin on my face.

I didn't need an official finish line with a signpost telling me I had crossed the Rockies. In that moment, I knew that I had completed my journey. Without giving myself time to overthink it, I pulled out my tracker and sent a message to my mom, letting her know I would be waiting at the side of the highway in a few hours.

*

In the months after the Rockies, I stayed in Canada during the next waves of the pandemic, which was an ultimately positive decision, as I set up home in the outdoor sports wonderland of Squamish, BC.

The episodes of fear that had begun occurring over the past year and were exacerbated multiple times in the Rockies continued to grow as an issue, until I eventually acknowledged there was an underlying problem. My fall in the Atlas Mountains had been a frightening could-have-been-much-worse episode that I never gave time to processing and, as they say, 'trauma is stored in the body'. That trauma forced its way out and, for a few months, I wondered if I would no longer be able to do the sports I loved.

The cure was simple: talking about it. I started telling people, for example, that I couldn't go skiing with them because I had fear issues sometimes. Almost everyone I unburdened my secret on nodded, accepted this as an injury, and told me their relatable stories. Once I saw the benefits of talking about it, I would tell almost anyone I came across. 'Hey! I get scared sometimes because of something that happened three years ago!' The 'fear episodes', as I called them, trickled off and, by the end of winter, I felt stronger than ever.

Of course, like everyone else, I had to wait a while, but when the vaccines came, I was ready to move again.

Baile Herculane

Sinaia

CHAPTER SIX

Being Brave:
The Transylvanian Alps

Arriving at the start, on each of these journeys, has been a memorable travel experience that always frames the run. The sixth and final leg may have been the best. In 2021, after winning the Silk Road Mountain Race (SRMR) for the second time, I travelled directly from Kyrgyzstan to Romania, and an overnight sleeper train delivered me to the small mountain town of Sinaia. I sat up in my single bunk, watching Romania whizz past the window, while clutching a glass of *fetească neagră* wine to calm my nerves (and give it a sense of occasion). I did not sleep well, each station we pulled into jolted me awake, worried I would sleep past my stop, where I was the lone passenger to depart the train at 5am.

'It's cold here, in the mountains,' the conductor nodded disapprovingly at my bare legs.

'It's not that bad,' I smiled back, but as the train left the station, leaving me there, alone in the dark in an unfamiliar and quiet town, I recognized that he was right – it was way too cold for shorts at 5am. Pulling on my extra layers before I even made it out of town, I wondered once again what I had gotten myself into – at the lowest altitude I would be at, I was finding it too cold. How was I going to survive the nights?

I had with me the most minimal setup I had tried yet – just a 24-litre backpack carrying next to no spare layers, a sleeping bag without a protective shelter, and my small stove. I was delighted by the small and lightweight pack size, but the reality of how committed I was to running fast was hitting home – I couldn't get caught out in bad weather, and that also meant I couldn't use the rest of the month. It was the second week of

September, and every night would be slightly colder than the last. The lightweight pack both allowed faster running and enforced it.

The Transylvanian Alps had never been on my radar. Europe is blessed with too many amazing options for mountain ranges, so as pandemic-related travel restrictions required me to cross some off my list, others remained, until I finally decided to go somewhere without a border crossing but with a likely stable situation. Transylvania popped up from the map like a beacon of hope – I would not delay my project, I would simply adapt my needs. The Transylvanian Alps were smaller and a shorter distance, and I saw this as an opportunity: I could really test myself as an *athlete,* and run these fast and hard. Once again making the bet against my legs that a logistically easier country would lead to faster trail days.

I picked up a cup of coffee from the only open gas station, and sipped it as I walked uphill through town, away from the train station and towards the ski lifts. The stars were still out, and only aggressive guard dogs barking as I passed their homes punctuated the calm night. I admired the charming buildings, many stone and some with elaborate wooden doors and windows, flowerpots bursting with colour and beauty. I walked the steep winding road, unsure when to truly 'start'. When I reached the parking lot for the ski lifts, I figured that was it: I stopped to take off my warm jacket, unfold my trekking poles and start my watch.

This was it.

NOW LET'S START

Before I even managed to 'start', I turned the corner and came face to face with a brown bear and her cub, digging through trash left out by the ski-lift cafe. I had been constantly warned about bears in Romania, to which I usually rolled my eyes and reminded the lecturer that I lived in Canada and had crossed the Rockies in grizzly season the previous summer. I was somewhat startled to realize there really *were* bears everywhere in Transylvania, but also quite vindicated to discover that they were as habituated as I had expected. A simple *clang* of my carbon trekking poles and a little verbal encouragement from me, and the mother and cub took off into the woods.

'Now let's start,' I softly said out loud, as if I had just cleared away some minor nuisance and was now fully ready to begin my sixth mountain range.

The winding trail in the middle of the ski piste snaked up the steep mountain, with a brief respite at the midway gondola station where I decided to wait for a cafe to open and enjoy a breakfast. The sun was now out, and I was becoming conscious of my sleepless night on the train. I watched tourists and mountain bikers file out of the first uplifts of the day, and wondered why I hadn't just had a few hours of sleep at the bottom and waited for the gondola to take me uphill. It wasn't cheating if the run hadn't started yet – right?

At the top of the climb, I summitted at just over 2,000m, an altitude I planned to stay above for the majority of the journey. The sky was clear and thankfully considerably warmer now, as I applied my sunscreen and prepared for my first downhill run. I was still navigating the ski slopes, with wide open runs to sprint down between the scars of resort development. The area in front of me was wide open – nothing obscuring my view of the project ahead, the Transylvanian Alps which stretched in a long ridge westward towards the Danube.

I knew that at 46km into the route, there was a mid-sized village with hotels and a pizza restaurant. I had set a target to make that my first day, and hoped to stay at roughly that sort of mileage throughout the journey, allowing me to finish this one off in just ten days. Still feeling good about myself from my recent win in Kyrgyzstan, I thought I now had what it would take to pull that off. I was addicted to feeling strong.

I've had a difficult relationship with the word 'athlete' since it started being thrown in my direction over recent years. I knew that the majority of this issue was rooted in my body image – that I didn't *look* like an athlete, so therefore I wasn't one. I also wasn't a very *good* athlete. Most of my social circle consists of bona fide athletes – winners and heroes and influencers who really push the limits of their chosen pursuit – so I always held back and simply classified myself as a writer with an enthusiasm for outdoor sport.

But I was trying to work on myself, in every way. My self-image had always been at the top of the list – the one thing I hadn't been able to shake. Enough of my friends – and total strangers – had by this stage given me the lecture that I did indeed qualify as an athlete, so the only person who wasn't qualifying me was myself.

Whether or not I could achieve this run, just two weeks after winning one of the toughest ultra cycling events in the world, would be my way of knowing. I wanted it. I really wanted it. I had tasted success and wanted more. But to be an athlete, I would have to think like one. This journey would have to be different from the previous five.

I followed a high run, ambling through well-marked European trails with the familiar red and white rectangles painted on trees marking the way, but when the big descent arrived – nearly the amount that I had already climbed that morning – it wasn't the freewheel I had planned out while calculating my expected arrival time at a hotel (and the pizza restaurant). A technical, rocky, overgrown, precipitous trail turned off from the lovely good one I had been using, and it took me hours of slow frustration to negotiate my way down the obstacles. Nettles constantly stung my legs and arms as I forged through overgrowth, and I was slowed to a crawl as I picked my way over rockslides, gently dropping myself down large ledges, careful not to break an ankle.

When the awful trail finally levelled out and reached the bottom, I could only let out a small *'hmmph'* as I joined the gravel road that led towards the village. The sun was setting rapidly, and I knew I would need to really up the pace to make it. My legs buckled and wobbled as I tried to force myself along the flat gravel road and took to mixing walking intervals. Eventually, the gravel road met a paved one, and the jolt of passing traffic inspired the highest speed my knackered legs could put in: a granny shuffle along the shoulder of the road.

Romanian traffic turned out to be the way I remembered it from a bike trip many years ago, so when I reached a cluster of *peninsueas* – guesthouses that frequently clustered the remote Transylvanian villages – well before the pizza restaurant, I resigned myself to not having pizza tonight: it would be nearly an hour of running with the chaotic drivers in the pure dark, and I just wasn't up for it. Defeated, I enquired at the first peninsuea that looked open.

The tourist season had ended only the week before, and many guesthouses had already shuttered their doors. I learned quickly that I wasn't going to be able to take chances with finding places, especially as I was waiting until so very late to call it a day. When I enquired with my host about a meal, I was told half an hour – and not asked what I would want. I took it as a good sign that I would be dining on authentic Transylvanian fare, and went upstairs to shower, plug in devices, and massage my feet until in no time my host was knocking on my door for dinner.

My meal, served to me in a completely empty restaurant with the Romanian TV blasting right in front of me, was a plate of barbecued red meat (perhaps mutton?), a whole fried fish and a ball of cheese-stuffed, fried polenta. My heart sank at the absence of vegetables, and I wondered if this was truly a traditional Romanian meal. As the host family sat down in their living room to enjoy the same bounty, I had to assume it was, along with wine glasses filled with cola, which was shared with me. I had hoped for healthier fare, but remembered that at least I was eating – only a week before, I had been quite ill in a Bishkek hotel room, and my shorts were fitting a lot looser than usual. If I wanted to keep my marathon-per-day pace, I was going to need to really *eat*. My exhausted body needed a lot of fuel to stay in the game.

I sat in bed looking at the map: I was 4km short of my goal on only the first day. If I missed goals by that much every single day, it added up. Knowing I had 4km extra the next day to get back on track didn't sound that bad – as long as I didn't let the problem exacerbate.

Following the difficult race in Kyrgyzstan, my lips were still cracked and bleeding from angioedema – an altitude-induced swelling – and the feeling hadn't returned to my toes. As I tried to pull myself out of the low bed in the morning, I acknowledged that I hadn't even begun to recover from the last event, but I still considered this my strength. I was on a high, and I wanted to hang on to it. Just long enough to get across Transylvania – my clear vibe was to achieve that as fast as possible.

YOU MUST BE CRAZY!

I didn't entirely succeed at my early-morning plans. The owners of my peninsuea weren't awake, so I used my own camp stove to make breakfast in my room and, after waiting long enough, left the money on the side table and crept outside, where it was already nearly an hour after sunrise. I tortured myself for the missed running time. I had slept wonderfully well for over eight hours – a huge upgrade from the schedule the recent race had had me on (three per night, if any) – but I knew I couldn't waste daylight like that.

I jogged steadily on the paved road, confirming that attempting the winding, busy road in the dark would have meant almost certain death, and arrived at my goal town shortly. Once again, I wasted more time – I had planned to fill up well at the grocery store here, and of course I wasn't going to go anywhere without stopping for coffee. The town of Rucăr held a distinct charm, with more elaborate wooden houses and lovingly tended gardens, built nestled into the lush valley between some of the highest peaks of Transylvania. I was gutted that I hadn't made it the previous night, even more so that I was doing my faff during good daylight hours. Hours I should be using to move, not to stay in one place doing logistics.

I stuffed my backpack to bursting with calories to last me through the next segment, one of the longer stretches without any supplies. Spotting a *fornetti* (bakery), I also grabbed some Eastern European pastries with my coffee, and found the owners to be a lovely couple who had just moved back home after a stint in Amsterdam, trying to improve their lives in Western Europe but ultimately missing their homeland.

'Where is your car? Or . . . bike?'

'I'm on foot.' For some reason, I held up one of my feet to fortify this statement.

'Wow! You must be strong . . .'

I beamed.

'. . . Alone?'

'Yep!'

'You must be crazy!!!' The nice man held his palm to his forehead dramatically. 'There are so many bad people out there . . . Going alone anywhere is simply crazy!'

I shrugged, and mumbled my usual, 'There are more good people than bad' and 'I'm very careful', etc., but then paid quickly and left with my bounty of pastries (much more than

I thought I had asked for) and coffee. I ducked around the corner to sit down and finish stuffing my bag while also stuffing my face with my second breakfast.

I left town at a walk, partly because I still had so many small pastries that I had to carry them in my hand, and partly because the town was bustling and I'm always embarrassed to run with my hiking bag in these situations. I'm not entirely sure why I find it so embarrassing – it's probably just that it attracts even more attention, and I shiver at being the centre of focus in public spaces.

The paved road turned to gravel, and the gravel turned to mud, and the mud turned left across a river without a bridge, directly into an incredibly steep, direct climb, back to the mountains. It took me nearly two hours to labour up the steep hill, which lacked any switchbacks despite the extreme gradient, and when I emerged above the treeline it was nearly noon. I had stopped to put duct tape across the pad of my foot, where a large blister had already formed and made putting weight on my left foot simply excruciating.

I crested the top of the climb to reveal my first proper ridge of the route. Before me sprawled a running fantasy: a trail undulating over the peaks, unhindered by trees or cliffs or any obstacles. I was free to *run*.

And run I did – for a while. My legs turned to jelly by mid-afternoon, my legs buckling and struggling impossibly and increasingly. I would use my poles to speed-walk up the climbs, but when the descents came, I could hardly coordinate my limbs. My knees would buckle as I lurched forward, and I was forced to stiffen my whole body to keep from falling over.

My options were either to freewheel completely out of control, or to slowly and delicately tiptoe my way down. I tried both, but the pain of putting weight on my blistered foot gave preference to the latter.

The only drawback to the ridge was the total lack of water – I hadn't seen a spring since the ascent I had made at midday, and it was now closing in on sunset. I had to keep pushing until I found a spring, so as the sun lowered I found myself climbing the summit of Peak Rosu.

The sky lit up in shades of rose and purple, and a sliver moon rose as I stood at the top, admiring only momentarily the view. I pulled out my head torch and donned my extra warm layers, as the night temperatures plummeted quickly. I had once again assumed I would make a rapid descent, and was once again extremely wrong. The narrow ridge sloping down to the north from the summit of Rosu was a steep scramble, with large boulders and unstable smaller ones littering the way down. The trail markers were not reflective and, in the dim light of my small head torch, hard to find. For two hours I crept down the trail, moving as fast as I safely could, which was not very fast at all. The initial descent of large boulders levelled only slightly, and then I was on a knife-edge ridge. At least it made navigation easy, but the potential consequences of a missed step in the dark were extremely worrying.

As I approached the saddle, the ridge widened and I managed to lose the trail a few times, it was such a faint line through the tall grass.

Finally, at nearly 10pm, completely exhausted and

frustrated, I approached the 'large river' marked on the map. It was hardly a trickle coming from a mountain spring. I explored the area, hoping to find any level ground to pitch my bivvy on. Jagged rocks threatened my air mattress, and the trail itself seemed like my best hope. Finally, I found a bit of grass that was angled, but workable, and set about making my camp. The trickle of water was difficult to fill a bottle from, but I was wildly dehydrated and grateful I had made it. I sat up in my bivvy, force-feeding myself some awful camping food that was so terrible I gagged a few times, while admiring the stunning starry sky. Under the silver moon, all was dark, and I hoped no bears would follow the smell of my 'veggie Mexican quinoa'.

Surprisingly, my slanted bed was amazingly comfortable and, with my stove nearby, I kept hot water going throughout the night, pouring it into the hard Nalgene bottle that I held next to my belly for warmth. In the morning, I woke to frost covering all of my belongings as well as my sleeping bag, and was pleased to realize that I was okay – I had been ruminating through anxiety for two days over my lack of spare layers, and even considering going back to Cluj, where my luggage was stored, to pick up my fleece tights or buy a new pair, even though there was no space in my pack (not to mention no spare time to take more Romanian trains).

FAGARAS

Starting Day 3, sitting upright in my frosted sleeping bag and enjoying my coffee, I felt at total ease. I had *barely* eked out my mileage targets for the first two days, my feet were in an incredible amount of pain, but I was making it. I was organized. I told myself things would get better as my efficiency improved and I settled in. I felt determined to stick to my ten-day ambition.

I was brimming with excitement: today was the day that I started the Fagaras Ridge. I had looked forward to this segment since I started planning (albeit not very long ago). With a clear weather forecast ahead, it was going to be the crown jewel in the experience. I also imagined it would lead to some fast-flowing miles, as once I completed the difficult ascent onto the ridge, I was *pretty much up there,* or so I thought.

My first day on the Fagaras was a day of summits. The only trail was a glorious, well-loved route that took in most of the highest mountains in Romania. What looked on my map like a smooth-ish line was in fact some of the slowest movement I could have done. Added to that, my feet were now both in excruciating pain. The left was already duct-taped, with a large bubble blister taking over the pad, but I could feel the right starting to go, too. Downhill sprints were almost out of the question, but I tried a few.

It was a Saturday, and a beautiful one at that, so after two long days of not meeting any other hikers, I was suddenly surrounded by them. All day, I passed groups, couples and a few solos, almost all carrying much larger packs than I was. I eventually nailed the casual *'Buna'* greeting, but preferred saying, 'Hello' to let them know I was a foreigner, which seemed to delight almost everyone I spoke to.

By the time the late-afternoon sun arrived, I had settled to a good steady walk – but only a walk. I passed endless men who either warned me that I couldn't possibly make the next hut (without knowing it was the hut *after that* which I was still aiming for), or declared amazement that I was alone.

The bivouac huts on the Fagaras Ridge are a wonderful series of refuges. Painted red and white like circus tents, they would easily be found in inclement conditions, and offer very basic shelter for hikers should the weather roll in, which was not a threat on that weekend. Inside, there is nothing but the dirt floor and the protective wood or metal walls, so I never planned to make use of them, always preferring the stars overhead and fresh air breezing over my sleeping bag. At one of the huts I stopped to search for water. I couldn't find it anywhere, but soon a Romanian girl called Miha noticed me and came in to help. She had pitched her tent far away from the hut in probably one of the most incredible campsites I'd seen all day – a flat pitch, away from the trail, looking out onto the stunning spiny ridge coming off Moldoveanu, the highest peak in Romania. I took an instant liking to her, and when she suggested I camp with her, I couldn't say no. There were two hours of sunlight left – two hours I had intended to use, and perhaps another hour after that – but not hanging out with Miha seemed ridiculous in that moment. Her friend, Kristina, was on the summit to the west of us, and when she arrived the three of us sat on the ledge enjoying our noodle dinners and gossiping like old friends. We were all the same age, and solo travel and outdoors enthusiasts. I can't get over how rare it is for me to have this kind of experience. A man who was staying in the hut came down to chat a little, and filled all of our mugs with a plum liquor from the north of the country. I initially declined the booze, but gave in easily and was so glad I did.

Kristina and Miha piled into their cosy tent after some stargazing, and I was left with my mountain perch. I had pitched my bivvy looking out over the ledge, and it was one of the best places I'd ever picked. The cost was, of course, the ripping wind that guaranteed cold, but the girls assured me I could jump in with them if it got too much. I knew I needed to get up a lot earlier than them, so kept my hot Nalgene going throughout the night once again. As a result, my fuel ran out as I was making my coffee in the morning, so I had a tepid coffee and oats, and accepted the fact that I really needed to make it to the highway that day.

I made it onto the trail before eight, the best I had done yet, and just swore to myself that I had to get the 23km ahead of me done as fast as possible. The first steps of the day solidified the thought that had been circling my mind – I needed new shoes. It seemed extravagant, but I also knew it was the 'athlete decision'. Keep going at any cost. Try everything to solve your problems. I also needed more camp fuel and food from town. Things were falling apart, and I needed a reset. My feet were the worst of all my problems, and covering both soles in duct tape wasn't enough this time – I needed shoes with more cushioning if I was to keep going.

I winced as I trundled down the rocky, steep descents. My legs wobbled and I cried as I pushed up the climbs. The route was truly stunning and spectacular but, as Miha had warned, it was some of the slowest movement I had done in Romania yet.

In some places cables offered hope of not falling off the mountain, and as the sun reached its full height more Romanians arrived to climb Moldoveanu, leading to wait times at these tricky sections as nervous hikers negotiated the *via ferrata*. Aside from these moments, I tried to avoid stopping all day. I needed to get to Sibiu. When I got phone signal, I booked a hotel room with a bathtub, willing to pay any price to help my wobbling legs. Again, trying to make the 'athlete decision'.

It was midday when I emerged at the famous Transfargarasan Highway. The last segment of rocky trail leading down from the mountains and to the busy parking lot at the top of the pass was cluttered with families and tourists making a day trip, most of them in inappropriate footwear for a hike and only travelling far enough to get a family photo of the iconic location. When I made it down to the parking lot and cluster of vendors, I delayed myself to eat a plateful of food from a barbecue vendor – not that I was very hungry, but I knew I needed to keep eating to keep this adventure dream alive. I then went to the gridlocked highway to hitchhike down the mountain. A kind family that spoke no English picked me up, and two hours later I was in my incredibly posh hotel room in the historic centre of Sibiu.

Gingerly, I tiptoed to the nearest chemist to get blister pads for my feet – recognizing the need to upgrade from duct tape – and some salts for my bath. That bathtub was worth every penny.

Unable to face any movement, I ordered a delivery dinner to my room, appalling myself that, of all the possibilities,

I went for a salad, as my body craved fresh vegetables after only a few days without any. I truly was destroying myself. In the morning, I went out in search of new shoes, and had only one option – a very sturdy and burly pair of French hiking boots. I had hoped for something a little more forgiving, but there was only one pair in my size and beggars can't be choosers. The change from barefoot to burly was significant, and immediately pleasing. With a bag full of fresh supplies, shiny new shoes on my feet, and legs with nearly 24 hours of pure luxury relaxation in them, I merely had to find my way back to the mountains. I could have lived in that hotel room for days, but the city was already making my skin crawl.

More than that, my vibe was still very much to just *get the thing done.* I couldn't face feeling like this a week from now. I needed to get to my finish line, and then I could go home and properly start my recovery. I knew I would be uncomfortable until that happened, so the only solution seemed to be to just *keep going, and go hard,* to get there faster. There was no way to make things easier. Only faster, so it could be over sooner.

This headspace dominated my mind through the most beautiful segments of the Transylvanian Alps. I hardly took my camera out, instead steadily pushing myself to keep moving. The technical trail and my physical state meant far too much walking, so I had to keep moving to eke out every hour of the day and maintain my hopes of 40km per day. I was not willing to compromise on that.

My mental space was burst by an oncoming solo guy, probably around my age.

'Are you alone out here?'

'Yep,' I smiled back.

'*Wowwww!!!* Go you!' It was admittedly pretty cool that I wasn't being warned off, for a change, and encouraged instead. But it was still patronizing.

'Are you alone out here?' I mimicked back.

'Well, yeah . . .'

'Wow, go you!' I smiled, teasingly. He knew what point I was making.

'Well, it's different because I'm a guy,' he blushed.

Patronizing comments (which were ubiquitous) aside, the small interactions with other people were really uplifting. I noticed how much I had changed, that although my natural tendency was to be alone and I mostly avoided people, I was starting to crave company on my journey. Knowing that in less than a week this whole challenge would come to an end and I would be 'free' to move on, I made lists in my mind of things I would do next year and who I would do them with. I had phone signal frequently, and left voice messages for friends as I moved along. When I came into signal and my phone buzzed, I regularly stopped to check it. Noticing the issue here, I finally put it on 'do not disturb' while I was trying to maintain my pace, and saved my social time for when I was either eating or in bed.

Despite my eager pace, I knew that only by taking care of myself would I be able to maintain it, so I tried my best to ensure I got a full night's sleep each night. If it was possible to get to a hotel room, I always aimed for it. As much as I yearned to camp out, it was also too cold to guarantee a good sleep, not to mention that the food was without exception terrible. Still, sleeping at least eight, often more, hours per night, I was waking every morning exhausted, feeling certain I could use another eight immediately.

Again, I resolved that the only way to deal with this would be to just get the whole thing done faster. I kept repeating to myself, *the sooner it's done, the sooner I can go into recovery*. In the mornings, I would roll out of my weird hotel beds and limp across the floor using only the outside edges of my feet, avoiding the huge blisters in the middle, reluctantly pulling on my clothes that I hadn't bothered to wash (I probably got in too late for anything to dry before I left again) and packing my bag for another day of very uncomfortable running.

While my hours and my focus were devoted entirely to knocking down the miles, not enough of my energy was being delegated to the place I was actually journeying through. I frequently forgot where I was, especially when I went for more than a day without a human interaction. It struck me how much was the same everywhere – my life was whittled down to the pursuit of water, a safe place to sleep, avoiding bears and keeping my solo self safe. It dawned on me most when I chanced upon some of the nicer mountain springs, where little monuments (often religious) appeared – sometimes along with a 'tap' that had been built into the mountainside. The small springs were important to far more travellers than just myself, and had been for a very long time. A lot of them had little cups left behind by someone, so anyone could take a drink from the source. I smiled at the shared experience – and shared need – that clean drinking water was, and it drew me back to the sense of place. Even after so much time isolated in the wilderness, these little touch points brought me back, and I felt connected to humanity more than ever – even if I had spent very little time interacting with it lately.

IS THIS FUN?

Leaving the Fagaras behind, the trails were quiet again. My burly hiking boots had got me moving once more, and I felt invincible with the hefty soles protecting me from the rocky trail. Winding through the woods on a gravel track, I was startled to meet a pair of hikers with an off-road vehicle. I saw their car first, and heard them calling from the woods. When I spotted them, they turned out to be two guys roving with a metal detector, hoping to find buried treasure. They jogged down from the forest to say hello properly, although only one spoke English.

'You're from Canada? And you came *here*??' It was a common astonishment I'd received. 'Why? How did you even hear about Transylvania??'

I was constantly amazed by the low esteem in which the people of Transylvania seemed to hold their land as a travel destination, although I hadn't met any other foreigners yet, so maybe they were just used to being overlooked.

'I love Romania, and I love mountains . . . so here I am,' I shrugged. It felt nice to see their national pride restored that I had come here on purpose.

Between the resupplies, my route was marked by long ridges, where I broke above the treeline and ran free, westwards, with Romania below me on either side. It was a strange feeling on the ridges. I felt isolated in every sense – I rarely saw anyone, or even any wildlife, and my senses were dulled. The ridges were silent, and my path was unbroken. In the valleys below I could see shepherd huts, campsites, even monasteries or lodges, but on the ridges themselves there was almost no human trace aside from the occasional trail marker. On the less popular routes, basically everywhere aside from the Fagaras, I got used to progressing without even a trail beneath my feet, and after hours of silent meditation moving along the grassy undulating ridge, I forgot the world completely. I had no ties to it up there, no reason to reconnect. I drifted away in my mind and entered a world of pure isolation.

I lost track of what day it was, what I was doing and who I was. I'd become so obsessed with being in Baile Herculane – a town I still can't pronounce – by Sunday that I just stumbled relentlessly forward from dawn until after dusk. I rarely stopped. I hardly took any photos. Was it Day 7 or Day 8? Or 12? Had I blown it? Was I killing it?

I fought with my inner dialogue.

Is this fun?

Yes, it's the most fun.

But you haven't stopped to explore, absorb, enjoy.

No, I'm being an 'athlete'. This is what it's like. I can go on holiday later. Finishing by Sunday leaves time for that.

It really hurts. Please stop.

No. It's fine. Be brave.

'Be brave' was my new mantra, and perhaps my favourite one yet. It had come to me on a cold night in the SRMR a few weeks earlier, when I found myself pedalling up to high altitude (nearly 4,000m) in the middle of the night, knowing my discomfort would only increase as I continued, but determined to perform well in the race. *To be like an athlete.* I realized that, while midnight ascents to such a height are not often considered advisable, there was no reason for me to hold back. I had the equipment, the skills and the physical capability to handle the mountain within any reasonable scenario it would throw at me – I would just probably be very uncomfortable. I can be uncomfortable. Anyone can be uncomfortable. It's just discomfort. You just need to be brave – brave enough to willingly enter that place that will not be comfortable. So, throughout the race, whenever my instinct to protect my body, hold back, get some extra sleep or wait for better conditions kicked in, I repeated to myself, 'Be brave' and forged ahead.

This mantra served me well in Transylvania. The discomfort started on only the second day, and I willingly set an intention to go deeper. To go as deep as possible and perhaps even beyond, if that's what was necessary to reach my goal. I knew that, while I was deeply – *deeply* – uncomfortable, that was the only danger I was really facing at that point. In the years of doing these things, I had honed my skills to the point that the mountains of Transylvania were well within my comfort zone, even if there was little skin left on my foot pads. I always knew how to keep myself safe. I just needed to be brave enough to let things get ugly. I figured that was the difference between a 'jolly' and an 'epic'. I have had plenty of jollies in my life, but this was the time for epic. This was the finale to a project that had been my world for five years. I wanted to do it proud. What were a few days of bravery against one of my life's great projects?

I pulled my head out of my determined isolation and tried to focus on some conscious reflection. In two days, hopefully, I would be finished. Not just with Transylvania, but with this entire project. I still had no idea how to feel. What to feel. Was I happy? Was I sad? Was I proud? Had I had enough? Did I still need more? Had I solved all of life's great questions?

The answer to the last of these was 'no', hence my conscious reflection time. I had only two days to figure it all out. People were going to ask me at the end, *'What did you learn, Jenny Tough?'* and I was going to have to say something. Something good. But I was drawing a total blank.

Some small commonalities made me smile. The reaction to being a solo woman – after six traverses, this remained the dominant conversation topic with the people I met. Whether it was passing on the trail, buying food for the next leg or deeper, more meaningful connections, the solo female aspect to my project was always the headliner. Sure, it differed – from the extreme of Morocco to the relative comfort of New Zealand – but it was always there.

The obsessive pursuit of water. The narrowing of my worldview to the essentials. The few possessions that mattered to me the most. The annoying clang of my trekking poles on the ground. The awkward transition from mountain to village. Although perhaps that one was getting worse over time.

CRAZY DOGS

Jogging through one village, a gang of stray dogs ran out to me. It's common, in Romania, although I was not getting any more comfortable with scary dogs barking at me and chasing me. I was swarmed by the mob of them, one even bit my arm (although I realize he meant it playfully, and it didn't puncture the skin, so I didn't need to rush off to a clinic). A couple of locals waiting for a bus watched in amusement, but no one really moved – this was village life. There were just lots and lots of crazy dogs.

I kept moving and, weirdly, four dogs followed. We reached the end of the village, and they were still with me. I jogged up a dirt track, away from civilization, and they still followed. Without any fuss, the four dogs had now filed into formation alongside me, and by the middle of the afternoon I accepted that I had unwittingly become the alpha of a pack of strays. The only thing to be done now was name them.

Rex took my heart first. Athletic and blonde, he was a good-looking pup. He also adored me, and ran at my heel at all times. He looked clean enough, so he was the first one I stroked. He loved it, and thereafter demanded more pets as often as possible. If I stopped for any reason, he rolled over on my feet hoping for a little love.

Love Bite was the one who bit me when we met. I had been scared of him – he was also athletic, and a very good-looking, strong dog, but I realized he was just a puppy. He also adored me, like puppies do, and when the initial fear from the bite wore off, I adored him back.

Gandalf was lovely. Tall, white, with long shaggy hair, he

had a particularly charming run and I loved to jog alongside him, admiring his effortless long legs. Long legs and messy hair – we were made for each other.

Hyena was the wild card for me. Named because she looked like a hyena, which I realize can't be a compliment no matter how you spin it, she'd clearly got some social issues going on. She'd come close, and looked to me for leadership, but absolutely refused to be patted. One or two times she accidentally brushed against me and the contact, even initiated by her, terrified her. Someone had obviously been mean to her once, so we kept a respectful distance. I admired her for coming on the adventure despite her trauma issues.

'Atta girl.

To my surprise, the dogs stayed with me all day. When I stopped for a break, all four of them collapsed to the ground, but when I rose to move again, they fell back into formation. They were self-sufficient, running off into the bushes now and then and lapping up water at the streams we passed. I didn't have enough food to share, but none of them begged.

A big thunderstorm was predicted for the night, and I had long since made my decision to push to the next peninsuea. I wondered how this would play out with the dogs. It was one thing to show up on someone's doorstep late, dirty and too exhausted to engage, but quite another to have four stray dogs at your heels.

Unfortunately, the situation never transpired. When I made the cluster of homestays that I had set as my goal – the goal I had worked so hard towards all day – the houses had all boarded up for the season. I had been told that summer had officially ended in Romania the previous week, but this was a killer reality. I tiptoed around each of the properties, confirming that they were indeed shut and empty. There was no hope of anyone even around to help me out. As thunder clapped in the distance, and my dogs who had all just run a little shy of a marathon looked up at me for our next move, I felt deflated. I simply couldn't keep going, and my ultra-light setup meant I was not equipped to be out in the storm.

I inspected each of the three boarded-up properties, looking for the best bivvy. The third one had a gazebo in the garden, and I wasted no time setting myself up there. I sat at the picnic table, boiling my last packet of noodles (so I really needed to finish tomorrow), hoping that perhaps the owners of the property would return now that it was sunset. Perhaps someone would arrive, anyone really, and invite me inside?

The dogs each found their own patches on the lawn – except for Love Bite, who always stayed at my feet – while I ate my noodles and massaged my faltering legs. By the time the sky went dark, I was well beyond ready for sleep, and decided not to wait any longer. I set up my air mattress and sleeping bag in the gazebo, hoping that if the home owners ever returned it would be totally cool that I was doing this – with my four weird dogs. Love Bite settled himself as my Little Spoon, and I drifted off in seconds. If anything stirred in the night, my four guard dogs were immediately on the case in a fit of howling. It was remarkably comforting, and I wondered why I had done all six ranges without a team of dogs? They had been nothing but an asset – pace buddies, guardianship and fantastic banter. And all they wanted in return were a few ear scratches.

I forced myself to wake up a couple of hours before dawn. I knew that, if I put in a really big day, I could finish – and that was an insanely tantalizing prospect. The thought that my next morning would be in a nice hotel bed and I wouldn't have to run *anywhere, ever again,* was drool-worthy. I needed it. I still had a long way to go, but I was desperate for the discomfort to be over. I didn't want to be brave any more. I whimpered and whined as I dragged myself out of my sleeping bag (Love Bite immediately moving into my warm spot) and onto the picnic table next to me to get breakfast going. My ankles were swollen and my head spinning. It was time to 'kick for home'. Time to put this thing to bed. Time to put me to bed.

THE FINISH LINE

I was packed up before the sun rose, and gingerly started my first steps of the day. *Be brave, be brave, be brave,* I repeated out loud in response to my full-body agony. I couldn't remember feeling this broken at any time during the past six mountain traverses, although I wondered if I had simply forgotten. I climbed up to the path, and soon found myself jogging. It was delightful to run on the last day, and I swore I wouldn't walk unless absolutely necessary. An athlete would finish strong. A brave person would run to the finish. I could do it.

And then I couldn't do it. After nearly two hours of steady jogging, a short uphill forced a slow down, and then I was walking again. The pain in my legs was too real now. Tears bubbled at the corners of my eyes as each footstrike on the trail sent shockwaves of pain up my thighs. Even my arms hurt from using the trekking poles. I had nothing left to give.

I checked my map and realized that my steady morning run had gained a good amount of mileage, but I still had a long day ahead of me. Baile Herculane stretched into the distance. *Be brave,* I commanded through gritted teeth and, with a hard push-off on the trekking poles, forced myself back into a jog. I did this on repeat every few minutes – forceful start to running, slow jog, then peter into a fragile walk again. It was like trying to kickstart a dead battery. The lights flicker on for a second, but then go blank again. There was nothing left in me.

The winding trail crossed through farmlands, and a team of sheep dogs chased off my pack of friends. The cacophony of barking summoned the farmer, who dispersed the animals and soon I found myself standing on the trail, alone. Standing still at any point left me feeling slightly dizzy, and I had to question whether the dogs had ever existed. I couldn't see them anywhere, and reluctantly kept moving forwards by myself. I hoped for hours that they would emerge from the trees and cheer me on to the finish line, but I knew I would need to get myself there. I had come this far on my own – from the first climbs of the Tien Shan to here, right now, I had learned to rely on my own strength to see me through. I had been so brave to get this far. I needed to push *myself* to my finish line now.

By the afternoon, the trail ahead of me sloped downwards, and there was no climbing left. It was all downhill from here. I wanted to soak the moment in – to know how it felt to complete a challenge that had taken five years of my life. A challenge that saw me through so much personal growth. A challenge that took me around the world to some of the best experiences I could have imagined.

But I couldn't feel anything. I was stumbling now. My knees constantly gave out and I was relying heavily on my trekking poles to save me from stumbling to the ground. I was back to using the edges of my feet to avoid the serious pain on the soles of my feet. My muscles literally wobbled and I couldn't hold a thought in my mind aside from how much pain I was in.

Be brave, be brave, be brave, I almost cried.

When my wobbling legs hit pavement, the pain shuddered up my joints and I nearly collapsed onto the hard ground. I stopped for a moment and looked ahead: hotels rose from the valley and the faint sound of traffic and civilization broke the silence of nature. I was finished. I pulled out my phone, made a hotel reservation and practically crawled along the road towards it.

Afterword

I have no natural talent for running, and it never made me properly skinny. I'm not very fast, and I haven't stuck to a training plan in over a decade. I'm no athlete, and I don't take this sport at all seriously.

But it saved my life, many times over, and has taught me almost everything I've learned so far about myself.

SELF-BELIEF IN THE TIEN SHAN

Through running I learned to believe in myself and be my own cheerleader whenever I needed one. I never thought I 'looked like a runner' (mainly thanks to magazine racks, not real-life runners, who look like pretty much anyone), so I always held back in describing myself as one. My 950km run across Kyrgyzstan pushed this lesson to the forefront and made me truly understand the importance of backing myself and cheerleading for myself. If I hadn't been able to do that, I wouldn't have completed that expedition. Is that lesson relevant to the rest of my life? More than anything, I would argue.

PERSEVERANCE IN THE ATLAS MOUNTAINS

Running anywhere in the world, as a woman, I will always hear advice and even criticism about safety. From a very young age, I learned that the world is not seen as a place for women. There are only certain hours and certain neighbourhoods we're allowed to exist in. But exploration, movement and self-expression should be available to everyone. It is never lost on me how fortunate I am – on many levels – to be able to run like I do. But my expedition across Morocco allowed me to almost walk that proverbial mile in the shoes of women in North Africa, who experience life in a far more disadvantaged way than I ever will. That journey fuelled my fire as a woman on this shared planet. It taught me my own personal strength to persevere, and reminded me of things that are important to persevere with: freedom for everyone. Freedom to move, freedom to be your true self, freedom to choose your own path.

OVERCOMING FEAR IN THE ANDES

Fear comes in many forms, and can exist in every setting. When I went for that first run, as a 'chubby' teenager with low self-esteem, I feared ridicule. I feared never being accepted, being ugly, being worthless. Running got me through that. My expedition in Bolivia showed me fear in every colour, and the lessons that journey taught me about myself and how to negotiate with fear have become some of the greatest assets for me navigating my adult life. From the threat of human danger to the very real physical risks of the environment and altitude sickness, I was practising living with fear every day. Just as any muscle that gets exercised becomes stronger, my fear-wrangling improved through use. We all fear something – or even lots of things. There is no such thing as fearlessness. But fear can be wrangled.

WRITING YOUR OWN TERMS IN THE SOUTHERN ALPS

If you start out as a runner through the usual channels, you will learn about pacing, drills, workout types, shoe types and target finish times for set distances. Sub-four-hour marathons and so on. But those numbers are irrelevant to the experiences I had. When I started this project, I was taking the sport of running and putting it into my own terms. This didn't make sense to many people I explained it to. Everyone wanted to know how many marathons I ran across New Zealand, as that was the only way to put that expedition into terms they worked with in their own heads. But this project was mine and mine alone. I did something that was important to me, and I made my own rules and routes. It's not a fastest known time or world record – I am aware I could have submitted myself to holding a few of those titles, but I never did. It wasn't a competition. Once I embraced that fact, it became far more enjoyable. I hope I always remember to live my life on my own terms.

RESILIENCE IN THE ROCKIES

Running teaches resilience right from the start. It's uncomfortable. There's a saying you hear a lot – 'It never gets easier, you just get better.' It's completely true. The discomfort never goes away, but you become more resilient to it. Resilience is perhaps one of the key traits that anyone should take into their life. There will always be discomfort, fear, challenges and the like. But a resilient person can weather all of that. The Rockies were uncomfortable, and they came at a time when burn-out from the pandemic was already weighing heavily on my shoulders. In terms of distance and isolation, it was the biggest range in my project, and in hindsight I'm amazed I was able to persevere through it. Every day posed new challenges, new discomforts or even just increases in the discomforts I was already experiencing. But a resilient mind can keep going, even getting stronger day by day.

BRAVERY IN THE TRANSYLVANIAN ALPS
Throughout this project, I learned to be brave. Actually, in hindsight, perhaps the lesson is that *I already was brave*. Maybe girls aren't raised to be brave – it's definitely a trait that was applied more often to boys in my generation. In Romania, 'bravery' became my new favourite word. What a fantastic key trait it is to adopt. Bravery isn't just about running through bear territory without enough warm clothing for the weather. Bravery is about being yourself and pursuing your own path. Tap into your bravery, and let it lead your life. It felt fitting to recognize my bravery at the completion of this project. After the first five expeditions had armed me with the skills and lessons I needed, all that was left was to become brave enough to use my strengths.

I think that relates to everyone. You probably know, even

deep down, what your strengths are. But being brave enough to show them to the world, that's the trick.

*

Did I solve all of life's big questions on this project?

No.

Did I figure out a few?

Actually, yes.

Every adventure teaches me something. That's the value of adventure. So, if you take anything away from this book, please believe in yourself, be brave and go have an adventure on your own terms. Solo.

You're tougher than you think.

Acknowledgements

I'm not sure which was more challenging: running across six mountain ranges or writing a book about them (and, consequently, myself). There are a few thanks owed to those who supported me throughout this challenge.

First and foremost, this book would not have happened without my brilliant publisher, Stephanie Jackson, who encouraged me to put my stories onto the page and guided me through the process of turning it all into a book. She coaxed me through my doubts and anxieties, always prodding me to keep going. To everyone at Octopus who has taken my manuscript (which went way past the desired word count) and turned it into a real book, thank you so much for your hard work and for applying your incredible skills to my story.

Thanks to John Summerton and *Sidetracked* magazine, who were the voice of encouragement by awarding me their Adventure Fund for my first expedition across Kyrgyzstan and continuing to publish the stories of my project up to the end. Being asked to write for your favourite magazine is a huge rite of passage for any creative, and that my solo project continued to receive attention through all six chapters was a massive honour for me. For the encouragement as both a friend and an editor, I owe John a great gratitude.

To all the friends who listened to me complain, let me talk at them over the phone while I tried to figure out what I was doing with this, read passages and gave their opinions, or took me out for bike rides to get me away from my computer for a few hours, the greatest thanks. Emily, Alex, Craig, Scott, Steven, Allan, Cat, Mom and so many more (basically anyone who saw me between 2020 and 2022). Thanks for not letting me go off the rails.

To all those who followed my journey online, your virtual support meant more than I could ever put into words. To those who read articles, came to public talks, watched the films, sent messages or simply liked an image I shared from the trail – thank you for encouraging me and making me feel so connected while I was 'solo'.

I would also, strangely, like to thank myself, for having the bravery to take on the project of my dreams and then seeing it through. This entire process, from landing in Bishkek for those first steps, to hitting 'send' on a final manuscript, has fostered huge personal growth and carried me through five years of my life and everything it threw at me. This project gave me the bravery to design the life of my dreams and start to live it. It was uncomfortable in so many places, and I'm proud of myself for showing up to the challenge day after day. So, to you, JT: I know I've never said this to you before, but I'm proud of you.

And finally, to all of the wonderful characters who I met at every stage along the way. There were far more friendly smiles, waves, conversations, acts of kindness, simple engagements and connections than I could ever fit in a book over the course of 4,582km and six countries. Some of the interactions were so small that I wouldn't have even half of your names, but to each person out there who touched my little runs in some way, thank you so much. I was a guest in so many lands over the course of this project, and it warms my heart that I was so heartily welcomed by you.